BOOST YOUR MENTAL A[...]

THE VEGAN SURVIVAL GUIDE

Your Guide to FUNCTIONAL VEGANISM

URSULA ESCHER
WITH GENE WEI, DOM

UEscher Publishing

The Vegan Survival Guide: Boost Your Mental and Physical Health
Your Guide to Functional Veganism
by Ursula Escher and Gene Wei, DOM

This book is intended as a reference volume only, not as a medical manual. The information given here is designed to help you make informed decisions about your health. It is not intended as a substitute for any treatment that may have been prescribed by your doctor. If you suspect that you have a medical problem, we urge you to seek competent medical help.

Mention of specific companies, organizations, or authorities in this book does not imply endorsement by the author or publisher, nor does mention of specific companies, organizations, or authorities imply that they endorse this book, its authors, or the publisher.

Our books may be purchased at special quantity discounts for business or special sales.
For information, please visit us at www.FunctionalVeganism.com.

Published by UEscher Publishing
Designs by Ursula Escher
Photographs by Ursula Escher and Gene Wei
All images and text copyright © Ursula Escher

ISBN-13: 978-1480229020 | ISBN-10: 1480229024 paperback

Proudly printed in the United States of America
First Printing: November 2013

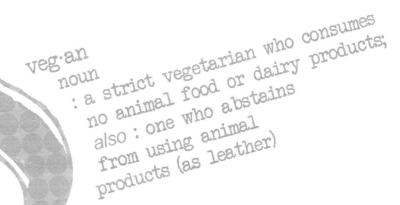

veg·an
noun
: a strict vegetarian who consumes
no animal food or dairy products;
also : one who abstains
from using animal
products (as leather)

Dedication

This book is dedicated to YOU, whether you are a new vegan, have been a vegan for a long time, or just wanted to give it a try.

Although I've been on a vegan-journey for over 30 years now, I still learn something new everyday.

The truth is that a vegan diet can be very healthy and healing, but it can also be full of disease causing ingredients. So *let's make the best choices* and take good care of our bodies, minds and souls - because we deserve it right? ;)

And though I know we live in the information age, I still hope that you will find at least one thing in this book that will make you say: *"Cool, I didn't know that!"*

— Ursula Escher

CONTENTS

❸ Vegan Survival: Brain

Vegan Survival: Immune

Vegan Survival: Body

Vegan Survival: Detox

Vegan Survival: For the Soul

❹ VSG Food for Function

INTRODUCTION

1

About the Author

"Being different can be challenging... and growing up vegan in a meat loving country like Brazil wasn't easy."

When it comes to life, "good old fashioned hardship" can often be the best motivator. Well, at least it was for me! Growing up vegan wasn't easy by any means. Even as a child, I had an aversion to animal based foods. That's just how I was born I guess. As a baby, milk made me sick; and while most kids loved to eat meat and cheese, I had to be forced and was even punished at times for refusing! Whenever I reluctantly ate something that wasn't vegan, I always felt sick and nauseas. So for me, growing up vegan really was all about survival.

Don't get me wrong, being born and raised in Brazil was great. I wouldn't trade it for anything in the world. From soccer and samba, to art, music and martial arts, it's such a unique country known for so many things. But anyone who is familiar with Brazilian culture knows that they love to eat meat and dairy. In fact, Brazil is world famous for their barbeque, also known as "churrasco."

So here I was, a Brazilian child who didn't even like being *near* a barbeque, let alone eat any of it. Even at family gatherings, I remember playing at the other end of the yard just to get away from the smell. I wasn't *trying* to alienate myself, I just didn't like the smell and the thought of cooking meat.

In fact, being vegan created many obstacles throughout my childhood.

A drawing I did when I was a kid. I loved Brazil for all its beauty, music, dance and martial arts. :)

Something I'll never forget was getting in trouble for refusing to finish my lunch at school. My teachers scolded me, saying that I would die if I didn't eat meat! They even punished me with dish duty at recess, while I watched the other kids play outside! Though situations like this were difficult for me at the time, they ultimately made me into a stronger person. If anything, I learned to stand up for what I believed in, *even* if it came at a cost.

Because meat and dairy are so integral to the Brazilian culture, raising a child on a vegan diet was basically unheard of at the time. To my parents I seemed like a difficult child. To my nanny, I seemed "spoiled" just because I didn't want to eat something. And there were many foods that I would have loved to try if they were made with vegan ingredients.

So instead of growing up on a well-balanced vegan diet, I was basically malnourished throughout my childhood.

My meals ended up including rice, tomato pasta, bread, carrots, and the occasional black bean stew when it was made without meat. In my household, there were so few dishes for me to eat that

< In Brazil many schools are religious and can be very strict. Since I didn't eat the meat portion of my lunch, I wasn't allowed to play during recess.

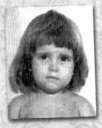

I was born lactose intolerant but didn't know. I only found out years later as an adult.

While family enjoyed BBQ on weekends, I usually stayed far away to avoid the smell, sometimes reading some books or drawing by myself.

> My classmates often encouraged me to *somehow* hide my food so I wouldn't get punished. But of course, being the hard-headed little girl that I was, I refused; and I was proud of my decision. :) I said to my friend: *"I didn't do anything wrong... I just don't like this food. It makes me feel sick! Why should I hide it?"*

Margarine contains man-made fats known to cause many diseases, including cancer. My parents and I didn't know about healthy oils and fats such as coconut and omega 3 rich flax oil.

PREMIO DE HONRA

Even while malnourished and chronically ill I was still able to be an A student!

I even remember being fed bread with margarine (hydrogenated). Things like coconut and flax oils were basically unknown to me and my parents at the time. In my household, there were so few options that I would sometimes give up and eat some cheese with my bread, or have some cake made with eggs. Even though I ended up feeling sick from these foods, chronic hunger has a way of making you eat!

I still remember the first time I heard about tofu. We had just installed cable TV at home, and I learned about it while watching Nickelodeon as a young teenager. I begged my mom to help me find some, and she tried but there was none to be found. I remember her taking me to every market in town, and asking for "tofu cheese," which I always thought was hilarious!

As you can see, my malnourished childhood was quite the ordeal. Things like migraine headaches, heart palpitations, depression, and chronic fatigue were all common for me. My doctors had no answers, and when they put me on anti-depressant medications, I became even more depressed. Feeling misunderstood made me an angry child.

Luckily, it also gave me a huge motivation to explore! I was dying to know what else was out there, especially outside of Rio De Janeiro, Brazil where I grew up. Then as I got into my teenage years, I realized for the first time, how close I was to freedom. Freedom to do what I wanted, eat what I wanted, and meet like-minded people who would understand my perspective! As soon as I turned 18, after fighting with my parents for nearly 2 years about going abroad, I was off to the United States to study animation.

I dreamed of the day that my food would be enjoyable and nutritious. I was delighted to learn about the growing vegan culture in the US.

Meeting like-minded people and finding your own tribe

Because my family was reluctant to let me go to the U.S., there was little support for me. I ended up going to school full-time, working part-time for pennies, and living like a starving artist. For a few months, I even lived on Ramen noodles and bananas because they were the cheapest foods at the market! *I'd always been an artist... and I was always starving anyways, so I guess it wasn't the worst transition!*

Regardless of all the challenges, I loved being abroad. For the first time in my life, I started to get a sense of "belonging." Just knowing that other vegans existed was such a great feeling!

I had never really heard of "veganism" (before coming to America), or things like natural food markets. I didn't even know about combining foods for complete protein, let alone the wondrous joys of vegan ice cream! Now I wanted to learn (and eat) everything that I could, and I loved it.

Going above and beyond

As my health began to improve, I wanted to learn more and more to see what else I could do. I've always had a deep interest in natural health and began researching healing diets. My animation career was hitting its peak and I also trained in martial arts. So I really needed nutritious foods to feed my mind and body.

I had also met Dr. Gene around this time, and we'd become very good friends. As a practitioner of Oriental, Functional and Natural Medicine, Dr. Gene guided me through the research process.

After many months working with Dr. Gene we ended up writing and publishing the healing diet book "A Day in The Budwig Diet," inspired by the work of Dr. Johanna Budwig, a German biochemist. But while in the process of researching and writing, *we found so many things that also related to the vegan diet.* I began to realize how many **things were often overlooked** by most of the vegan community! It was so ironic to me because veganism is usually associated with health.

Learning, for example, about the dangers of margarine, and seeing it used in many vegan cookbooks was a complete shock! The wonderful research we did, and all the things I learned, would ***forever change my outlook on the vegan diet.*** I also began to follow a vegan form of Dr. Budwig's protocol, and started to feel better than ever. My energy greatly increased, I could work much longer without getting headaches, and my overall outlook was much happier. All of these things made me reassess what I thought I knew as a vegan. And I also began to see how much valuable information there was to bring to the vegan community.

A new diet lifestyle

Researching and working with Dr. Gene brought great improvements to my health. He guided me on what foods to incorporate into my diet, what to avoid, and which supplements to take. Now up until then, I had never taken any supplements. I always wanted to be as "natural" as possible, so Dr. Gene helped me maximize my diet, and take only the supplements that I *really* needed. I was a bit reluctant to supplement at first. But there's nothing more convincing than feeling good, and my health improved greatly. I realized that a "high stress" lifestyle can deplete anyone of their health and vitality. And though "burning out" was also common for his omnivore patients, I had to be even more careful as a vegan.

This is the book I wish I had growing up!

It explains many important dietary guidelines I've learned as a lifelong vegan. Follow the principles of *The Vegan Survival Guide* and you'll be planning your ultimate vegan diet with ease. Whether or not you have the luxury of shopping at markets like Whole Foods, once you understand the nutritional strengths of foods, and how to synergize them, you can get the most out of every meal. We've also made it a point to highlight many everyday ingredients because they are so common, accessible, and affordable. ***Ironically, many of these everyday foods are actually super-foods...*** especially when you know how to unlock their nutritional potential! Half the battle is also knowing what **_not_** to eat.

Grass skiing in Brazil. ;)

If you've had any challenges growing up, you would understand... As a child I wanted so badly to be active. But my diet could not sustain me, so I often had low energy. I didn't get to play sports much, and often took medical leaves of absence instead.

There are so many dangerous chemicals, pesticides, GMO's, and even toxic oils in our foods today. While some of these hazards are more obvious, others can be quite illusive. So it's important to know how to navigate the supermarket and avoid these dangers.

But before I forget... a quick disclaimer. For me, it's not about following every single nit-picky thing in this book all the time. Let's face it... sometimes you just have to live life! **Rather,** these are just nutritional guidelines that you can apply to your life, when and where you feel they're needed. Here is an example. Most restaurants use poor quality oils in their cooking which many experts would consider toxic. *Does that mean you can never, ever eat out?* That would be unrealistic for most. Rather, when you understand the advantages of naturally produced oils, and how much healthier they are than commercial cooking oils, you can decide *how often* you want to eat out. If perhaps you've been eating out too often, you could slow down, and cook more at home for instance. If you have been eating too many oily restaurant foods, you could choose a low fat vegan option instead, and then supplement with healthy oils.

If you suffer from chronic illness for instance, it's very important to eat mostly vital nutritious foods. On the other hand, if you're a very healthy and active person, you can be a little less cautious. It's up to you to decide how you want to balance your diet. But, when you start noticing the benefits of eating high quality vital foods on a regular basis... seeing

how it affects your skin and hair... noticing how it affects your exercise endurance... your "ideal balance" may shift. Our goal is to make you aware of potential dangers, and to show you what to look for when selecting your foods. When you know more of what's happening, you can plan more effectively.

The information in this book has helped me in so many ways. I hope it can also help you improve your life, even if it's in a small way. Whether you've been a lifelong vegan, or you're just starting out, this book will give you the perfect foundation for planning your diet. Eating vegan is not always easy. There are many factors to consider for us to live and perform at an optimal level. Yet once you know what these factors are, it's actually really easy! So sit back, relax, flip through some pages, and start with any section that interests you. No need to start from the beginning. ■

The ABCs
of the VSG

2

Why Vegan Survival?

The search for a perfect book title.

We know that a complete vegan diet can give the body mostly everything that it needs... *So why did we decide to call our book The Vegan Survival Guide?*

Does the term "Vegan Survival" sound a bit alarmist to you? If so, then... awesome! :)

There was one day a few years back... I was looking through some of my friend's vegan cookbooks and I noticed something that absolutely shocked me! There was margarine in the recipe ingredients! No way!

Having been a vegan since childhood in Brazil, margarine was an everyday thing in our household. But I had just recently learned about the dangers of trans-fats in margarine, and had just eliminated them from my diet. And there I was looking at them in vegan cookbooks!

I had assumed that vegans, being the health conscious group that we tend to be, would have known not to include this in their recipes. With so many illnesses created by the modern food production, it is so important to know what you should, and shouldn't put into your body. And though we now have "margarine type products" that are made of completely natural oils, it's so important to know how to spot these dangers in the marketplace.

I also realized how common it was for people to think of vegan diets as "automatically" clean, pure, and healthy. *But this is definitely not the case!* From pesticides and genetically modified foods, to poorly regulated blood sugar and trans fats, the vegan diet is still vulnerable to many of the pitfalls that all diets can encounter.

Most importantly, any diet can be sub-optimal if we don't choose the most nutrient rich ingredients. We live in such a high-performance world that's full of stress, toxins, and processed foods. And it was during my own search for optimal health that I realized the power of food and nutrition. I saw how health practitioners were recommending certain ingredients to promote certain functions in the body, and I realized how much this could benefit the vegan community.

Ultimately, there are vegan ingredients that are "not very healthy." There are also ingredients that are basically "hazardous." There are vegan diets that are "good enough," and there are vegan diets that are highly optimal. I wanted to create a book to show you this optimal path, and guide you around these ever-present pitfalls.

Believe me, choosing the name for this book was no easy task. "The Flourishing Vegan" was super cheesy, well "vegan" cheesey I guess... and "Functional Veganism" sounded overly ambitious.

So voila! The Vegan Survival Guide, it was!

Hopefully you'll find some interesting bits of information that can help you optimize your vegan diet. ■

To Cook or Not to Cook?

The raw foods diet debate.

The raw foods diet has become a popular choice for many. Plus many of our recipes are completely raw, mostly raw, or have raw options. But there's still so much debate about the health benefits of a raw foods diet... *so what's the deal?*

Well, one thing is for sure... adding more raw foods to your diet is definitely a good thing for everyone. Higher heat cooking in general can create toxic by-products and reduce some of the nutrients in your foods. Some of the enzymes that get destroyed in cooking can also leave you with less than the optimal amount of nutrients. An example of this is the enzyme *myrosinase* in broccoli, which is required to form *sulforaphane,* a well known anti-cancer nutrient. Cooking your broccoli for too long will destroy this enzyme, and unless you add it in with another ingredient (i.e. mustard, horseradish, broccoli sprouts), you're not going to get the health benefiting effects of sulforaphane.

On the other hand, cooking can also increase certain health boosting nutrients. A great example of this is *lycopene* found in tomatoes, which is made more bioavailable by heating. Research done with long term raw foodists found that they were commonly deficient in lycopene. But other studies showed that taking watermelon juice on a regular basis was just as good as tomatoes. So if a raw foodist doesn't know to include other lycopene containing foods in their diet, they may not be getting the optimal nutrition for their body.

For some people, eating only raw foods may also be straining to their digestive system. In fact, eating raw vegetables is one of the first things that Oriental Medicine practitioners will eliminate when a patient complains of digestive issues. These are replaced with lightly steamed vegetables instead.

So the bottom line?

People who eat cooked foods:

- ☑ Don't overheat or overcook your foods too often.
- ☑ Try to cook more w/ water (steam, soups, stews)
- ☑ Incorporate more raw foods in your diet in general.
- ☑ Include more high vitamin C & B foods in your diet, especially in raw form.

People who enjoy, and feel healthy eating an all raw foods diet should be aware of some nutrients that may require extra attention. There are also certain ingredients that should be reduced or avoided on a raw foods diet.

People who only eat raw foods:

- ☑ Incorporate more lycopene rich foods and juices with ingredients like watermelon, red grapefruit, pink grapefruit, apricots, papaya, guava, and sun-dried tomatoes.
- ☑ If you eat large amounts of raw cruciferous vegetables, make sure to get enough iodine in your diet. These vegetables contain beneficial nutrients called glucosinolates. But for people who are low in iodine, these same nutients can also cause thyroid issues if eaten in large amounts.

Because so much of a raw foods diet can come from vegetables, sprouts, and legumes, here are some common foods (and their inherent toxins) to be careful of or avoid altogether.

Don't Overeat

- ☑ Raw Celery (psoralens/ furocoumarins)
- ☑ Parsnips (psoralens/ furocoumarins), peeling can reduce toxins by 30%.
- ☑ Buckwheat Greens and Sprouts (fagopyrin)
- ☑ Alfalfa Sprouts (cavanine)
- ☑ Raw Large Beans/ Sprouts (phytohaemag-glutinin): such as White Kidney Beans, Black Beans, Black Eye Peas.

Avoid!

- ☑ Raw Kidney Beans/ Sprouts (phytohaemagglutinin)
- ☑ Raw Cassava/ Yucca/ Manioca (linamarin)
- ☑ Raw Lima Beans/ Sprouts (linamarin)
- ☑ Raw (or Cooked) Green Potatoes (solanine) ■

What To Choose For Cooking Oil?

The topic of cooking oils is filled with lots of debate. There are so many options and opinions when it comes to choosing "the healthiest cooking oil," and some even advise none at all! *So what's the story?*

One thing is for sure. High heat cooking damages fatty acids, and some fats are more sensitive than others. Some oils are great for cooking, while others should never be heated. There are also oils that should be avoided all together. But any oil will produce toxins if exposed to very high temperatures. Beyond the damaged fatty acids, the foods themselves can also generate toxins when exposed to higher temperatures.

Let's face it though, most of us like to cook with heat and oil because it makes our food taste good. Fortunately, your body is designed to withstand a variety of toxins within reasonable amounts. And it's practically impossible to avoid them all. Even if you never heat anything and eat only raw foods, your body can still be exposed to naturally occurring plant toxins like *psoralens* in celery and *oxalates* in a wide variety of foods. Controlling the amount and frequency of toxin exposure is really the key.

So in terms of cooking and cooking oils, it's really up to you to see what fits your needs and lifestyle the best. The healthier you are, the more your diet will have some wiggle room to work with. But if you suffer from any chronic inflammatory conditions for example, the more you should work to reduce the toxins and damaged fatty acids that may be coming from your diet.

Because of this, we're going to talk about a wide variety of options. This way you can choose the best path for your lifestyle.

The list starts with the lowest potential for damaged fatty acids, first. So the more you want to, or need to optimize you health, **the more you should stick to the beginning of the list.** But most importantly... we will talk about the oils *that we should all definitely avoid!*

Raw Foods Diet

There's no need to talk about cooking oils if you are not going to cook at all. If you end up choosing a raw foods diet, you can get your fats from vegetables, fruits, grains, legumes, nuts, and seeds in their natural state. But even a raw foods diet is vulnerable to damaged fatty acids. Even if you never use heat, sensitive fatty acids like those found in many seeds and nuts, can also be damaged by air and light exposure. *Ever had a raw walnut that tasted a little strange? Like an oil paint kind of flavor?* That's a sign of oxidation, and you should discard them. So make sure your fatty foods don't show any signs of rancidity, and store them in the refrigerator in light sealed containers. And because of their sensitive fatty acids, it's still best to choose seeds and nuts in their raw form, even if you aren't on a raw foods diet.

Cooking With Water

Some people will choose to cook without any oil at all. In this case, cooking with water and water-based ingredients like vegetable broth, will generally be the best solution. It's a very healthy way to prepare your food, and should be used more often in general. But because healthy fats are important for the body to function optimally and absorb fat-soluble nutrients, it is still important to get fats in your diet from foods themselves. Unless you feel best on a very low fat diet, you can also add healthy oils to salads, to foods after they've been cooked, and even to soup and stew recipes once the water has already been added. This way they will not be exposed to such high heat. And even if you do cook with oil, it is still good to incorporate more steamed, boiled, and stewed recipes into your diet. This helps to minimize the amount of toxins produced from over heating oils. You can always use creative sauces and seasonings to add more flavor to your food!

Cold Pressed Oils

In terms of oils, unrefined, cold-pressed oils are the closest to nature that you can get. Having the highest nutrient value and the least potential for fatty acid damage from production, cold pressed oils can be a very healthy addition your diet. Proper cold pressing is done under temperature-controlled conditions (under 120 degrees F), and is usually reserved for very sensitive oils (i.e. flax), or for oils where flavor is key (i.e. extra virgin olive oil). Due to the fragility of these oils and the plant matter that they still contain, they should generally not be heated. Flax oil in particular should never be heated. So try these oils on a salad, or add them to a dish after it has cooled. Cold pressed oils are also more vulnerable to damage from *light and air* during storage. So be sure to keep them refrigerated in light blocking bottles. Cold pressed oils are also great for raw foodists! *But beware: S*ome companies take advantage of loopholes in US regulations by using the term "cold pressed" deceptively. They often label their products cold pressed because there is "no added heat," even when there are no temperature controls. Just the pressing process itself can result in higher temperatures.

Expeller Pressed Unrefined Oils (Lower Heat Cooking)

Expeller pressed, unrefined oils can also be a great choice. Unlike "mass market" cooking oils, which use toxic chemical solvents during oil extraction, expeller pressed oils are mechanically extracted with a machine, much like an auger juicer! These oils still retain their nutrients and original flavor, but are still vulnerable to heat damage. Though these types of oils are generally recommended for medium heat cooking, using the lowest heat possible will ensure the least damage. Also, for highly sensitive oils like flax oil, expeller pressing (without temperature control) is not ideal. Unlike coconut oil, which is naturally more resistant to heat, flax oil can be damaged by the standard expelling process.

"Optimal" basically ends here...

If you want to maximize health and minimize inflammation, try not to go beyond this point.

Expeller Pressed, Naturally Refined Oils (Higher Heat Cooking)

Many people will cringe when they hear "refined oil." And while refined oils aren't the most nutritious oils in general, they are not all created in the same way... *not even close.* The term "refined oil" makes many people think of "mass market" cooking oils, which are indeed refined. But these oils are also extracted and refined with toxic chemical processes. They are also exposed to very high heat, pressure, and have to be deodorized because of the amount of damaged caused to the oil during the process.

On the other hand, there are companies that use expellers to mechanically extract their oils. They then use gentler, natural chemicals like citric acid (as in citrus fruits) to refine their oils under low temperatures. While these refined oils are not the best for their nutrient contents, they are useful for cooking. The same plant matter that gives unrefined oil their flavor and nutrition, also make them vulnerable to higher heat cooking. Ultimately, it is best to cook with lower heat, but if you are cooking with higher heat, expeller-pressed, naturally refined oils *are the way to go!*

"Healthy" ends here...

If you suffer form any chronic inflammatory disorders and need to minimize inflammation, definitely do not go beyond this point.

- - - - - - - - - - - - - - - - - - -

Let's Choose Healthy Cooking Oils!

"Mass Market-Commercial" Chemically Extracted, Chemically Refined, High Heat, High Pressure Treated Oils

DANGER!

These are oils that should be avoided in general. On a practical level, these are very difficult to avoid if you ever eat out, *as most restaurants will use these kinds of oils.* If you use common cooking oils from a "normal" rather than a "natural foods" market, it is also more likely that you are using this kind of oil. Ultimately, even if your food is vegan, it's hard to consider it "healthy" if it is cooked with these kinds of oils. As we mentioned above, these oils are usually extracted and refined using toxic chemicals, and are subjected to high heat and high-pressure deodorization processes. In fact, researchers have found many of these oils to contain high concentrations of "trans fats" even though they have not been hydrogenated! Trans fats are fatty acids that have been altered in a way that is very unhealthy for the body. Trans fats are intentionally made with the hydrogenation process. But even just the high heat + high pressure manufacturing processes themselves can create trans fats in commercial oils. Do your best to avoid these oils as much as possible *or avoid them all together!*

Beyond this point is definitely hazardous.

This line should never be crossed, at all costs!

- -

Hydrogenated Oils & Trans Fats

EXTREME HAZARD!

These oils are made with all of the unhealthy processes used to make mass-market, commercial oils... *and worse.* The process of hydrogenation and partial hydrogenation intentionally created trans-fats so that food companies could increase the shelf life of their products. It also makes vegetable oils solid at room temperature, where they would have naturally been a liquid. Though food companies have been using these less and less over the years, there are still hydrogenated oils in many products. These oils are especially common in fast food restaurants, and in a variety of products mostly found at conventional supermarkets. In terms of vegan foods, these may include peanut butter, microwave popcorn, chips, bread, breakfast cereals, margarine, shortenings, French fries, cocoa mix, noodle soup cups, and sauce mixes. Even when these foods are vegan, they are definitely hazardous to your health. *Also,* food producers are legally allowed to say "no trans fats or 0g trans fats" as long as there is less than 0.5g in a serving. So regardless of the nutrition facts, be sure to still look at the label for any "hydrogenated" or "partially hydrogenated" oils before you buy. *Avoid these at all costs!*

Products that commonly contain hydrogenated or partially hydrogenated oils

Fortunately for vegans, most of the trans fat containing products that we found at the market also contained milk. *So vegetarians should be extra careful!* Here are the vegan products that we found to contain hydrogenated or partially hydrogenated oils at our local conventional markets.

1 **Peanut Butter:** Every peanut butter from a major manufacturer that was not a "natural version" contained hydrogenated oils.

2 **Cookies:** Including vegan peanut butter sandwich cookies, shortbreads, and graham crackers.

3 **Cereals:** Many of the kids cereals contained hydrogenated oils.

4 **Microwave Popcorn:** Many brands contained hydrogenated oils.

5 **Oils:** Including margarine and shortening "baking" sticks.

6 **Non-Dairy Coffee Creamer:** Though these also contained milk products like sodium caseinate.

All of these products that we found said "0 grams trans fats" on their nutrition facts!

Now that you know what to avoid, let's get back to the oils that you can use. If you are going to be cooking with oil, you should definitely use expeller pressed, rather than chemically extracted oil. So the only questions left are: "*What kind of expeller pressed oil? Should I get (naturally) refined, or unrefined?*"

There are so many kinds of oils, and besides a few of the more unique oils which we will discuss, the kind of oils you choose will mostly depend on 2 things:

1 The oils' heat resistance.

2 The amount of sensitive polyunsaturated fats that they contain.

If you can limit yourself to low temperature cooking, then *unrefined oils are the best choice,* as you will be getting the most nutrition from the oil itself. But with unrefined oils you will also be getting the flavor of the oils which may or may not be a good thing depending on the recipe. The flavor of coconut for example may be great for some recipes, but may taste strange in others. So if you don't mind the taste of the oil you are using, and are cooking at lower heat, use *expeller pressed unrefined oils.* You'll be getting the most nutrition and the least amount of toxins!

If you are going to cook at higher heat, *naturally refined oils* are the best choice. After all, it is better to get less nutrition from naturally refined oils, than to get toxic byproducts from over-heating an unrefined oil. These higher heat cooking oils will mainly be of two types: (plant based) saturated fats like those found in coconut oil, or oils with a high fraction of oleic acid (monounsaturated Omega 9 fatty acid). These fatty acids are the least vulnerable to oxidation and heat damage.

Oil Smoke Points

Here is a chart of smoke points for some common oils. Choose the ones that best fit your needs.

Oil Smoke Points Chart

OILS	Smoke Point Temperature
Avocado, Refined	510F
Almond Oil, Refined	495F
Apricot Kernel Oil, Refined	495F
High Oleic Sunflower Oil, Refined, High Heat Variety	460F
High Oleic Safflower Oil, Refined, High Heat Variety	460F
Canola Oil, Refined, High Heat Variety	460F
Peanut Oil, Refined	460F
Olive Oil, Refined	450F
Palm Fruit Oil, Refined	450F
Sesame, Refined	445F
Grapeseed Oil, Refined	425F
Avocado Oil, Unrefined	390F
Coconut Oil, Refined	365F
Sesame Oil, Unrefined	350F
Peanut Oil, Unrefined	350F
Coconut Oil, Unrefined	280F
Extra Virgin Olive Oil, High Quality	200–325F

Many of these oils can also be found **in organic form.**

Note: Because of the way each oil is refined, and the breed of the actual crop tested, smoke point lists are far from exact. Keeping your cooking temperatures *well under these values* will keep you in the clear. When in doubt, lower the temperature, or call the manufacturer and ask for the smoke point of their particular oil.

Did you know?

Canola Oil...

Canola oil is at high risk for being a GMO product. Organic canola oil on the other hand comes from a breed of rapeseed that has been hybridized (natural breeding) to produce an edible product. Though organic canola oil is acceptable, there are many other oils that are we prefer over canola.

Sunflower and Safflower Oils...

"High Oleic" and "High Heat" versions of sunflower and safflower oils come from a special breed of these plants. These have been naturally bred to produce an oil that's higher in monounsaturated fatty acids which are less sensitive to heat. "High Linoleic" versions of these oils on the other hand, are higher in sensitive polyunsaturated fatty acids. These should be cold pressed, never heated, and should be treated like flax oil.

Coconut Oil and Palm Fruit Oils...

Coconut Oil and Palm Fruit Oils are two common sources of plant based saturated fats. Unlike animal based saturated fats (long chain), these plant based versions are of the short and medium chain variety. Research is showing that they are metabolized differently and can be a very healthy addition your diet. Being a saturated fat also means that they are less prone to oxidative damage. "Palm Kernel Oil" on the other hand can only be extracted with chemical methods and should be avoided.

Laser Gun?

 Get a *laser thermometer gun* at your local hardware store. It's an easy and effective way to keep your cooking temperature under control, based on the oil that you are using.

Oils That You Should *Never Heat*

✓ Flax Oil
✓ Borage Oil
✓ Evening Primrose Oil
✓ Wheat Germ Oil
✓ Pumpkin Seed Oil
✓ High Linolenic Sunflower Oil
✓ High Linolenic Safflower Oil

Using flax oil is a great way to get the ideal Omega 3:6 ratio in your diet, which is about 1:1. Oils like borage and evening primrose are also a great source of anti-inflammatory "gamma-linolenicacid" (GLA).

Still Not Sure What To Choose?

There is so much information about oils... *but which ones do we choose?* Based on health and practicality (cost and availability) we would generally recommend: **Coconut Oil, High Oleic (high heat) Sunflower, High Oleic (high heat) Safflower Oil, and Sesame Oil.**

Coconut oil is a unique source of immune supporting lauric acid. And being that it's a healthy form of saturated fat (medium chain), it is also less prone to oxidation from heat. Coconut oil and high oleic oils are especially low in polyunsaturated fats, which are the most prone to heat damage. These polyunsaturated fats (like Omega 3 and 6) should come from raw foods, or unheated cold pressed oils to ensure minimum fatty acid damage. **Sesame oil** is also unique in that it contains heat-activated anti-oxidants called "sesamin" and "sesamol."

Now if cost and availability are less of an issue, **avocado oil and almond oil** are some of the best choices due to their high heat resistance. As you can see, these two oils top the list in terms of heat resistance and are the best choice for high heat cooking. Olive oil can also be a good choice for cooking, but it is important to choose lighter color versions (more refined), rather than extra virgin olive oils, which are easily damaged by heat. Extra virgin olive oils are best on salads, or can be added after cooking.

And don't forget... moderation is key with cooking oils. Choose naturally (not chemically) refined oils for higher heat cooking, stay well below the oil's smoke point, and when in doubt, reduce the heat. ■

Sweet and Savory

Choose Your Flavors Wisely

Sweeteners

Much like cooking oils, there are many choices of sweeteners available today. *But which ones are best? Are they all vegan?*

Two things are for sure. Eating too much of any sweetener is not a good idea. Reducing added sugars in your diet is a great idea. But nevertheless, certain sweeteners are richer in nutrients, while others may be gentler on your blood sugar. There are also those that are trickier to understand, while some should be avoided altogether.

Though some sweeteners can be exceptional sources of certain nutrients, especially minerals, they still come with a lot of sugar. So ultimately, nothing beats moderation when it comes to sweeteners. But since we tend to choose sweeteners based on health vs. taste and function, here are some things to consider.

Nutrient Rich Sweeteners

Blackstrap Molasses:

Exceptionally great source of selenium. Great source of potassium, magnesium, manganese, and vitamin B5. Good source of iron, calcium and vitamin B6.

Maple Syrup:

Great source of zinc and selenium, anti-oxidants, and anti-inflammatory compounds. Make sure to use 100% maple syrup, as others can contain high fructose corn syrup.

Coconut Palm Sugar:

Good source of potassium, zinc, and magnesium. Of all these sweeteners, coconut palm sugar may be the best for blood sugar control. Though it is often approved for people with diabetes, it should still be used with caution.

Brown Rice Syrup:

Best avoided by children and pregnant women as it can contain arsenic taken up from the soil.

Barley Malt Syrup:

May contain traces of gluten.

Natural Low and No Calorie Sweeteners

Stevia:

How "natural" this sweetener is, will depend on the brand, its manufacturing process, and any additives that may be included. Stevia is one of the best sugar substitutes, but make sure to look for whole leaf and water extracted stevia products.

Monkfruit / Lo Han:

Like stevia, monkfruit sweeteners can be processed in different ways and can also contain additives. Fortunately, some of the most common brands use natural water extraction to create their product. The sweetening compounds in monkfruit are also said to have anti-oxidant effects.

Yacon Syrup:

This sweetener is usually created with natural processes. Though it is not a zero calorie sweetener, its "fructo-oligosaccharides" (FOS) have little effect on blood sugar. And unlike fructose, it passes through the body undigested and has little effect on blood triglycerides. FOS also feeds the friendly bacteria in your body!

Xylitol:

High risk of GMO if made from corn, and is highly processed in general. Eating too much can cause digestive distress, but is no problem in smaller amounts. If you use xylitol, look for it in non-GMO form and keep away from pets (toxic for dogs and other animals).

Erythritol:

High risk of GMO if made from corn, and is highly processed in general. Erythritol is also gentler than xylitol on the digestive system for most people. Make sure to get it in non-GMO form.

These sweeteners have little to no effect on blood sugar or calorie intake. But be careful of additives, and when in doubt, contact the manufacturers to ask about their manufacturing processes. Some people may also be sensitive to some of these sweeteners, especially xylitol and erythritol, so be sure to use them with caution. Taste can also vary between brands, so try a few to see which ones you like best. You can also combine these with sugar-based sweeteners for reduced calories and better taste. If you use these low calorie sweeteners in general, try rotating or blending them so your body doesn't get overloaded with any one particular compound.

Fructose Rich Sweeteners

Agave:

Exceptionally great source of calcium. Because agave has a very high percentage of fructose, it has the lowest impact on blood sugar, but the biggest impact on the body via fructose metabolism.

Dates:

Exceptionally great source of potassium. Great source of calcium, magnesium, manganese, vitamin B6 and vitamin B3. Also a good source of fiber, which can also help to balance blood sugar.

Sweet Fruit Juices:

Can be a good source of nutrients and polyphenols depending on the type of juice being used. Like all fruits and fruit juices, its impact on blood sugar will depend on the percentage of fructose it contains.

These sweeteners tend to be very natural, but can also be a bit deceptive. Because of their higher fructose content, they can have a lower impact on blood sugar because of how fructose is metabolized. This is why agave is often approved for people with diabetes. But, fructose can potentially cause things like fatty liver, elevated blood triglycerides, and insulin resistance, when eaten in excess. *Because of this, moderation is key.*

Good Old Sugar

Unrefined Brown Cane Sugars
(Sucanat, Turbinado, Muscovado, Demera)

Raw Cane Sugar

Refined Vegan White Sugar

Refined Vegan Powdered Sugar

These sweeteners all have relatively little to no nutrient value and will also raise blood sugars quickly. However, darker sugars will have more minerals than lighter sugars in general.

Not Always Vegan

Though there are now vegan producers, refined sugars are often processed with cow bone char so they generally aren't vegan. Be sure to look on the package to make sure.

Refined Sugar:
High risk of being a GMO product from sugar beets. Buy vegan organic.

Powdered Sugar:
High risk for being a GMO product from sugar beets and cornstarch. Buy vegan organic.

Brown Sugar:
Can also be at risk of being a GMO product from sugar beets. Also can be processed with bone char. Buy vegan organic.

Danger!

High Fructose Corn Syrup:
High risk for being a GMO product, and could contain traces of mercury from the manufacturing process. Corn syrup has shown to induce weight gain beyond the calories that it provides, and at a much greater rate than standard sugar.

Sucralose:
Artificial sweetener with the potential to cause anemia, male infertility, and kidney damage.

Aspartame:
Artificial sweetener implicated in a wide range of disorders including fibromyalgia, hypertension, migraine headaches, and other brain disorders.

These sweeteners can cause a wide variety of health issues over time. It is best to eliminate them from your diet completely!

There are so many choices when it comes to sweeteners. Maple syrup, molasses, and dates stand out because they are rich in nutrients and are widely available. But for those who need to control their blood sugar very carefully, stevia, monk fruit, and yacon syrup will be best. If you want a balance of blood sugar control, nutrients, and taste, coconut palm sugar also makes a great choice. So give some of these a try to see which ones you like best!

Salt

Salt is often the last thing that comes to mind when talking about a vegan diet. After all, beyond the fact that salt mines and ocean water will have some traces of animal particles, all salt is basically vegan. *So why does it matter?*

Well just like everything else in food, there is high quality and low quality salt. And what you choose will have an impact on your health. For decades, refined and iodized salt has been the norm. But more and more, we are now seeing artisan salts, even on the shelves of conventional markets! Products like Celtic Sea Salt, Himalayan Pink Salt, and Real Salt have become increasingly popular. *Is this just a fad? Or should we all be switching to these kinds of salts?*

Here's something to consider. Researchers have tested these salts for their mineral content in comparison to normal refined salt. *The results are rather shocking!* Refined salt contained little to no beneficial minerals and contains various anti-caking conditioning agents. This kind of salt is also processed with toxic chemicals and has altered molecular structures from the high heat, high pressure refining process.

Because of these things, it's also better to get your iodine from food sources other than refined iodized salts. Anything labeled "sea salt" can also be highly refined in many cases. So if you do use a certain brand of sea salt, make sure it is unrefined and mineral rich.

On the other hand, the unrefined artisan salts were found to contain up to 80 different trace minerals! From pH balance to a wide variety of bodily functions, we all know how important minerals are for supporting optimal health. And because these salts are naturally produced, you are getting salt that is as close to nature as possible.

So the quality of the salt we take in is just as important as the amount of salt. And because vegan athletes have to pay more attention to their salt intake, this is even more important for them. Though artisan salts may be a bit pricier than conventional salt, you only use a little at a time. So the extra dollars will go a long way! *So if you haven't already, start phasing conventional salt out of your life. Your body will thank you for it.* ∎

Known and Lesser Known Dangers

Being the health conscious people that vegans often are, you may have already reduced or eliminated these ingredients on our "vegan foods to avoid" list. *But a survival guide just wouldn't be complete without it! So here we go!*

Bisphenol-A

Also known as BPA, Bisphenol-A is a chemical that is often found in cans and plastic bottles. This substance leeches especially into foods that are acidic, or high in fat, and can disrupt the hormone system. Things like tomato products and coconut milk are especially vulnerable. If using canned products, look for "BPA Free" cans. Glass jars and paper cartons are a better choice whenever available.

Microwave Popcorn

Microwave popcorn is a double whammy. Not only do many brands of microwave popcorn contain hydrogenated oils, but the paper bags are also lined with chemicals that include "perfluorooctanoic acid" (PFOA). Though it's meant to prevent oil from seeping through the bag, this chemical can also leach into your food. PFOA has been shown to disrupt the hormone system, and has also been implicated in a wide range of serious diseases. So make sure to prepare your popcorn the old fashion way with some healthy oil in a pan. *You'll be glad you did!*

Free Glutamates

We've all heard of "monosodium glutamate" (MSG) and how unhealthy it can be. Many people are already aware of this ingredient, *but there may be more to this story.* The problem with MSG is related to a substance called "free glutamate." Unlike glutamate that is found in protein (bound glutamate), free glutamate is metabolized very quickly by the body. Many researchers have found it to be toxic to the brain and nervous system in high concentrations (i.e. MSG). But many are now looking into the presence of free glutamates in a variety of "natural ingredients" and have sounded the alarm about this potential health issue. In many cases, these "natural ingredients" are basically used as "natural MSG substitutes," adding flavor to food products.

Common Natural Flavor Enhancers & MSG Substitutes

☑ Yeast Extract
☑ Autolyzed Yeast
☑ Brewer's Yeast
☑ Nutritional Yeast

Common Free Glutamate Containing Ingredients

☑ Textured Protein
☑ Hydrolyzed Vegetable Protein
☑ Soy Protein
☑ Soy Protein Concentrate
☑ Soy Protein Isolate

Now to be clear, free glutamates do occur in whole vegan foods, like tomatoes for example. And one popular company that produces vegan meat substitutes (with autolyzed yeast and textured protein) publicly stated that their products contain no more free glutamate than other whole foods, based on their lab tests.

All in all, the problem is likely the amount and concentration of the free glutamate being eaten, relative to the rest of the food. MSG itself can be 80-100% free glutamates, while an ingredient like autolyzed yeast is usually 5-10% free glutamates.

The danger lies in the amount being used. If a company for example, uses 10 times more autolyzed yeast than they would MSG to achieve a strong flavor, then you still have a similar problem. Since the ingredients don't tell you how much is added, it is very difficult to know. This same thing is also possible if you sprinkle a huge amount of nutritional yeast on your popcorn.

So the key here is to be aware of the potential dangers. If you want to be extra safe, or find yourself to be sensitive to free glutamates, you can avoid these ingredients all together. But overall, it may be best to reduce them in your diet. If you find one of these ingredients in a product that you absolutely love, you can always contact the company and see if they have measured the free glutamates in that product. *As clients and consumers, we have the power! If enough of us ask for these tests, then they are likely to do one eventually!*

GMO Foods Lists

As if it wasn't enough to deal with pesticides and chemicals in food packaging! Now we have to be careful of genetically modified ingredients as well! These artificially manipulated crops have been shown to cause a huge variety of illnesses and health damaging effects. This ranges from infertility, immune disorders, and accelerated aging... all the way to major mutations in various organs and the digestive system! These may be especially problematic for pregnant mothers and small children. We must definitely avoid these at all costs, and support initiatives that work to identify and protect consumers from these crops.

Potential Risk GMO Crops

- ☑ Acorn Squash
- ☑ Bok Choy
- ☑ Chard
- ☑ Delicata Squash
- ☑ Flax
- ☑ Garden Beet
- ☑ Mizuna
- ☑ Napa Cabbage
- ☑ Patty Pan
- ☑ Rapini
- ☑ Rice
- ☑ Rutabaga
- ☑ Siberian Kale
- ☑ Tatsoi
- ☑ Turnip
- ☑ Wheat

Support The Non GMO Project:
http://www.nongmoproject.org

High Risk GMO Crops

EXTREME HAZARD!

- ☑ Alfalfa
- ☑ Canola
- ☑ Corn
- ☑ Cotton
- ☑ Papaya
- ☑ Soy
- ☑ Sugar Beets
- ☑ Zucchini
- ☑ Yellow Summer Squash

Pesticides

Dangerous pesticides are often used to grow conventional crops. Yet, some crops carry more pesticide residues than others. While some foods can be purchased in conventional form, there are many that you should only eat in their organic form. Follow this list to reduce your pesticide exposure. ■

	Dirty Dozen Plus™			Clean Fifteen™
1	Apples		1	Onions
2	Celery		2	Sweet Corn
3	Sweet bell pepper		3	Pineapples
4	Peaches		4	Avocado
5	Strawberries		5	Cabbage
6	Nectarines (imported)		6	Sweet peas
7	Grapes		7	Asparagus
8	Spinach		8	Mangoes
9	Lettuce		9	Eggplant
10	Cucumbers		10	Kiwi
11	Blueberries (domestic)		11	Cantaloupe (domestic)
12	Potatoes		12	Sweet potatoes
+	Green Beans		13	Grapefruit
+	Kale/ Greens		14	Watermelon
			15	Mushrooms

+ May contain pesticide residue of special concern

Dirty Dozen Plus and Clean Fifteen are registered trademarks of the *Environmental Working Group* and are updated annually. Support them at *www.ewg.org*.

Nutrient Focused

Maximizing Vegan Nutrition

All people, vegan or not, can become deficient in certain nutrients depending on their diet. And a well-designed vegan diet can give your body nearly everything it needs. But unfortunately, there are many factors in modern day life that are far from naturally optimal. Some may be able to live a more natural and balanced lifestyle all the time. But for many, even things like gardening, walking in nature, and making optimally nutritious meals have to be squeezed into already busy schedules.

As modern humans we also tend to spend a lot of time indoors, away from the sun. Many will find themselves sitting on computers and pushing their brains to the max for long periods of time. And if that wasn't enough already, the soil that produces many of our crops can also be low in beneficial micro-organisms and the vitamins that they produce.

But just like plants, us vegans are highly adaptable! In order to keep our bodies in tip-top shape, there are some tips and tricks that we should all know. It's important to keep track of how your body is doing, and there are also times when supplementation may be best. *So here are some nutrients that we should all pay attention to.*

Vitamin B12

Most vegans know about the importance of vitamin B12. This vitamin is crucial for a healthy brain, nervous system, and cardiovascular system. Yet in the vegan diet debate, it's often known as the vitamin that "isn't provided by plant foods." But as you'll see, there's definitely more to this story.

Researchers have found that plants can indeed be a source of B12. Organic crops were also found to contain more B12 than their conventional counterparts. This is largely due to the healthy presence of micro-organisms in organically fertilized soil. These produce the B vitamins for the crops to absorb.

Unfortunately, not all crops are grown in super optimized soil and it's hard to know how much B12 these "super-organic" crops could even provide. We also know that plant sources can have reduced bioavailability because of "B12 analogs" like methylmalonic acid found in seaweed. Researchers have also shown that B12 produced by gut bacteria is mostly eliminated, rather than absorbed by the body. So probiotics are good for the body, but not so much for your B12 status. Because of all these things, it's good to supplement with B12 on a regular basis.

One of the best forms of B12 to take is in the form of "methylcobalamin." About 1000 mcg per day taken sublingually will be enough to get most people out of vitamin B12 deficiency.

The best way to optimize B12 levels is to get your levels tested. Though serum B12 tests can be useful, there is now a test called the "methylmalonic acid" (MMA) test which is even more precise. *Getting tested will help you bring your B12 levels into the optimal range!*

Vitamin D

From calcium absorption and immune function, to cancer prevention and muscle health, vitamin D is getting more attention than ever before. And unlike vitamin B12, there are non-supplement ways to get your optimal dose of vitamin D!

Because your body can produce its own vitamin D, the easiest way to increase your levels is by getting regular exposure to the sun! But be careful, because this will depend on where you live, the time of day, and your skin tone. With full direct exposure to overhead sunlight, a lighter skin person will only need about 10-15 minutes over large areas of skin. A darker skin person on the other hand may need up to an hour of sun. But remember not to over-expose your skin to prevent burning. You can always space out your sun-bathing sessions if necessary.

But what if there's not much sun in my area? Can I just expose my food to the sun to get some vitamin D?

As crazy as this may sound, you can actually do this with mushrooms! Researchers have found that fresh mushrooms produce huge amounts of vitamin D when exposed to sunlight. To give you an idea of how much vitamin D was produced, just a handful of fresh shiitake mushrooms (100g) created over 45,000 i.u. of vitamin D with just 12 hours of sunlight! And shiitake mushrooms aren't the only ones. You can do this with a wide variety of mushrooms, even common button mushrooms, making this a very practical solution.

How to Make Vitamin D Rich Mushrooms:

1. Slice your fresh mushrooms into thin slices.

2. Spread them over a tray or screen, and expose them to direct sunlight for 6 hours (10 am to 4 pm is optimal).

3. Put them back in the refrigerator in the evening, and repeat the process the next day.

4. Then you can use them immediately or finish drying them in a food dehydrator and store for up to a year.

So boost your vitamin D levels by adding a handful of sun-dried mushrooms to your next meal. A conservative daily dosage for vitamin D is about 1500 i.u. per day. So even just a few slices will give you the vitamin D you need!

Regardless of the methods you choose, the best way to optimize your vitamin D levels is to get your levels tested. Then you can use sunlight, sun-dried mushrooms, or vitamin D supplements to bring your levels in range.

Iodine

From supporting thyroid health to proper immune function, iodine is an important nutrient that can't be overlooked. And though it is important for health in general, there are many reasons to make sure that you're getting enough. Iodine is especially important if you eat a lot of raw cruciferous vegetables, as these can cause thyroid dysfunction in people with low iodine. Bromine compounds are another reason to optimize your iodine intake. From *methyl bromide* pesticides on conventional strawberries, to *potassium bromate* in baked goods, bromine containing substances can reduce iodine uptake in the thyroid.

But much like vitamin D, you don't have to take supplements to get your daily dose of iodine. *Luckily for us, many of the richest iodine sources are vegan!* From seaweed and navy beans, to cranberries and strawberries, iodine can be found in a variety of vegan foods. You just need to know what these foods are so you can include them in your diet. *Use the following charts to get your dose of daily iodine!*

Kelp and other sea vegetables are one of the richest sources of Iodine

Iodine Rich Sea Vegetables

☑ 1g Kombu Kelp (2700 mcg)
☑ 1g Arame (540 mcg)
☑ 1g Wakame (250 mcg)
☑ 1g Dulse (100 mcg)
☑ 1g Nori/ Laver Seaweed (20 mcg)

Hiziki should be avoided as it may contain high levels of arsenic.

Other Iodine Rich Foods

☑ 1 cup Cranberries (400 mcg)
☑ 1 medium Potato with Skin (60 mcg)
☑ 1/2 cup Navy Beans (32 mcg)
☑ 1/2 cup Corn (14 mcg)
☑ 1 cup Strawberries (13 mcg)
☑ 5 Prunes (13 mcg)

While iodized salt is an option, it may be better to use higher quality salts for their other mineral contents. Just make sure to get your iodine from other sources.

Your daily iodine should be a minimum of at least 150 mcg. Up to even 800 mcg per day is still very safe. **But be careful, too much iodine over long periods can cause thyroid dysfunction.**

DHA Omega 3's

Though vegan diets should prioritize omega 3 fatty acids, these will generally come from ALA rich foods like flax, walnuts, and chia seeds. DHA and EPA omega 3's on the other hand have generally been associated with fish and fish oil. Though your body can convert some of the ALA from plants into DHA and EPA, it can still be beneficial to add some through supplementation, especially DHA. Fortunately we don't have to get it from fish oil because algae makes it too! *In fact, these can be even better than fish oil because they are highly sustainable, and are at lower risk for containing pollutants!*

DHA omega 3's can help to optimize your health in so many ways. It's important for cancer prevention, anti-inflammation, brain function, memory, and can even improve the brain's response to stressful events! This form of omega 3 is also important for people who are battling depression. EPA on the other hand, while beneficial, may not be as beneficial as DHA. In terms of the vegan forms of these supplements, you can get DHA and EPA together, or DHA alone. Either one is ok, but DHA is really the priority. If you choose to supplement with vegan DHA in your diet, 200-600 mg per day is a good target zone. Make sure to also keep these oils in the refrigerator to prevent rancidity. And don't forget... it is still important to get your plant based omega 3's.

DHA (Docosahexaenoic Acid)
EPA (Eicosapentaenoic Acid)

Long-chain Omega 3 fatty acids.

☑ Supplements made from Algae

ALA (Alpha-Linolenic Acid)

Short-chain Omega 3 Fatty Acid in a variety of vegan foods.

☑ Chia Seed Oil   ☑ Hempseed Oil
☑ Chia Seeds   ☑ Hempseeds
☑ Flax Oil   ☑ Walnut Oil
☑ Flax Seeds   ☑ Walnuts
☑ Hemp Milk

Prepare To Be Nourished

There are also nutrients that can be optimized by choosing certain foods on a regular basis. Minerals like calcium, zinc, and iron are often considered the "weaker" links in the vegan diet. But unlike vitamin B12, these are more about the foods you choose, and how you prepare them. Plant foods often contain substances like "phytates" and "oxalates" that can prevent the bioavailability of these minerals. Fortunately there are some things you can do to minimize these substances in your diet.

Choose calcium, zinc, and iron rich foods on a regular basis, and prepare them to reduce anti-nutrients.

Calcium vs. Oxalates:

Here are some calcium rich foods that you should include in your diet on a regular basis. But to reduce the calcium blocking oxalates in these foods, you can boil them in water for 1 minute, drain the water, and continue using as you would normally. This will help to reduce the oxalates while maintaining maximum nutrition.

Calcium Rich Foods

- ☑ Beet Greens
- ☑ Cellery
- ☑ Collards
- ☑ Dandelion Greens
- ☑ Kale
- ☑ Okra
- ☑ Spinach
- ☑ Swiss Chard

Minerals vs. Phytates:

These are some zinc and iron rich foods that should be included in your diet on a regular basis. But to minimize the mineral reducing phytates in these foods, you can soak them for 24 hours before cooking as you normally would. Be sure to change the water at least once during soaking. For even more phytate reduction, let them germinate for 3-5 days before cooking.

Mineral Rich Foods

- ☑ Adzuki Beans
- ☑ Black Beans
- ☑ Garbanzos
- ☑ Kidney Beans
- ☑ Lentils
- ☑ Mung Beans
- ☑ Pinto Beans
- ☑ Quinoa

All of these mineral rich grains and legumes can also be combined with the vitamin C rich foods on the next page to increase their iron bioavailability.

Did you Know?

Tempeh is another great source of bioavailable minerals because the process of fermentation also reduces phytates significantly.

Iron + Vitamin C

Vitamin C increases the absorption of iron from plant sources. Here is a list of some iron rich foods vs. vitamin C rich foods. Try combining some of these wonderful ingredients to get the most from your meals!

Iron Rich Foods

- ☑ Asparagus
- ☑ Barley
- ☑ Beet Greens
- ☑ Cashews
- ☑ Collard Greens
- ☑ Granola
- ☑ Oats/ Oatmeal
- ☑ Pine Nuts
- ☑ Pumpkin Seeds
- ☑ Spinach
- ☑ Sunflower Seeds
- ☑ Swiss Chard
- ☑ Tempeh
- ☑ Tofu
- ☑ Wheat Germ

tip Women experiencing heavy menstrual bleeding should consider iron supplementation. Getting your iron levels tested can help you adjust accordingly.

Vitamin C Rich Foods

Try to minimize cooking of these ingredients, or eat them raw for maximum vitamin C content.

- ☑ Bell Pepper
- ☑ Broccoli
- ☑ Cantaloupe
- ☑ Cauliflower
- ☑ Grapefruit
- ☑ Guava
- ☑ Kiwi
- ☑ Lemon
- ☑ Lime
- ☑ Mangos
- ☑ Oranges
- ☑ Papaya
- ☑ Pineapple
- ☑ Raspberries
- ☑ Strawberries
- ☑ Tangerines

Tailored to Your Needs

We designed the VSG recipes with a fine balance of health consciousness *and* deliciousness in mind. After all, what good is a cookbook if the recipes don't taste amazing? :) Because of this, we chose to explain each recipe like a "normal" cookbook, with "normal" cooking techniques.

Yet, there are many things that can be done to optimize each recipe, even beyond the VSG functions. For example, if the instructions say to "sauté on medium-high heat" you can always sauté on a lower heat to ensure the lowest amount of toxins generated by cooking. If a recipe says to simmer for 45 minutes, you can always reduce to 10 minutes to retain more nutrients. Cooking for longer can make the recipes taste better, *but reducing the cooking time will get you the most nutrients possible!*

And because each person is unique, with different sets of dietary needs, we wanted our recipes to be adaptable. Because of this, you will find options for gluten free, soy free, and raw variations if the recipe isn't like that already. We also included small amounts of maple syrup in some of our recipes for balance of flavor. We chose this sweetener because it's widely available and contains many beneficial nutrients. But if you want to eliminate added sugars in your diet, you can always omit it, or use one of the many natural no-calorie sweeteners instead.

In terms of the cooking oils, we often sauté with coconut oil because it contains the least polyunsaturated fats, which are easily damaged by heat. But feel free to use the oils that best fit your needs. Those who like to cook without oil can also omit it, and cook their food dry or with water instead.

tip *For those who choose a very low fat diet, many of our recipes can be made this way just by eliminating the cooking oil.*

Overall, there are many little adjustments you can make to tailor these recipes to your needs. *So be sure to look at some of our recipe variations, and choose the ingredients that best compliment your diet!* ∎

The VSG Formula

Functional Veganism is a method of creating recipes with special functions. Using ingredients that maximize certain nutrients, you can make every meal support your mind and body, so you can always feel your best!

Our modern lifestyles can demand so much from the body and mind. Multitasking to the max, exposure to toxins, and even a lack of sun exposure... the human body is facing a whole new set of challenges that it has never seen before. The days of waking up with the sun, working on the land, and eating foods that were naturally organic are things of the past for most people. Even whole and unprocessed foods can be lower in nutrients when grown in depleted soil.

All these things put immense stress on our bodies. In modern day society, we must take great care of ourselves to live at our best and prevent ourselves from burning out.

The human body is an ecosystem of biochemical reactions. The foods that you eat are crucial to how well your body functions, and ultimately how good you feel. Your brain for instance requires certain amino acids, B-vitamins, and minerals to produce neurotransmitters, keeping you motivated, happy, and sharp.

Health practitioners often use nutrients in higher "therapeutic doses" to help the body recover from illness. These nutrients can also be used in specific combinations to create a synergistic effect in the body. But while supplementation can be an important aspect of health, we can't forget about the foundation... **_food!_**

The VSG formula shows you how to get the highest amount of the right nutrients in specific combinations. This helps you fine-tune your meals to support your mind and body in the ways that you need. From boosting the brain, to detoxifying the body, the VSG covers the most important aspects of our health. *And let's not forget, we also have to nourish the soul with some tasty treats!*

What's better than supporting your health with tasty foods that you can eat everyday? The road to optimal health should be fun and enjoyable. The VSG will show you how. :)

How to Navigate the VSG

All of the recipes contained in the book have been "pre-optimized" for each of the VSG functions. When we first started designing these recipes, we looked at each ingredient separately, and chose them for their maximum nutrient contents. But after weeks of painstakingly comparing one ingredient to another, we realized the huge need to compile all of this information in one place.

So in the last section of the book, you will find our lists of all common vegan ingredients, ranked by their nutrient contents. You will also find detailed charts for each of the VSG formulas and functions.

These took us weeks to create, and you'll have them all in one book, right at your fingertips!

You can *create your own* mind-body optimized meals and let your creativity run wild! You'll also be able to check your favorite recipes to see if they are fully optimized. You may find that your favorite recipe is great for a particular function! Or it may just need an additional ingredient to give it everything that you need! As we like to say, "The VSG is like GPS for your vegan diet!" So check out some of our recipes, take a look at the charts in the back, and most importantly... Enjoy! ∎

VSG RECIPES

3

VEGAN SURVIVAL: Brain

Feed your Mind...

Many of the best brain boosters
are already in your kitchen!
We'll show you some of the
wonderful possibilities!

From pumpkin seed pesto and
chocolate pancakes, to our tasty
vegan gumbo, boosting your brain
has never been so delicious!

Let's get started!

VSG: Brain

A healthy brain helps us mentally, emotionally, *and* physically.

Optimal brain function is crucial to healthy living. The brain and nervous system control everything in the body, acting like the master computer. But most importantly, it can affect the way you feel, your behavior, and even your outlook on life. This section of the VSG is divided into four parts, one for each of the four primary brain chemicals, also known as neurotransmitters. Though all of these brain chemicals are important, each person's brain is unique. Because of this, some may benefit from supporting one brain chemical more than another.

So which ones apply to you?
Read more below to find out.

The four main neurotransmitters are: Dopamine, Serotonin, Acetylcholine, and GABA.

Dopamine: Controls things like energy and alertness, mental focus and responsiveness, planning and goal setting, and libido. Imbalance of dopamine can result in low energy, mental sluggishness, lack of motivation, lack of focus, and low libido.

Serotonin: Regulates things like emotional wellness, rest and regeneration cycles, and appetite control. Imbalance of serotonin can result in irregular sleep cycles, addictive tendencies, and emotional instability.

Acetylcholine: Regulates things like sensory input (smell, sight, touch etc...), memory, learning, and creativity. Imbalance can lead to forgetfulness, diminished creativity and diminished sensory sensitivity.

GABA: Regulates things like consistency, dependability, and sociability. Imbalance can lead to anxiety and nervousness.

Brain Boosting Nutrients + Foods

Here are some foods that support your brain. Make sure you get them all!

Staying sharp has never been so easy! The top Overall Brain Boosters include: **Chickpeas, Pumpkin Seeds, Oats and Wheat Germ.** ■

Top Overall Brain Boosters for all 4 neuro transmitters include: Chickpeas, Pumpkin Seeds, Oats and Wheat Germ

Examples of some top foods in this category:

Dopamine:
Tyrosine + B6 + Folate + Vitamin C + Iron + Zinc

Tofu, Tempeh, Peanuts, Spelt, Adzuki Beans, Lentils, Split Peas

---

Serotonin:
Tryptophan + B6 + Magnesium + Zinc + Calcium

Tofu, Tempeh, Sunflower Seeds, Sesame Seeds, Quinoa, Pinto Beans, Kidney Beans

---

Acetylcholine:
Choline + B1 + B5 + Manganese

Broccoli, Brussels Sprouts, Collard Greens, Swiss Chard, Cauliflower, Artichokes

---

GABA:
Glutamic Acid + Inositol + B1 + B3 + B6

Tofu, Tempeh, Almonds, Split Peas, Lentils, Adzuki Beans, Millet

Sesame Noodles

SERVES: **4** PREP TIME: **25 MIN**

Ingredients:

Sauce:
- ¼ cup **tahini,** raw if available*
- 4 teaspoons **water**
- ¼ cup **rice wine vinegar**
- ¼ cup **soy sauce**
- 4 teaspoons **dark sesame oil**
- ½ teaspoon **real maple syrup**
- 1 teaspoon **salt**
- 2 teaspoons **chili paste with garlic** (Sambal Oelek = Sirracha's cousin)**
- 4 **garlic cloves,** crushed
- ½ teaspoon **white pepper**

Noodles:
- 8 ounces **thin udon noodles,** or Chinese wheat noodles***
- 1 cup **edamame,** shelled and frozen
- 1 cup **cucumber,** grated into noodle-like strips
- 1 cup **carrots,** grated into noodle-like strips
- ½ cup **green onion,** thinly sliced
- ⅓ cup **fresh cilantro,** chopped
- ¼ teaspoon **salt**

Directions:

1. Prepare the sauce by thoroughly mixing all the sauce ingredients in a medium bowl. Set aside.

2. In a large pot, boil edamame for 4-6 min or until tender. Remove from water, set aside, and save the water to cook noodles.

3. In a large mixing bowl, add grated cucumbers, grated carrots, green onion, edamame, and cilantro. Mix and set aside.

4. Cook noodles according to packaging. When ready, rinse very briefly in cool water, drain thoroughly, and combine with the rest of the vegetables in the large mixing bowl.

5. Combine all ingredients with sauce (to taste) and mix thoroughly. Serve alone or as a main dish.

If you can't find raw tahini, normal tahini from roasted sesame seeds is also ok because it contains heat activated anti-oxidants (known as sesamin and sesamol).

"Sambal Oelek" is the lesser known cousin of "Sirracha" hot sauce. You can find it online or at your local asian market (right next to its famous cousin!)

*** Many types of noodles can be used. If you want the exact one used in this recipe, do a Google search for "Eden Organic Kamut Udon Pasta."*

see recipe

Healthy **Brain**, Healthy **Body**

Carrots are a great source of vitamin B6. Your body uses this vitamin to produce a variety of brain chemicals including dopamine.

Carrots are also rich in anti-cancer "polyacetylenes" including "falcarinol." Studies have demonstrated the ability of this phytonutrient to inhibit the growth of cancer cells in the colon.

Edamame: Focused and Motivated

Edamame is a rich vegan source of the amino acid tyrosine. This is the building block of dopamine, a brain chemical that helps us withstand stress, keeps us motivated, and focused. *It's also packed with complete protein to keep you going through your day!*

Variations

Gluten Free: Replace wheat noodles with gluten free buckwheat noodles. Use gluten free tamari.

Soy Free: Substitute soy sauce with coconut aminos. Replace edamame with your favorite sprouted legume. Sprouted mung beans, lentils, or garbanzo are a great choice.

Raw: Omit chili paste. Substitute wheat noodles with zucchini grated into noodle-like strips. Use coconut aminos (raw) or unpasteurized soy sauce (Nama Shoyu) and unpasteurized vinegar. Replace edamame with your favorite sprouted legume. Use raw agave in place of maple syrup.

Maple Syrup: Sweet and Nutritious

Maple syrup, rich in zinc and manganese, is one of the most nutrient dense sweeteners available. Though zinc is known for its immune functions, it is also important for dopamine production in the body. Sugars, in general, are best in moderation. But don't worry, the maplesyrup used in this recipe amounts to a 1/2 gram of sugar per serving.

Nutrition Facts
Recipe makes 4 servings

Amount per serving	
Calories	**196**
Total Fat	**8.5g**
Saturated Fat	1.5g
Total Carbohydrates	**25g**
Carbohydrates from Fiber	5.5g
Sugars	**3g**
Protein	**8g**

Indian Split Pea Stew with Potatoes and Cauliflower

GF GLUTEN FREE **SF** SOY FREE

Ingredients:

- 2 ½ cups **water**
- 1 ½ cups **vegetable stock**
- 1 cup dried **yellow split peas**
- 1 **bay leaf**
- 2 cups **cauliflower,** cut into florets
- 1 cup **potatoes,** cut into 1/2 inch cubes
- 1 tablespoon **coconut oil**
- 1 cup chopped **onion**
- 1 ½ teaspoons minced peeled **fresh ginger**
- 2 **garlic cloves,** minced
- 1 tablespoon **cumin seeds**
- 1 tablespoon **black mustard seeds** (yellow if not available)
- 1 ½ teaspoons **ground coriander**
- 1 teaspoon **ground turmeric**
- ½ teaspoon **ground red pepper**
- 1 teaspoon **maple syrup** (optional)
- 1 teaspoon **lemon juice**
- **Salt** to taste

Directions:

1. Using a large saucepan, combine 2 ½ cups water, split peas, bay leaf, and salt to taste. Bring to a boil, reduce heat, and simmer for 40- 50 minutes or until tender.

2. As the peas are cooking, heat coconut oil to medium-high heat in a small skillet. Add mustard seeds and cumin. When seeds begin sputtering, add onion, ginger, and garlic and sauté for 3-5 minutes until the onions are translucent. Add the rest of the dry spices, mix thoroughly, and continue cooking for 3-5 minutes on low heat, stirring occassionally. Set aside for step 3.

3. When the peas are tender, add 1 ½ cup vegetable stock, cauliflower, potatoes, sautéed onion mixture, and bring to a boil.

4. Reduce heat, and simmer for 25 minutes or until cauliflower and potatoes are tender. Stir occasionally. Salt to taste.

5. Serve as a main dish over a bed of rice or your favorite grain.

see recipe

Dried Peas:
Brain Booster, Sulfite Buster

Dried peas are rich in amino acids and minerals involved in dopamine production. But they have even more to offer!

Are you sensitive to sulfites found in products like dried fruits, wine, and prepared foods?

Peas are rich in a mineral called molybdenum, which is used by your body to break down these sulfite preservatives. _Add more peas to your diet to boost your body's sulfite detoxifying mechanisms!_

Potatoes:
More Than Meets The Eye

Most people think of potatoes as the un-nutritious source of junk foods like _French fries and chips_. But potatoes are actually one of the richest sources of B6 which is important for brain function.

Plus, researchers have found potatoes to contain blood pressure lowering compounds called "ku-koamines"! _Wow!_

Nutrition Facts
Recipe makes 6 servings

Amount per serving	
Calories	195
Total Fat	3.5g
Saturated Fat	2g
Total Carbohydrates	16.5g
Carbohydrates from Fiber	11.3g
Sugars	7.6g
Protein	10.5g

Spelt Salad with Artichoke and Herbs

Ingredients:

- 1 ½ cups **dry spelt**
- 6 cups **water**
- 1 large **clove garlic,** crushed
- 1 tablespoon **lemon juice**
- ¼ cup **extra-virgin olive oil**
- ¼ teaspoon **black pepper**
- 1 cup **tomatoes,** seeded, diced small
- 1 cup **sweet onion,** chopped
- ½ cup **flat-leaf parsley,** chopped
- ¼ cup **fresh basil,** chopped
- ½ cup **cucumbers,** chopped
- ½ cup **marinated artichoke,** chopped
- **Salt** to taste

Directions:

1. Add spelt, water, and 1 teaspoon salt to medium-sized pan. Bring to a boil, reduce heat to medium- low, cover and simmer until spelt is al dente, about 45-50 minutes. Drain thoroughly and set aside to cool.

2. In a mixing bowl, add garlic, lemon juice, olive oil, and pepper. Mix thoroughly.

3. Add the rest of the salad ingredients, spelt, and toss to combine. Add sea salt to taste.

Gluten Free Variation:

Use wild rice in place of spelt.

see recipe

Did You Know?

Lack of folate may be involved in Parkinson's disease. Parkinson's, which can lead to tremors and stiffness in the limbs, is related to a lack of dopamine function.

So make sure you get enough folate, and other dopamine supporting nutrients, *so your body can work at its best!*

Spelt:
Better Than Whole Wheat?

Spelt, the ancient cousin of wheat, is rich in dopamine supportive tyrosine, iron, and zinc. Plus, it has 50% more folate than its well-known cousin! But if you are sensitive to gluten, make sure to avoid both and opt for another option instead.

Artichoke:
Folate Champion

Amongst commonly available foods, artichokes dominate the field when it comes the B-vitamin folate, also known as folic acid. This nutrient is super important for your health, especially for your brain and blood vessels.

Nutrition Facts
Recipe makes 4 servings

Amount per serving

Calories	**384**
Total Fat	**15g**
Saturated Fat	2.2g
Total Carbohydrates	**57g**
Carbohydrates from Fiber	10g
Sugars	**9g**
Protein	**11g**

Dopamine Support Smoothie

GF GLUTEN FREE **SF** SOY FREE **R** RAW

Ingredients:

- 1 **banana**
- 1 cup **spinach**
- ¼ cup **wheat germ** or **oats** (gluten free)
- 1 cup **strawberries**
- 2 cups **almond milk**
- (optional) **Dates** or favorite sweetener to taste

Directions:

1. Combine all ingredients in a blender and blend until smooth.

Gluten-Free Variation:

Be sure to use gluten free oats.

Raw Variation:

Be sure to use raw wheat germ and raw almond milk. If raw almond milk is not available, you can make it yourself by blending raw almonds with water, and filtering through cheesecloth. Adjust the water to nut ratio until desired level of creaminess is achieved!

see recipe

Vitamin C: *Triple Play*

The strawberries in this smoothie provide more than just a wonderful flavor, they're also a huge source of vitamin C. This ubiquitous vitamin has so many properties when it comes to supporting health... yet... there are three particular aspects of vitamin C that stand out in this recipe. Not only is vitamin C involved in dopamine synthesis, it also helps the body absorb iron from the spinach, wheat germ, and/or oats!

And if you choose the gluten free oats instead of wheat germ, vitamin C has also shown to boost the cholesterol protective effects of oats! *So make sure to add the strawberries in this recipe. Your smoothie will be better in every way!*

Wheat Germ: *Friend or Foe?*

Wheat germ does an exceptional job when it comes to supporting dopamine synthesis. This nutrition powerhouse sits at the top of the list for nearly all dopamine boosting nutrients. *But is this ingredient your best friend? Or could it be your worst enemy...?*

Well, if you have any kind of wheat or gluten allergy, or even sensitivity, you may want to opt for gluten free oats instead. Though wheat germ is much richer in B6 and folate than oats, it also contains something called wheat germ agglutinin (WGA). This substance can cause digestive troubles for some people. So if you decide to try wheat germ, pay attention to your body to avoid any unwanted reactions. *If you have any doubts at all, try oats instead!*

Nutrition Facts
Recipe makes 4 servings

Amount per serving

Calories	**81**
Total Fat	**2g**
Saturated Fat	0.1g
Total Carbohydrates	**14g**
Carbohydrates from Fiber	3g
Sugars	**5g**
Protein	**3g**

Chocolate Granola with Raw Seeds and Nuts

SERVES: **6** PREP TIME: **1h 10 MIN**

GLUTEN FREE · **SOY FREE**

Ingredients:

- ¼ cup high quality **cocoa powder (cacao)**
- 4 ½ cups **rolled oats**
- 3/4 cup **apple sauce**
- 2 teaspoons **ground cinnamon**
- 1 teaspoon **ground ginger**
- ¼ cup **brown rice syrup**
- ¼ cup **maple syrup**
- ¼ cup **light brown sugar**
- 1 ½ cups **dry pineapples,** unsweetened and chopped
- 2 tablespoons high oelic **sunflower oil**
- 1 teaspoon **sea salt**
- 1 tablespoon **white sesame seeds**
- ½ cup **pumpkin seeds,** raw
- ½ cup **sunflower seeds,** raw
- 1 cup **walnuts,** raw

Directions:

1. Set oven to 310 degrees F.

2. Add all ingredients, except nuts and seeds, to a large mixing bowl. Mix together thoroughly.

3. Spread ingredients over a large baking tin, and bake for about 30 min. Then turn the granola over and continue baking for another 30 min.

4. When finished, allow the granola to cool, and then mix in the nuts and seeds.

5. Serve alone as a snack, or with your favorite vegan milk or yogurt!

Nuts and seeds contain delicate fatty acids. Leaving them raw ensures that these fats don't get oxidized.

see recipe

Cocoa:
Delicious Stress Reducer

Cocoa can help your brain in more ways than one. This ingredient is rich in tyrosine, which supports dopamine production to keep you motivated, focused, and effective.

But researchers have also found cocoa to combat stress and anxiety by reducing stress hormones in the body.

Pumpkin Seeds:
Overlooked Superfood

Pumpkin seeds often get overlooked in today's superfood craze. This humble seed is one of the richest ingredients available for supporting dopamine production by supplying dietary, zinc, tyrosine and iron.

Walnuts:
Good Fats, Good Decisions

Walnuts are a great source of Omega 3 Alpha Linolenic Acid (ALA). Researchers found that animals deprived of this healthy fat showed severely reduced levels of dopamine in the frontal cortex. This part of the brain is related to judgment, problem solving, and decision-making.

So get more walnuts in your diet and perform at your best!

Nutrition Facts
Recipe makes 6 servings

Amount per serving

Calories	**723**
Total Fat	**29g**
Saturated Fat	3.6g
Total Carbohydrates	**99g**
Carbohydrates from Fiber	11g
Sugars	**42g**
Protein	**16g**

Chickpea Pumpkin Seed Stir-Fry

SERVES: **4** PREP TIME: **15 MIN**

GF GLUTEN FREE **SF** SOY FREE

Ingredients:

- 1 tablespoon **coconut oil**
- 2 **garlic cloves,** minced
- 1 cup **onions,** chopped
- 3 cups **plum tomatoes,** chopped
- 2 cups **garbanzo beans,** cooked, drained
- 2 cups **baby spinach**
- ½ cup **vegetable broth**
- ¼ cup **raw pumpkin seeds,** crushed
- **Salt and pepper** to taste

Directions:

1. In a large pan, bring coconut oil to medium-high heat.

2. Add minced garlic, onions, and fry for 2-3 min until fragrant.

3. Add chopped tomatoes, garbanzo beans and continue cooking for another 5 minutes. Add salt to taste and ¼ cup of vegetable broth if too dry.

4. Then add spinach, ¼ cup vegetable broth, and cook for 1-2 minutes.

5. Remove from heat, sprinkle with crushed pumpkin seeds, salt and pepper to taste, and mix thoroughly.

6. Serve over a bed of rice, quinoa, or your favorite grain.

see recipe

Chickpeas:
Tasty and Satisfying!

Not only are chickpeas delicious and versatile, they can also help to reduce our appetites. Researchers found that people who included chickpeas in their diet were more satisfied with their meals and had reduced appetites overall.

This effect may be from chickpeas' ability to regulate digestion with its unique combination of protein and fiber.

Pumpkin Seeds and Spinach:
Powerhouse Combo!!!

Pumpkin seeds and spinach are both exceptional sources of tyrosine, iron, and zinc.

And when you combine these ingredients with the vitamin C in tomatoes and lemon juice, you ensure the best possible absorption of iron from your meal!

Nutrition Facts
Recipe makes 4 servings

Amount per serving	
Calories	**300**
Total Fat	**11.5g**
Saturated Fat	4g
Total Carbohydrates	**38.5g**
Carbohydrates from Fiber	9g
Sugars	**11g**
Protein	**15g**

Miso Tempeh Green Beans

Ingredients:

Miso Sauce:
- 1 teaspoon **sesame oil**
- 1/8 cup **scallions,** sliced
- 1 1/2 cups **shiitake mushroom,** hydrated and sliced
- 1 1/2 cups **vegetable broth**
- 3/8 teaspoon **black pepper**
- 3/8 teaspoon **white pepper**
- 2 tablespoons **cornstarch** (organic)
- 3 tablespoons light **miso paste** (organic)
- 3 tablespoons **warm water** or **vegetable broth**

Tempeh and Vegetables:
- 1 tablespoon **sunflower oil**
- 1 (8 ounce) **package tempeh,** sliced
- 2 tablespoons **tamari** or **soy sauce**
- 2 1/4 cups **package green beans**
- 1 **bell pepper,** sliced
- 1 teaspoon **sesame seeds**

 tip Tamari is generally a wheat and gluten free soy sauce.

Miso Sauce Directions:
1. Bring sesame oil to medium heat in a small saucepan. Add scallions and sauté for 2-3 minutes until fragrant. Add mushrooms and continue sautéing for another 2-3 minutes.

2. Then add vegetable broth, black and white pepper, bring to a simmer, and continue simmering for 5 min.

3. As the sauce simmers, dissolve cornstarch in a small amount of water in a small bowl. Then slowly stir the cornstarch mixture into the simmering sauce. Continue cooking until the sauce thickens, then remove from heat.

4. In a small bowl, combine miso paste with 3 tbsp warm water or vegetable broth. Mix until smooth, and stir into sauce.

Tempeh and Vegetables Directions:
1. Bring sunflower oil to medium-high heat in a medium saucepan. Add tempeh slices and sauté for 3-5 minutes. Add tamari or soy sauce and mix to season tempeh evenly.

2. Add green beans, bell pepper, and continue sautéing for another 5 minutes.

3. Stir in miso sauce, mix to evenly coat tempeh and veggies, and remove from heat.

4. Serve over bed of rice or even quinoa!

see recipe

Shiitake Mushrooms:
Special Iron Booster

Beyond the brain boosting B6 and zinc found in shiitake mushrooms, this wonderful ingredient can also boost your iron stores in a unique way. Researchers are finding that the iron in shiitake mushrooms may be just as bioavailable as a special form of iron called "ferrous gluconate." This makes shiitake mushrooms especially important for a healthy vegan diet.

Hidden GMO?

Since corn and soy are some of the most widely genetically modified crops, be sure to get them in their organic, non-GMO forms just in case!

Gluten Free Variation:
Be sure that the tempeh you choose has no gluten containing grains added. Choose gluten free tamari over soy sauce.

Tempeh:
Protein Rich Brain Support

Tempeh is rich in dopamine supporting amino acids tyrosine and phenylalanine. For those who have difficulty digesting protein rich plant foods, tempeh can be a great choice. The fermentation process makes tempeh *easy to digest, and can also increase mineral bioavailability!*

Nutrition Facts
Recipe makes 4 servings

Amount per serving

Calories	**268**
Total Fat	**12g**
Saturated Fat	3g
Total Carbohydrates	**30g**
Carbohydrates from Fiber	11g
Sugars	**5g**
Protein	**14g**

Brain Boosting Pancakes

SERVES: **2** PREP TIME: **15 MIN**
GLUTEN FREE SOY FREE

Ingredients:

Pancakes:
- 1 ½ cups **gluten free oat flour**
- ½ cup **chickpea flour**
- ¼ cup **cocoa powder**
- 1 tablespoon **baking powder**
- 1 teaspoon **vegan sugar** (optional)
- ¼ teaspoon **salt**
- 1 ½ cups **coconut milk beverage,** or your favorite vegan milk
- 4 teaspoons high oleic **sunflower oil**

Toppings:
- ¼ cup **bananas,** sliced
- ½ cup **strawberries,** sliced
- ¼ cup **raw walnut pieces**
- ¼ cup **maple syrup** or to taste

Directions:

1. Combine all dry ingredients in a large mixing bowl and mix together thoroughly. Sift if necessary.
2. Set a lightly oiled pan to medium heat.
3. Combine all wet ingredients with the flour and mix thoroughly.
4. Ladle about a ⅓ cup of batter into pan. Spread evenly over the pan, and cook for about 2 minutes or until pancakes are puffed, dry around the edges, and bubbled. Flip carefully and cook other side for about 2 more minutes.
5. Top with sliced bananas, strawberries, walnuts, and serve with a side of maple syrup.

tip If the batter becomes too thick, add more vegan milk ½ teaspoon at a time to achieve desired texture.

tip You can use any vegan milk, but try coconut milk beverage to create the best texture.

see recipe

Chickpea and Oat Flour: *A Dynamic Duo*

Chickpea and oat flours make more than just a delicious pancake... they're also loaded with health supporting effects! Not only are they rich in tyrosine and dopamine supporting minerals, they also create a complete protein source to power you through your day.

Combine this with vitamin C rich strawberries, vitamin B6 packed bananas, *and you've got yourself a super brain-supporting combo!*

Cocoa: *Delicious, Exciting and Confused?*

Cacao is more than just delicious, it can also boost the brain in so many ways. This ingredient is rich in tyrosine, an amino acid that supports optimal dopamine synthesis. Cacao also contains compounds that have shown to affect mood and alertness in a drug like way! *But have you ever wondered about the difference between cacao and cocoa?*

Don't worry... you're not or alone! Cacao and cocoa actually refer to the beans of the same plant. Though this bean can be processed in a few different ways, "cacao" is basically the way it is spelled and pronounced in South America, where much of it is produced. And be careful not to overdo it... cacao can have stimulant like effects that shouldn't be abused.

Nutrition Facts
Recipe makes 2 servings

Amount per serving

Calories	**842**
Total Fat	**35g**
Saturated Fat	2g
Total Carbohydrates	**122g**
Carbohydrates from Fiber	17g
Sugars	**37g**
Protein	**26g**

Happy Pumpkin Seed Pesto

SERVES: **10** PREP TIME: **10 MIN**

GLUTEN FREE · SOY FREE · RAW

Ingredients:

- ½ cup **olive oil**
- 2 cloves **garlic,** chopped
- 2 cups **fresh basil leaves,** tightly packed
- ½ cup **raw pumpkin seeds**
- ¼ cup **raw pistachios**
- 1 teaspoon **lemon juice**
- ½ teaspoon **salt,** or to taste

Serve as a dip with bread, toast or chips!

Or add to your favorite sandwich or pasta.

Directions:

1. Combine basil, garlic, and olive oil into a strong blender, pushing all ingredients into the oil. Cover with lid and pulse the blender 6-7 times or until all ingredients are roughly chopped.

2. Then add all remaining ingredients, and pulse the blender until all ingredients are rendered into a course puree.

Lower Fat Variation: Reduce olive oil to ¼ cup, reduce salt to ¼ tsp, and add ¼ cup vegetable broth, 2 tsp miso, and ¼ tsp black pepper.

see recipe

Pistachios:
Protein + Brain Function

Pistachios are known as a great source of lysine, an important amino acid for vegans to get complete proteins in their diet.

But pistachios are also one of the richest vegan sources of vitamin B6, a very important nutrient for your brain to produce most of its neurotransmitters, including serotonin.

Along with vitamins B12 and folic acid, B6 is also protects your cardiovascular system by reducing homocysteine, a chemical in the body that can damage blood vessels.

Basil:
A Tasty Brain Booster

Basil's rosmarinic acid, and its metabolite caffeic acid, can have anti-depressant like effects by boosting brain chemicals like serotonin and dopamine.

Add more of this delicious herb to your diet to stay happy, calm, and focused!

Pumpkin Seeds:
Nature's Mood Boosting Powerhouse

Pumpkin seeds are one of the richest vegan sources of tryptophan, magnesium, and zinc. All of these are serotonin boosting nutrients making pumpkin seeds an important ingredient for regulating mood, sleep, and even appetite!

Nutrition Facts
Recipe makes 10 servings

Amount per serving

Calories	**165**
Total Fat	**16g**
Saturated Fat	0.9g
Total Carbohydrates	**2.2g**
Carbohydrates from Fiber	0.7g
Sugars	**0.2g**
Protein	**3g**

Tempeh Pita Pocket Sandwich

SERVES: **4** PREP TIME: **35 MIN**

Ingredients:

Tahini Sauce:
- ½ cup **vegan sour cream**
- 2 tablespoons **tahini** (raw is best)
- 2 cloves **garlic,** smashed
- 4 teaspoons **lemon juice**
- **Salt** to taste

Tempeh Filling:
- 2 teaspoons high oleic **sunflower oil**
- 2 cups **tempeh,** crumbled (= 1 tempeh pack, or 8oz)
- 2 cloves **garlic,** minced
- 1 cup **onion,** chopped
- ½ teaspoon **dried oregano**
- ½ teaspoon **ground cumin**
- ½ teaspoon **dried rosemary**
- ½ teaspoon **black pepper** plus **salt** to taste

Pita:
- 4 large **whole grain pita breads**
- 2 **plum tomatoes,** diced
- 1 **cucumber,** diced
- 1 ½ **large ripe avocados,** sliced
- 1 cup **alfalfa sprouts**
- 1 cup **baby spinach leaves**

Directions:

1. Using a large pan, bring oil to medium-high heat. Add garlic, onions, and sauté for 3-5 min until fragrant.

2. Then add tempeh, all dry spices, mix thoroughly and continue cooking for about 3 min. Then add ½ cup of warm water, set heat to low, cover, and let cook for 5 more minutes to infuse flavors. Stir regularly.

3. As the tempeh is cooking, mix all sauce ingredients in a small bowl until blended. Set aside.

4. Once the tempeh is done, use a medium mixing bowl, combine tempeh, tomatoes, spinach, ¼ cup of the tahini sauce, and toss to mix.

5. Cut each pita in half and open carefully. Spoon tempeh mixture into each pocket, top with sprouts, cucumber, and avocado.

6. Drizzle each sandwich with tahini sauce before serving.

Gluten Free Variation:
Use your favorite gluten free pita bread.

Soy Free Variation: Substitute tempeh for lentils boiled to al dente. Omitt vegan sour cream, and substitute with an additional 2 tbsp of tahini, 1 tbsp of lemon juice, 1 tbsp of water, and salt to taste.

see recipe

Avocado: *Boost Your Nutrient Absorption*

While avocados are rich in serotonin boosting B6, they have many other health benefits as well. In fact, the healthy fats in avocado help your body absorb more fat-soluble nutrients found in other foods... 3-5 times more according to some researchers!

Also, researchers have found that the dark green avocado, closest to the peel, is the richest in nutrients. So make sure you get all!

Organics are always best, but if you have to be thrifty, conventional avocados are an acceptable option.

Spinach: *Quick and Nutritious*

Spinach is one of the richest sources of serotonin boosting magnesium.

And to save time, you can try using pre-washed spinach in ready to eat containers. Researchers have actually found the constant light exposure at the market to increase the nutritional value! So save yourself some time and give (organic) pre-washed spinach a try.

Dirty Dozen vs Clean 15: *Save Your Health and Some Money*

Conventional spinach is on the *Dirty Dozen* list as it's often loaded with pesticides. So make sure to get this in its organic form.

Avocados on the other hand, are on the Clean 15 list. They are protected by a thick skin and are one of the safest fruits to get in the conventional form.

Nutrition Facts
Recipe makes 4 servings

Amount per serving	
Calories	**456**
Total Fat	**20.5g**
Saturated Fat	3g
Total Carbohydrates	**55g**
Carbohydrates from Fiber	10.5g
Sugars	**10.5g**
Protein	**22g**

Spicy Kidney Bean Curry

SERVES: **4** PREP TIME: **50 MIN**
GLUTEN FREE   SOY FREE

Ingredients:

- 4 cups **onion,** chopped
- 5 cloves **garlic,** chopped
- 1 ½ teaspoons **ginger root,** peeled and chopped
- 3 tablespoons **coconut oil**
- 1 tablespoon crushed **red pepper**
- 1 teaspoon **cumin seeds**
- 6 **cloves,** whole
- 1 teaspoon **ground coriander**
- 1 teaspoon **ground turmeric**
- 1 teaspoon **ground cumin**
- 2 **tomatoes,** chopped
- 1 cup **tomato sauce**
- 1 ½ cups cooked **red kidney beans**
- 1 cup **bean water** (from kidney beans)
- 1 cup **peas**
- 1 teaspoon **maple syrup**
- 1 teaspoon **garam masala**
- ¼ cup **cilantro leaves,** chopped
- **Salt** to taste

Directions:

1. Using a food processor (or mortar and pestle), combine onions, ginger, and, garlic. Grind into a paste. Set aside.

2. In a large pot, bring coconut oil to medium-high heat. Add crushed red pepper, cumin seeds, cloves, and fry for 2-3 minutes until fragrant. Lower the temperature if the ingredients start to brown too quickly.

3. Once the cumin seeds begin to sputter, add the onion, ginger, garlic paste. Add turmeric, ground cumin, and coriander. Stir frequently and sauté for 7-10 minutes until fragrant.

4. Add chopped tomatoes and continue to sauté for another 7 minutes.

5. Then add tomato sauce, kidney beans, peas, and bean water. Salt to taste, bring to a boil, then set to simmer for 20 minutes.

6. Add garam masala and let simmer for 5 more minutes.

7. Top with chopped cilantro before serving.

8. Serve over rice for a delicious meal.

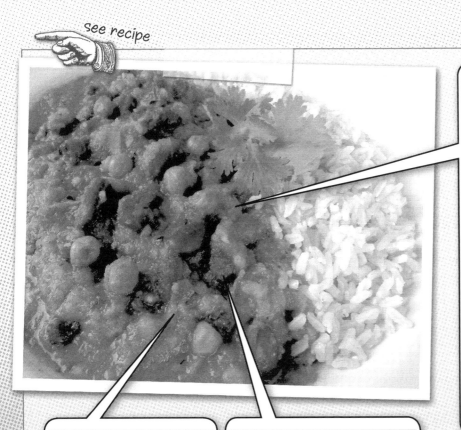

see recipe

Peas:
Increase Health, Decrease Cancer

B6 is very important vitamin that is also necessary for serotonin production in the body. Green peas are a great source of this multi-tasking nutrient.

Peas are also rich in a polyphenol called "coumestrol." Researchers have found this phytonutrient *to be protective against stomach cancer!*

Cumin:
Happy Brain... Happy Stomach

Cumin seeds are a good source of calcium, a mineral that is important for serotonin production.

Cumin seeds have also been used to stimulate digestion after meals in the Indian culture. Researchers now understand that this may be from cumin's ability to stimulate bile acids and digestive enzymes.

Tomato:
Culinary Chemistry at Its Finest

Though some ingredients are healthiest in the raw, tomatoes are the opposite when it comes to lycopene. This anti-cancer nutrient is actually increased as the tomato gets broken down during cooking. And because it is fat soluble, researchers found that cooking it with oil makes it even more available! *What a delicious combination!*

Nutrition Facts
Recipe makes 4 servings

Amount per serving

Calories	**395**
Total Fat	**12g**
Saturated Fat	9g
Total Carbohydrates	**67g**
Carbohydrates from Fiber	13g
Sugars	**19g**
Protein	**14g**

Veggie Barley Casserole

SERVES: **4** PREP TIME: **1h 30 MIN** **SF** SOY FREE

Ingredients:

- 3 tablespoons **coconut oil**
- 1 cup **onion,** chopped
- 1 cup **barley**
- ½ cup **peas**
- ½ cup **broccoli,** chopped
- 1 cup **chunky salsa** of choice
- 3 cups **vegetable broth**
- **Salt & pepper** to taste
- Your favorite **vegan cheese** (optional)

Directions:

1. Preheat the oven to 350 degrees F.

2. Bring coconut oil to medium-high heat in a large pan, add onions, and sauté until fragrant. Add barley and continue sautéing for 3-5 minutes stirring frequently.

3. Pour onion-barley mixture into a large casserole dish; add peas, broccoli, salsa and vegetable broth. Add salt and pepper to taste.

4. Cover with foil, place in the oven, and cook at 350 degrees F for 1 hour.

5. Then remove covering (optional: top with your favorite vegan cheese) and cook for 15-20 more minutes, or until most of the liquid has evaporated.

tip Be careful with the salt in step 3, as the dish becomes saltier when the liquid evaporates. You can always salt to taste at the table to be extra safe!

see recipe

Broccoli: *Nature's Wonder-Veggie*

Broccoli is rich in B6, magnesium, calcium and tryptophan... all of which support optimal serotonin production in the body.

But this wonder-veggie has even more tricks up its sleeve. Because it is so rich in vitamins A and K, broccoli also helps us metabolize vitamin D. So if you are taking higher dose vitamin D supplements, be sure to eat lots of broccoli.

Onion: *Cleanest of Them All*

Onions don't need much spraying when it comes to pesticides. Because of this, they were found to be the #1 cleanest conventional crop according to the Clean 15 list. Organic is always best, but if you must, buying conventional onions is a safe way to save.

Barley: *Better Digestion*

Barley can help keep your body happy in more ways than one. It's not only rich in tryptophan to support serotonin production, the fiber found in barley *also feeds the friendly bacteria in your digestive tract!*

Keep your friendly bacteria happy and they will help you out when you need it most.

Nutrition Facts	
Recipe makes 4 servings	
Amount per serving	
Calories	**325**
Total Fat	**12g**
Saturated Fat	9g
Total Carbohydrates	**50g**
Carbohydrates from Fiber	12g
Sugars	**6.5g**
Protein	**10g**

Chickpea and Herb Salad

SERVES: **4** PREP TIME: **15 MIN**
GLUTEN FREE   SOY FREE

Ingredients:

- 1 ½ cups cooked **chickpeas,** drained and rinsed
- ½ cup **red onion,** sliced extra thin
- 3 **tomatoes,** deseeded and chopped
- 2 tablespoons **fresh coriander leaves,** chopped
- 2 tablespoons **fresh peppermint leaves,** chopped
- 3 tablespoons **tahini** (raw is best)
- 2 cloves **garlic,** crushed
- ¼ tablespoon **lemon juice**
- 2 tablespoons **water**
- **Salt** to taste

Directions:

1. In a small mixing bowl, combine tahini, crushed garlic, lemon juice, and water. Mix thoroughly and set aside.

2. In a large mixing bowl, combine chickpeas, onion, tomato, coriander and mint. Add dressing to taste and toss.

3. Salt to taste.

4. Serve with pita bread for a complete meal, or use as an appetizer or side dish.

Raw Variation: Substitute cooked chickpeas for fresh green or sprouted chickpeas.

see recipe

Onions:
Rich in quercitin

Onions, especially red onions, are one of the richest sources of quercitin. Though this antioxidant is mostly known for its anti-inflammatory effects, researchers found that it may help improve mood *by slowing the breakdown of serotonin and other neuro-transmitters!*

But most of the quercitin is found in the outer layers of the onion. So be sure to peel off as little skin as possible when preparing your onions.

Peppermint:
A "cool" stress reducer

Peppermint is not only tasty, it may also help in reducing stress

Researchers found that the anti-stress effects of peppermint extracts come from its ability to regulate hormones and neuro-transmitters involved in the stress response.

Chickpeas: *A nutrient dense vegan food*

Fresh chickpeas (raw and never been dried), also known as "green garbanzos" are much more nutritious than their dried counterparts. *In fact, these are some of the most nutrient dense vegan foods available!*

They can often be found fresh at your local ethnic market, or frozen at many specialty markets.

Nutrition Facts
Recipe makes 4 servings

Amount per serving	
Calories	**215**
Total Fat	**6g**
Saturated Fat	1g
Total Carbohydrates	**33g**
Carbohydrates from Fiber	3.5g
Sugars	**5g**
Protein	**8g**

Quinoa with Black Bean and Summer Squash

SERVES: **4** PREP TIME: **60 MIN** **GF** GLUTEN FREE **SF** SOY FREE

Ingredients:

- 1 teaspoon high oleic **sunflower oil**
- 1 **onion,** chopped
- 3 **cloves garlic,** peeled and chopped
- 1 cup **tomatoes,** chopped
- 1 cup uncooked **quinoa**
- 2 cups **vegetable broth**
- 1 teaspoon **ground cumin**
- ¼ teaspoon **cayenne pepper**
- **Salt and pepper** to taste
- 3 cups **summer squash,** chopped
- 1 cup **spinach,** chopped
- 1 cup **peas**
- 2 cups **black beans** cooked and drained
- ½ cup **fresh cilantro,** chopped

Directions:

1. Bring oil to medium heat in a medium saucepan. Sauté garlic and onions for 2-3 minutes until translucent. Then add tomatoes and continue cooking for another 2-3 minutes.

2. Add quinoa to the saucepan with half of the vegetable broth (1 cup). Add cayenne pepper, cumin, black pepper, and salt to taste. Bring to a boil, cover, reduce heat, and let simmer another 15 minutes.

3. Add 1 more cup of vegetable broth, summer squash, spinach and peas. Bring to a boil, then reduce heat, and simmer for 5 minutes. Stir regularly.

4. Mix in the black beans and cilantro, and continue cooking for 3-5 minutes on medium heat or until heated through.

5. Serve as a main course or side dish.

see recipe

Black Beans:
Black Beans Promote Bacteria Growth?

Black beans are rich in tryptophan, magnesium, and folate for serotonin production. But interestingly... they can also support bacteria growth. But don't worry; we're talking about good bacteria! Even more so than lentils or chickpeas, black beans support your gut bacteria with its large "indigestible fraction." These bacterias are an important part of your immune and digestive systems. They can also help to ward off the bad bugs. *So give you brain and gut bacteria a boost by eating more black beans!*

Summer Squash:
Making The Cut

Though summer squash didn't make the top 12 most contaminated conventional produce list, it did make the Dirty Dozen Plus List as a special addition. Summer Squash was found to contain residues of the exceptionally toxic organochlorine pesticides. So when it comes to summer squash, *you should definitely go organic at all costs.*

Quinoa:
More Than Complete Protein?

Quinoa is so popular amongst healthy foodies, and rightfully so! Quinoa is famous for being one of the only grains that provide a complete vegan protein. But this super grain has even more to offer! Besides being a great protein source, quinoa is also packed with flavanoids like quercitin and kaempferol. *In fact, it has the same amount, and sometimes more flavanoids, than anti-oxidant rich cranberries!*

Nutrition Facts
Recipe makes 4 servings

Amount per serving

Calories	**409**
Total Fat	**5.2g**
Saturated Fat	0.2g
Total Carbohydrates	**73.5g**
Carbohydrates from Fiber	18g
Sugars	**9g**
Protein	**20g**

Raw Sunflower and Walnut Pâté

SERVES: **6** PREP TIME: **Overnight + 15 MIN** **(GF)** **(SF)** **(R)**
GLUTEN FREE • SOY FREE • RAW

Ingredients:

- 1 cup **raw sunflower seeds,** sprouted
- 1 cup **raw walnuts**
- 4 **cloves garlic**
- ½ cup **parsley**
- 2 tablespoons **raw tahini**
- 3/8 cup **lemon juice**
- 1 tablespoon **cumin powder**
- 1 teaspoon **paprika**
- 2 tablespoons **water**
- **Salt** to taste

Directions:

1. Using raw sunflower seeds (without hulls), soak in water for 8-10 hours. Then drain, and let rest 3 to 4 hours to sprout. After sprouting is complete, rinse, drain, and remove inner husks that come off of the sprouts (optional).

2. Using a food processor, first process the garlic and parsely well. Then add sunflower seeds, walnuts, tahini, lemon juice, cumin, paprika, salt, water, and process into a smooth paste.

Serving Suggestions:

Serve as a dip for sprouted crackers, vegetables, or as a spread on a sandwich.

see recipe

Garlic:
A Vegan's Best Friend

From boosting the immune system to benefiting the brain, garlic is a tasty ingredient with so many functions. But it doesn't stop there!

Garlic may also help with iron metabolism by increasing a protein called "ferroportin." This cellular protein transports iron for your body to use. So add some garlic to your next meal and give your body the boost it needs!

Sunflower + Sesame Seeds:
Optimize Serotonin, Reduce Cholesterol

Sunflower and Sesame Seeds are exceptionally rich in nearly all serotonin-supporting nutrients. But these tasty ingredients have another function. Researchers have found these foods to be rich in substances called "phytosterols."

These healthy cholesterol like compounds not only reduce blood cholesterol levels, but they may also reduce the risk of cancer.

Nutrition Facts
Recipe makes 6 servings

Amount per serving

Calories	**186**
Total Fat	**17g**
Saturated Fat	1.5g
Total Carbohydrates	**6.7g**
Carbohydrates from Fiber	2.5g
Sugars	**1g**
Protein	**5g**

Happy Serotonin Smoothie

SERVES: **4** PREP TIME: **5 MIN**

(GF) GLUTEN FREE **(SF)** SOY FREE **(R)** RAW

Ingredients:

- 2 cups **frozen mangos**
- 1 **frozen banana**
- ½ cup **raw cashews**
- 2 tablespoons **dates,** pitted
- 1 cup **almond milk**
- ½ tablespoon **lemon juice**
- ½ cup **ice**

Directions:

1. Combine all ingredients in a blender and blend until smooth.

Raw Variation:

Be sure to use raw almond milk and cashews.

If raw almond milk is not available, you can make it yourself by blending raw almonds with water, and filtering through cheesecloth. Adjust the water to nut ratio until desired level of creaminess is achieved!

see recipe

Mango:
Ultra Convenient and Economical!

Besides being rich in brain boosting vitamin B6, mangos, are also proving to be one of the more convenient fruits available. Being in the Clean 15 list means that you can buy conventional mangos without putting your family at risk. But researchers also found that pre-cut mangos lose less vitamin C than other fruits! Compared to pre-cut cantaloupe, which lost 25% of its vitamin C in 6 days, mangos only lost 5%. So *if you need to save some time, pre-cut mangos are a great option!*

Cashews:
Non-Dairy Goodness for the Brain and Heart!

Cashews are a great way to add some non-dairy creamy goodness to your smoothies.

Not only are they rich in serotonin boosting amino acids and minerals, they are also rich in mono-saturated oleic fatty acids. Much like the healthy fats in olive oil, these fatty acids benefit the cardiovascular system to keep your heart happy, healthy, and strong.

Nutrition Facts
Recipe makes 4 servings

Amount per serving

Calories	**275**
Total Fat	**14g**
Saturated Fat	0g
Total Carbohydrates	**36g**
Carbohydrates from Fiber	3.6g
Sugars	**22g**
Protein	**6.5g**

Rosemary Navy Bean Soup

SERVES: **6** PREP TIME: **1h 20 MIN**
GLUTEN FREE **SOY FREE**

Ingredients:

- 1 lb **navy beans,** dry
- 1 cup **fresh spinach**
- 1 cup **crimini mushrooms,** sliced
- 3 cloves **garlic,** chopped
- 6 cups **vegetable stock**
- ¼ cup **parsley,** chopped
- 1 teaspoon **rosemary**
- 2 tablespoons **coconut oil**
- 1 tablespoon **lemon juice**
- **Salt and pepper** to taste

tip To maximize the nutritional benefit of the mushrooms, add them to the recipe during step 4 instead of step 2.

tip Using (BPA free) canned navy beans for this recipe makes it a very quick and easy meal!

Directions:

1. Clean and soak beans overnight in water. Drain and rinse thoroughly.

2. Heat 2 tablespoons of coconut oil in a large pot, sauté minced garlic on medium heat for about 10 seconds until fragrant. Add ¼ cup chopped parsley, 1 cup mushrooms, and continue to sauté for another 3-5 min. Add 5 cups vegetable stock, navy beans, rosemary, salt and pepper.

3. Bring soup to a boil, cover, reduce heat and simmer over low heat for about 45 min.

4. Once the navy beans are soft, puree the soup using an immersion blender. Then add 1 cup of spinach, 1 tablespoon of lemon juice, and more salt and pepper to taste if necessary. Simmer on low heat for another 5-10 min stirring frequently. Add some additional vegetable stock if mixture becomes too thick.

5. Serve with your favorite bread, or as a great compliment to any meal.

see recipe

Crimini Mushrooms:
Maximizing Nutrients

Crimini mushrooms are a great source of choline and vitamin B5. Exotic mushrooms have gotten most of the attention in the media today. Yet, this common mushroom has proven to be just as good, and even better than its glamorous cousins, for benefiting the immune system.

But to maximize nutrients in the crimini mushroom, be sure to always store them in the refrigerator immediately, and cook them for no more than 7 minutes.

Spinach:
Popeye knows...

Spinach is one of the richest vegan sources of acetylcholine promoting nutrients including choline, vitamins B1 and B5. Besides supporting brain function, acetylcholine is also used when you activate your muscles. Because of this, getting plenty of dietary choline is important for people with active lifestyles, especially for endurance athletes.

Navy Beans:
Brains and Brawn

Navy beans are one of the richest vegan sources of choline. This nutrient is required by the body to form acetylcholine, a neurotransmitter responsible for a wide variety of functions, including memory and cognition.

It's also a great source of protein to support you throughout the day!

Nutrition Facts
Recipe makes 6 servings

Amount per serving

Calories	**303**
Total Fat	**5.5g**
Saturated Fat	4g
Total Carbohydrates	**58g**
Carbohydrates from Fiber	20g
Sugars	**11g**
Protein	**19g**

Cabbage Lentil Curry

SERVES: **4** PREP TIME: **40 MIN** **(GF)** GLUTEN FREE **(SF)** SOY FREE

Ingredients:

- ½ tablespoon **coconut oil**
- 1 ½ **medium onion,** chopped
- 1 tablespoon **garlic,** crushed
- 1 cup **tomatoes,** diced
- 1 cup **cabbage,** finely sliced
- ½ cup **celery,** chopped
- ½ cup **carrots,** diced
- 1 cup **cauliflower florets**
- 2 tablespoons **curry powder**
- ¾ cup **red lentils**
- 3 cups **vegetable stock**
- 1 ½ tablespoons **fresh cilantro**
- **Salt and pepper** to taste

Directions:

1. Sort, rinse, and strain lentils. Set aside.

2. Bring coconut oil to medium-high heat and sauté onion and garlic for 5 minutes until fragrant.

3. Then add tomatoes and continue cooking for another 5 minutes.

4. Add cabbage, celery, carrots, curry powder, and continue to sauté for another 3-5 minutes until soft.

5. Add lentils and vegetable stock, bring to a boil, cover, reduce heat, and let simmer for 15 minutes.

6. Stir in the cilantro and season with salt and pepper to taste.

7. Serve over a bed of rice, quinoa or your favorite grain!

see recipe

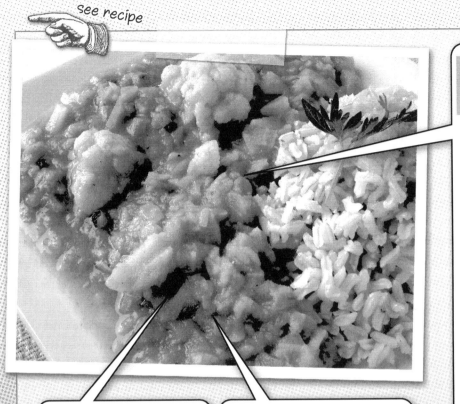

Cabbage and Lentils:
A Great Choline Boosting Combo

Both cabbage and lentils make a great combination for boosting dietary choline. Lentils are especially rich in vitamin B1 and manganese to support optimal acetylcholine production in the body.

Celery: _Avoiding The Conventional_

Celery came in at #2 on the Dirty Dozen list, making it one of the most heavily contaminated conventional crops. So _avoid conventional celery at all costs and buy it organic!_

Curry Powder:
Bringing Out The Essence

Curry powders add wonderful flavors to our food. But this combination of spices may offer more than just flavor!

Researchers found that the extracts of many curry spices, contained "large" amounts of the neurotransmitter acetylcholine, as well as its nutrient precursor, choline. They also found the greatest neurological effect when the spices were roasted. _Delicious!_

Nutrition Facts
Recipe makes 4 servings

Amount per serving	
Calories	**122**
Total Fat	**2g**
Saturated Fat	1.5g
Total Carbohydrates	**22.5g**
Carbohydrates from Fiber	5.5g
Sugars	**12g**
Protein	**7g**

Marinated Vegetable Salad

SERVES: **4** PREP TIME: **45 MIN + Overnight**   (R)
GLUTEN FREE **SOY FREE** **RAW (Option)**

Ingredients:

- ½ tablespoon high oleic **sunflower oil**
- ½ lb **crimini mushroom,** sliced (1 pack)
- ½ **head medium cauliflower,**
  broken into florets
- 7 **stalks asparagus,** cut into 2 inch pieces
- 1 cup **marinated artichoke hearts,**
  quartered, with the water that it comes in
- ¼ cup **olive oil**
- 2 **cloves garlic,** minced and exposed
  to air 5-10 mins
- ½ cup **apple cider vinegar**
- ¾ cup **water**
- ¾ teaspoon **salt**
- ½ teaspoon **cracked peppercorn**
- ½ teaspoon **dried thyme**
- ½ teaspoon **oregano**

Directions:

1. Bring ½ tablespoon sunflower oil to medium-high heat in a large saucepan. Add mushrooms, cauliflower, asparagus, and sauté for 5-7 minutes, or until just tender.

2. In a large bowl, combine all sautéed vegetables, olive oil, minced garlic, apple cider vinegar, water, salt, and all spices. Mix thoroughly and make sure everything is covered. Then top with artichoke hearts including the water that it comes in.

3. Cover and marinate overnight in the refrigerator.

4. Serve as a tasty side dish with your favorite meal.

Raw Variation:

Omit step 1 and marinate all vegetables raw. Use fresh artichokes trimmed until only tender parts are left. You can also slice the artichoke hearts thin for better marinating. Peel the lower portions of the asparagus to avoid the fibrous skin.

see recipe

Mushrooms and Asparagus: Clean 15

Both mushrooms and asparagus made it onto the Clean 15 list of the cleanest conventional crops.

So when you need to save some money, go ahead and get these crops in their conventional form.

Asparagus: A Neuro-Multitasker

Not only is asparagus rich in acetylcholine supporting B1, it is also being investigated for its anti-inflammatory compounds called asparagus saponins.

One of these compounds in particular, sarsasap-ogenin, is being investigated for its effect on a neurological disease called amyotrophic lateral sclerosis, also known as "Lou Gehrig's Disease."

Nutrition Facts	
Recipe makes 4 servings	
Amount per serving	
Calories	**365**
Total Fat	**17g**
Saturated Fat	2g
Total Carbohydrates	**55g**
Carbohydrates from Fiber	12.5g
Sugars	**4g**
Protein	**9g**

Roasted Broccoli and Brussels Sprouts

SERVES: **6** PREP TIME: **25 MIN**

GF GLUTEN FREE   **SF** SOY FREE   **R** RAW (Option)

Ingredients:

- 4 cups **broccoli florets**
- 3 cups **brussels sprouts,** halved
- 2 ½ tablespoons high oleic **sunflower oil**
- 3 **cloves garlic,** minced and exposed to air 5-10 min
- 1 teaspoon **oregano**
- 1 ½ tablespoons **fresh lemon juice**
- 2 tablespoons **raw pine nuts**
- **Salt and black pepper** to taste

Raw Variation:

Chop all vegetables and serve as a salad-like dish.

Directions:

1. Preheat oven to 350 degrees F.

2. In a large mixing bowl, combine broccoli, Brussels sprouts, 2 tablespoons sunflower oil, salt and pepper to taste. Toss to coat ingredients evenly.

3. Spread vegetables over a large baking sheet, and roast for 10-15 minutes until tender. Turn vegetables over once, half way through cooking.

4. As the vegetables are roasting, heat ½ tbsp of sunflower to medium heat in a small saucepan.

5. Add the garlic, oregano, and heat for 1-2 min. Remove from heat, let it cool slightly, then add lemon juice and mix thoroughly.

6. When the vegetables are done roasting, put into a serving bowl, add the garlic-lemon mixture, and toss to coat. Salt and pepper to taste.

7. Sprinkle pine nuts on top before serving.

see recipe

Brussels Sprouts:
Protein Rich Cancer Fighter

Amongst its vegetable counterparts, Brussels sprouts are a great source of protein coming in at 0.96 grams of protein per ounce.

And... compared to other cruciferous vegetables, *Brussels sprouts top the list in anti-cancer glucosinolates!*

Brussels Sprouts and Broccoli:
All In The Family!

Brussels sprouts, and its cousin broccoli, are both in the top 5 when it comes to choline. But when it comes to acetylcholine supporting B vitamins, broccoli is super rich in B5, but not as much in B1.

Good thing brussels sprouts are the opposite! *Where one cousin falls short, the other cousin excels!*

Nutrition Facts	
Recipe makes 6 servings	
Amount per serving	
Calories	**123**
Total Fat	**3.7g**
Saturated Fat	0.6g
Total Carbohydrates	**8.5g**
Carbohydrates from Fiber	3.5g
Sugars	**2.7g**
Protein	**4.5g**

Mashed Sweet Potato with Hazelnuts and Sesame

GF GLUTEN FREE **SF** SOY FREE

Ingredients:

- 4 cups **sweet potatoes,** peeled and cubed
- 2 tablespoons **raw hazelnuts**
- 2 tablespoons **raw sesame seeds**
- 2 tablespoons **apple cider**
- 2 tablespoons **almond milk**
- 2 tablespoons **coconut milk**
- **Salt and pepper** to taste

Directions:

1. Using a large pot, bring sweet potatoes to a boil with a pinch of salt. Then reduce to a simmer for 10 min until soft. Drain completely and set aside.

2. Meanwhile, use a coffee grinder to coarsely grind hazelnuts and sesame seeds together and set aside.

3. Mash sweet potatoes until smooth, then stir in the hazelnut sesame seed mixture, apple cider, almond milk, coconut milk, and mix thoroughly. If the potatoes are too dry, add almond milk until desired consistency is achieved.

4. Add salt and pepper to taste and mix thoroughly.

Reduced Fat Variation:

To make a lower fat version, replace the 2 tbsp of coconut milk with the same amount of almond milk.

see recipe

Brain

Sweet Potatoes:
A Purple Surprise

Though sweet potatoes are often orange colored on the inside, they can sometimes exhibit a beautiful purple tone! This purple surprise is more than just pretty... it turns out to be a healthy surprise too!

Scientists have found these purple fleshed varieties to contain certain types of anthocyanins. These were found to be protective against heavy metal toxicity when passing through the digestive tract.

Hazelnuts:
The Richest Tree Nut

Not only are hazelnuts super rich in brain boosting choline, they are also the richest in proanthocyanidin of any tree nut. This substance gives hazelnuts their unique flavor and may also help reduce the risk of urinary tract infection.

Nutrition Facts
Recipe makes 4 servings

Amount per serving

Calories	**299**
Total Fat	**4.5g**
Saturated Fat	2g
Total Carbohydrates	**55g**
Carbohydrates from Fiber	8g
Sugars	**23g**
Protein	**6g**

Low Fat Vegan Gumbo

SERVES: **8** PREP TIME: **2h 15 MIN** **GF** GLUTEN FREE **SF** SOY FREE

Ingredients:

- 1 tablespoon **coconut oil**
- 2 cloves **garlic,** minced
- 1 cup **onions,** diced
- ½ cup **celery,** diced
- ½ cup **green pepper,** diced
- 1 cup **okra,** sliced
- 1 cup **mushrooms,** sliced
- 1 ½ cups **tomatoes,** chopped
- 3/4 teaspoon **black pepper**
- 3/4 teaspoon **thyme**
- 1 ½ teaspoons **oregano**
- 3 teaspoons **smoked paprika**
- ¼ teaspoon **cayenne pepper,** or to taste
- 2 **bay leaves**
- 6 cups **vegetable broth**
- 2 cups **collard greens,** sliced thin
- ¼ cup **oat flour**
- 3 cups **of your favorite vegan protein,** such as lentils (cooked), tempeh or tofu
- ½ tablespoon **filé powder**
- **Salt** to taste

Directions:

1. Using a large pot, bring 1 tbsp of coconut oil to medium-high heat. Add garlic, onions, bell pepper, celery, okra and sauté for 5-7 min, or until the vegetables are soft.

2. Add the mushrooms, tomatoes, black pepper, thyme, oregano, smoked paprika, cayenne pepper, bay leaves, and cook for an add'l 5 min.

3. Add the vegetable stock, collard greens, bring to a boil, cover, set on low heat, and simmer for 35-50 min or until collard greens are soft. Stir occasionally.

4. Prepare your choice of vegan protein as the stew is simmering. Legumes should amount to 3 cups after boiling. Tempeh and tofu can be steamed or pan fried. Set aside after cooking.

5. When the stew is done simmering, slowly sift in the oat flour a little at a time, while stirring constantly. *Then add your choice of vegan protein.* Continue to simmer on medium heat for another 15-20 min. If oat flour turns into clumps, simmer until gone. Add salt to taste.

6. Then add filé powder while stirring constantly. Cover and let settle for about 10 min before serving.

7. Serve over a bed of rice.

see recipe

Collard Greens:
Black List or Dean's List?

Collard Greens are amongst the top 5 richest in brain support-ing choline. But... It's also on the Dirty Dozen+ list. Though it didn't actually make the top 12 most pesticide ridden crops, it was added to the list because of the exceptionally neuro-toxic residues that were found on do-mestically grown collard greens.

So to get the most out of collard greens' brain supporting proper-ties, make sure to get it organic.

tip This recipe is very versatile when it comes to complete protein. Try adding 3 cooked cups of lentils, tempeh, tofu or your favorite vegan protein.

tip You can also serve over a bed of quinoa for a complete protein.

Also note that the nutrition facts do not include the rice, protein, or quinoa, just the gumbo.

Spices:
Spice Up Your Life, And Your Health

Spices can make your recipes more than just delicious. They can also benefit your health in many ways. Take a look at the spices in this recipe, and how they can benefit you.

Thyme: Contains "thymol" which can increase the amount of healthy fats in cellular structures.

Oregano: Contains powerful anti-biotic and anti-oxidant compounds.

Cayenne: Contains anti-inflammatory, im-mune boosting, and fat burning properties.

Nutrition Facts
Recipe makes 8 servings

Amount per serving

Calories	**123**
Total Fat	**5.6g**
Saturated Fat	0.1g
Total Carbohydrates	**15.5g**
Carbohydrates from Fiber	3g
Sugars	**5g**
Protein	**7.6g**

Fiesta Bean Salad

Ingredients:

SERVES: 5 PREP TIME: 20 MIN
GLUTEN FREE · SOY FREE · RAW (Option)

Dressing:

- 2 tablespoons **extra-virgin olive oil**
- 2 tablespoons **lime juice**
- 1 **clove garlic,** crushed
- ¼ teaspoon **chili powder**
- ¼ teaspoon **cumin**
- ⅛ teaspoon **black pepper**
- ¾ teaspoon **salt,** or to taste

Salad:

- 1 cup **pinto beans,** boiled and drained
- 1 cup **fresh sweet corn kernels** (about 1 ear)
- ½ cup **yellow bell pepper,** finely chopped
- ¼ cup **sweet onion,** finely chopper
- 1 small **avocado,** chopped
- 1 cup **tomatoes,** seeded and chopped
- ¼ cup **fresh cilantro,** chopped
- **Salt and pepper** to taste

Directions:

1. Mix all dressing ingredients in a small bowl. Mix thoroughly and set aside.

2. In a large mixing bowl, toss the beans, corn, bell pepper, and sweet onions. Then add the dressing, tomatoes, avocado, cilantro, salt and pepper to taste. Mix these remaining ingredients gently to cover with dressing.

3. Serve as a side dish or have as a delicious main course.

Raw Variation:

Replace cooked beans with equal amount of sprouted or green garbanzos.

see recipe

Avocado and Corn:
B5 Super Team

This nutrient rich combo is often used in your favorite Mexican recipes. But they offer more than just a great dining experience.

Both corn and avocados are super rich in vitamin B5. Not only is this good for boosting your brain, it also turns carbohydrates into energy to fuel your day!

Corn:
Beyond Dirty Dozen? Beware!

Corn is something that you must get in its organic form. Though corn is not on the Dirty Dozen list, it is at high risk of being genetically modified. Over 70% of conventional corn in the United States has been genetically modified to be pesticide resistant, insect resistant, or pesticide producing. Though the adverse effects are not fully understood, *it is best to steer clear of GM corn and go organic!*

Nutrition Facts
Recipe makes 5 servings

Amount per serving	
Calories	**233**
Total Fat	**12g**
Saturated Fat	2g
Total Carbohydrates	**28g**
Carbohydrates from Fiber	8g
Sugars	**4.5g**
Protein	**6.5g**

Anti-Stress Breakfast Oatmeal + Green Tea

SERVES: **1** PREP TIME: **1h 15 MIN**
GLUTEN FREE **SOY FREE**

Ingredients:

- 1 cup cooked **oatmeal**
- 1 cup **cantaloupe**
- ⅓ cup **mix of pistachios, sliced almonds, and walnuts** (raw is best)

Optional: Add your favorite natural sweetener and sea salt to taste.

tip I love making this recipe with steel cut oats made a little bit al dente.

Directions:

1. Combine all ingredients together in a bowl and enjoy with a cup of green tea.

This breakfast recipe soothes your mind by increasing your brain's anti-stress chemical GABA.

see recipe

Pistachios:
Slow That Sugar Down!

Protein rich pistachios are in the top 3 richest common foods when it comes to GABA supporting B6. But this wonderful ingredient can also help maintain your blood sugar balance. Researchers found that including pistachios in your carbohydrate rich meals can significantly reduce blood sugar spikes, giving you sustained energy, and reducing your risk of diabetes!

With the lysine rich pistachios and a balanced ratio of omega 3s and 6s from walnuts and almonds, *you've got yourself a delicious power breakfast!*

Cantaloupe:
Number 1 Pick!

Cantaloupe leads the pack by a long shot when it comes to GABA supporting inositol. In fact, it contains almost 3 times more inositol than the next richest source, rutabagas!

But be careful... Researchers found that pre-cut cantaloupe can lose much more vitamin B when compared to other pre pack fruits... up to 25% in 6 days! So next time you feel like having some cantaloupe, make sure to get it whole and cut it yourself.

Nutrition Facts	
Recipe makes 1 serving	
Amount per serving	
Calories	**730**
Total Fat	**25g**
Saturated Fat	4g
Total Carbohydrates	**83g**
Carbohydrates from Fiber	13g
Sugars	**16g**
Protein	**21g**

Millet Flax Seed Casserole

Ingredients:

- ½ cup **dry millet**
- 2 ½ cups **coconut milk beverage**
- 2 tablespoons **dates,** chopped
- 2 cups **pears,** chopped
- 1 teaspoon **cinnamon**
- ¼ teaspoon **salt**
- ¼ cup **flax seeds**
- 1 tablespoon **maple syrup**

Directions:

1. Preheat oven to 375 degrees F.

2. In a casserole dish, combine millet, coconut milk beverage, dates, pears, and cinnamon. Cover with foil and bake for 35 min at 375 F.

3. As the casserole is baking, grind flax seeds into a course power with a pinch of salt (optional) in a coffee grinder. Using a small bowl, combine with maple syrup and mix to coat evenly.

4. Remove casserole and stir. Let cool, and top with flax seed-maple syrup mixture before serving.

see recipe

Millet:
Gluten Free and More!

Millet is becoming an increasingly popular gluten free option.

A grain rich in glutamine precursors, and GABA supporting B vitamins, millet is a great choice for keeping your brain healthy and calm.

This awesome grain has also shown to reduce triglycerides and inflammatory markers significantly better than white rice.

Pear:
Save The Best Part

Pears are a rich source of GABA supporting inositol. Though the fruit itself is full of health boosting phytonutrients, pear skin was found to have 3 to 4 times the nutrients than the flesh.

So next time you have a pear, be sure to save the skin. It's the best part!

Nutrition Facts	
Recipe makes 4 servings	
Amount per serving	
Calories	**231**
Total Fat	**10.5g**
Saturated Fat	0.5g
Total Carbohydrates	**36g**
Carbohydrates from Fiber	6g
Sugars	**13g**
Protein	**5g**

Indian Lima Bean Rice

SERVES: **4** PREP TIME: **25 MIN**
GLUTEN FREE SOY FREE

Ingredients:

- 1 cup **dry brown basmati rice**
- ½ tablespoon **coconut oil**
- 1 cup **onion,** chopped
- 1 teaspoon **garlic paste**
- 1 teaspoon **ginger paste**
- 1 **green chili**
- 1 teaspoon **curry powder**
- 1/2 teaspoon **garam masala**
- 1 teaspoon **turmeric powder**
- 1 cup **baby lima bean**
- 1 cup **tomato,** chopped
- ½ teaspoon **salt** or to taste

Directions:

1. Fill a medium-sized pot with 5 cups of water and bring to a rolling boil.

2. Add the rice, let return to a boil, lower to medium high heat and boil for 25 min uncovered. Rice should feel tender on the outside, but slight al dente.

3. Drain the rice and allow it to sit in a strainer draining for 5 min, allowing the rice to continue steaming. Fluff the rice and let sit for another 5 min.

4. In a large saucepan, bring coconut oil to medium-high heat. Add the onions and sauté 2-3 min until translucent. Add the garlic paste, ginger paste, green chilies, curry powder, garam masala, tumeric powder, and sauté for another 1 min.

5. Add the tomatoes and continue sautéing for another 2-3 minutes or until the tomatoes are soft.

6. Add the lima beans, lower to medium heat, and continue sautéing for 5 min.

7. Add the cooked basmati rice, 1 cup of warm water, and sauté for another 5 min on medium heat, stirring constantly. Salt to taste.

8. Serve as a main course or as a tasty side dish.

see recipe 👉

Lima Beans:
Control The Sugar and The Sulfites

Lima beans are a good source of all the GABA supporting nutrients. But this humble ingredient has even more to offer! Because of its high fiber content, lima beans can help stabilize blood sugar increases after meals.

And because it is rich in the mineral molybdenum, *it may also help the body detoxify itself from sulfite preservatives!*

Brown Rice:
Lost In The Process?

We all know that brown rice is healthier than its refined and polish counterpart. *But how much of the naturally occurring nutrients are lost in rice processing?* Look at this graph to find out. ▶

Though some of these nutrients are re-added to "enriched" white rice, many are not. Also, these nutrients are not in their natural form.

Brown to White Rice
Nutritional Loss...

White Rice	Loss
B1	- 80%
B3	- 67%
B6	- 90%
Manganese	- 50%
Phosphorus	- 50%
Iron	- 60%
Fiber	- 100%
Essential Fatty Acids	- 100%

White rice is rice that had its outer layer removed. This process increases storage life, however it *also removes all its fiber and essential fatty acids.*

Nutrition Facts
Recipe makes 4 servings

Amount per serving

Calories	**269**
Total Fat	**3.2g**
Saturated Fat	0.4g
Total Carbohydrates	**52g**
Carbohydrates from Fiber	5g
Sugars	**4.7g**
Protein	**8g**

Lemon Zest Artichoke Salad

GLUTEN FREE SOY FREE RAW (Option)

Ingredients:

Dressing:
- 1 teaspoon **lemon zest**
- 1 ½ tablespoons **lemon juice**
- 2 tablespoons **olive oil**
- 2 **cloves garlic,** crushed
- ¼ teaspoon **pepper**
- **Salt** to taste

Salad:
- 2 ½ cups **long grain brown rice,** cooked
- 2 cups **artichoke hearts,** drained and quartered
- ¼ cup **sweet onions,** finely chopped
- ½ cup **bell pepper,** chopped
- ¼ cup **flat leaf parsley,** chopped

Raw Variation: Use sprouted lentils instead of brown rice. Use fresh artichokes trimmed until only tender parts are left. Slice thin.

Directions:

1. In a small mixing bowl, mix all dressing ingredients and set aside.

2. Using a large mixing bowl, combine and mix all salad ingredients.

3. Whisk dressing into salad bowl and mix until evenly coated. Cover and let marinate for 10-15 min before serving.

4. Serve as a delicious side dish for any meal.

This is an easy and delicious way to use leftover rice from a previous meal!

Brown Rice:
Natural Support

When using rice for GABA support, make sure to use brown rice instead of white rice. Most of the GABA supporting nutrients in rice are lost during processing. And while some of the nutrients are added back during the "enrichment" process, they are not in their natural form. *Plus, many of these nutrients, including brain boosting B6, are never replaced at all.*

Artichoke:
Calm and Clean

The artichoke is a unique vegetable that is rich in the GABA supporting nutrient inositol. Besides helping to keep your brain calm and collected, artichokes can also help your body's detoxification systems. Much like the popular detoxification herb milk thistle, artichokes are rich in a flavonoid called "silymarin." This protects your liver against toxins so it can effectively detoxify your body.

Nutrition Facts
Recipe makes 4 servings

Amount per serving

Calories	259
Total Fat	7g
Saturated Fat	1g
Total Carbohydrates	43g
Carbohydrates from Fiber	10g
Sugars	4g
Protein	6g

Oven "Fried" Veggies with Sundried Tomato Buckwheat

SERVES: **4** PREP TIME: **45 MIN**

GLT FREE
(Option)

SOY
FREE

Ingredients:

Breading:

- ⅔ cup unsweetened **coconut milk beverage**
- ¼ cup **mustard**
- 2 teaspoons **onion powder**
- 2 teaspoons **garlic powder**
- 1 ½ cup crushed **Ezekiel cereal** or **unsweetened rice cereal** (GF)
- ½ teaspoon **black pepper**
- ½ teaspoon **sea salt** or to taste

Vegetables:

- 1 medium **eggplant,** sliced into ½ inch pieces
- 1 **zucchini,** sliced into ¼ inch pieces
- 1 tablespoon high oleic **sunflower oil**
- **Sea salt and black pepper** to taste

Buckwheat:

- 1 tablespoon high oleic **sunflower oil**
- 3 **cloves minced garlic**
- 2 cups **vegetable stock**
- 1 cup **buckwheat groats**
- ½ cup **sun-dried tomato,** chopped
- **Salt** to taste

Directions:

1. Preheat oven to 385 degrees F.

2. In a medium size bowl, mix unsweetened coconut milk beverage with mustard, onion powder, and garlic powder. Using a separate bowl, mix cereal crumbs, pepper, and salt. Mix both thoroughly to ensure even distribution.

3. Dip both eggplant and zucchini slices in coconut milk and mustard mixture. Let the excess liquid drip off, then dip to cover in cereal crumb mixture.

4. Using an lightly oiled baking sheet, lay breaded eggplant and zucchini slices and bake at 385 degrees for 30 min, turning once, until golden brown.

5. As the vegetables are baking, begin preparing the buckwheat. Using a large sauce pan, bring sunflower oil to medium high heat. Add minced garlic and sauté for 1 min until fragrant. Then add buckwheat, sundried tomatoes, and sauté for another 2-3 min.

6. Add vegetable stock, bring to a boil, cover and let simmer for 10-15 min until all the liquid is absorbed. Add salt and pepper to taste.

7. When the breaded eggplant and zucchini are done baking, remove from oven and let cool for 2-3 min.

8. Serve breaded vegetables with side of buckwheat for a delicious meal.

see recipe

Buckwheat:
Unique and Gluten Free

Buckwheat is getting increasingly popular with so many people going gluten free. Though many people may think that buckwheat is a type of cereal grain, it is actually a fruit seed!

And here's a tip for the raw foodies out there. If you are going to use buckwheat in your recipes, make sure to avoid the "kasha" variety as these have already been roasted.

tip We use unsweetened coconut milk beverage to make the breading because its fats are more heat stable. If this is not available to you, you can use your favorite vegan milk instead.

Eggplant:
To Soothe and Protect

There's more to eggplant than just deliciousness and GABA supporting nutrients. Researchers have also identified a nutrient in eggplant called nasunin.

This awesome anti-oxidant has the ability to protect cell membranes, especially in the brain!

Nutrition Facts	
Recipe makes 4 servings	
Amount per serving	
Calories	**224**
Total Fat	**6.5g**
Saturated Fat	0.3g
Total Carbohydrates	**48g**
Carbohydrates from Fiber	13g
Sugars	**12.5g**
Protein	**7.5g**

Garlic Spinach and Green Beans

SERVES: **4** PREP TIME: **15 MIN**

GLUTEN FREE | **SOY FREE** | **RAW (Option)**

Ingredients:

- 1 tablespoon **coconut oil**
- 1 tablespoon **garlic,** minced
- 2 cups **green beans,** trimmed
- ¼ cup **water**
- 4 cups **fresh spinach**
- **Sea salt and pepper** to taste
- 1 tablespoon **sliced almonds**

Raw Variation:

This recipe can be made into a salad like recipe for those on a raw food diet. But be careful of "raw" almonds sold on most store shelves. Many of these have been pasteurized or blanched, and are not actually raw. A more accurate label for these almonds is "not roasted." If you want truly raw, unpasteurized, sproutable almonds, the internet is a good place to look.

Directions:

1. Using a medium saucepan, bring oil to medium-high heat. Add garlic and sauté until for 1-2 minutes until fragrant.

2. Add green beans, sauté for an additional minute. Then add ¼ cup of water to the pan, cover, and let steam for 4-5 min until the green beans are tender.

3. Then add spinach, toss with garlic and green beans, and let cook until wilted. Add salt and pepper to taste. Remove from heat and sprinkle with sliced almonds before serving.

4. Serve as a side dish for a delicious meal.

see recipe

Spinach:
Good at Everything

Spinach is one of those vegetables that's just good at everything. In terms of GABA support, spinach is not only rich in glutamine precursors, but all of the GABA related B vitamins as well. As if this isn't enough, researchers have found another beneficial aspect of spinach.

By inhibiting something called the angiotensin 1 converting enzyme, *scientists found that spinach can actually reduce blood pressure!*

Green Beans:
Fresh or Frozen?

Fresh produce is always best. But sometimes we can only find things in the frozen food section. *With inositol rich green beans, you shouldn't worry.*

Studies have found that frozen green beans can retain up to 90% of its nutrients. But try to avoid canned green beans... *These can lose about 30% of their nutrients during canning.*

Nutrition Facts
Recipe makes 4 servings

Amount per serving	
Calories	**72**
Total Fat	**4g**
Saturated Fat	0.3g
Total Carbohydrates	**7g**
Carbohydrates from Fiber	3g
Sugars	**1g**
Protein	**2.5g**

Calm and Collected GABA Smoothie

Ingredients:

- 2 cups **almond milk**
- 1 cup **frozen blackberry**
- 1 cup **frozen mango**
- ¼ cup **raw walnuts**
- 2 tablespoons **flax seeds**
- ½ cup **ice**
- **Dates** or **vegan sweetener** to taste (optional)

Raw Variation:

Be sure to use raw almond milk if available. If not, you can make it yourself by blending raw almonds with water, and filtering through cheesecloth. Adjust the water to nut ratio until desired level of creaminess is achieved!

SERVES: **4** PREP TIME: **2 MIN**
GLUTEN FREE **SOY FREE** **RAW (Option)**

Directions:

1. Combine ingredients in blender. Blend until smooth.

Try adding another 1/2 cup of ice to make an icy treat!

see recipe

Walnuts + Flax:
Bitter Sweet Benefits

Much like flax seeds, walnuts are rich in brain supporting omega 3 fatty acids and glutamine precursors. But be careful when you are preparing your walnuts. Researchers have found that up to 90% of the walnut's phyto-nutrients come from skin. Though the skin may have a bit of a bitter flavor, do your body a favor and leave it on. With all of the wonderful fruits in this smoothie, your taste buds will never know the difference.

Mangos:
Complementary Nutrition

When you're craving something sweet, mangos can really hit the spot. Rich in inositol and B vitamins, mangos makes a great complement the glutamine precursors in walnuts and flax seeds. But it doesn't end there! When eating something as sweet as mangos, combining it with seeds and nuts *can reduce the blood sugar spikes and give you sustained energy!*

Nutrition Facts
Recipe makes 4 servings

Amount per serving	
Calories	290
Total Fat	16.5g
Saturated Fat	1g
Total Carbohydrates	31g
Carbohydrates from Fiber	14.5g
Sugars	20g
Protein	7g

VEGAN SURVIVAL: IMMUNE

Boost Your Defenses!

Your immune system is constantly working around the clock.

Giving it the nutrients it needs will keep your defenses balanced, and on high alert!

Nature's medicine cabinet is full of surprises!

VSG: Immune

A strong and balanced immune system is a foundation of great health.

Whether you're at the office, on a plane, or sitting in class, your immune system is constantly being bombarded with bugs and pathogens. And an immune system out of balance can just as quickly become your biggest adversary! Keep your immune system strong and balanced, and you'll be the one who doesn't get sick.

Modern diets can often be lifeless, overly processed, and fail to support our immune defenses. But nature has provided us with so many immune boosting and balancing ingredients! It should be easy, tasty, and enjoyable to keep ourselves healthy.

From vitamin C and beta-glucans, to a huge variety of polyphenols, the plant kingdom is like a natural pharmacy of immune supporting compounds. Portobello mushrooms, coconut milk, kiwis, strawberries... nature's medicine cabinet is practically endless. But some of these foods get less than the attention that they deserve!

We've all been told to squeeze some lemon into our tea when we're feeling down. While this is definitely beneficial, think about this... One cup of fresh strawberries has *3 times* more vitamin C than a quarter cup of lemon juice! This is also true of broccoli, bell peppers, and brussels sprouts! And if you can get your hands on some fresh (or frozen) guava, just one cup give syou over 10 times the vitamin C! *And who would have thought, over peeling a red onion can cause it to lose over 70% of an important polyphenol!*

So whether your immune system is running low, or just out of control, the plant kingdom is here to help! You can make so many wonderful combinations and recipes to keep yourself strong. We'll show you just some of the tasty possibilities! ∎

Immune Boosting Nutrients + Foods

Examples of some top foods in this category:

Vitamin C: Guava, Broccoli, Bell Pepper, Brussels Sprouts, Strawberries, Payapa, Pineapple, Kiwi, Oranges, Cantaloupe

---

Zinc: Granola, Pumpkin Seeds, Wheat Germ, Chickpeas, Pistachios, Pine Nuts, Cashews, Sesame Seeds

---

Beta Glucans: Barley, Oats, Shiitake Mushrooms, Button Mushrooms, Crimini Mushrooms, Portabello Mushrooms

---

Lauric Acid: Coconut Oil, Coconut Milk, Coconut Flesh.

Allicin: Garlic, chopped and exposed to air 10-15 min

Vitamin D: Mushrooms sliced and exposed to sun for 12 hrs before drying

Immune Balance Nutrients + Foods

Examples of some top foods in this category:

Omega 3's: Walnuts, Flax Seeds, Chia Seeds, Hemp Seeds

Polyphenols: Berries, Pomegranate, Rosemary, Turmeric, Onions, Green Tea

It should be easy, tasty and enjoyable to keep ourselves healthy!

Garlic Cashew Broccoli Stir-Fry

SERVES: **2** PREP TIME: **20 MIN**
GF
GLUTEN FREE

Ingredients:

- ½ pound **broccoli florets,** cut into small pieces
- ½ tablespoon **coconut oil**
- 2 cloves **garlic,** minced
- ½ teaspoon ground **black pepper**
- ¼ teaspoon ground **white pepper**
- 1 cup **vegetable stock**
- 2 tablespoons **tamari** (or **s**oy sauce)
- 1 teaspoon **rice wine vinegar**
- 1 tablespoon **real maple syrup**
- 1 tablespoon **whole oat flour**
- 2 tablespoons **water**
- ¼ cup **cashews** (raw is best)

Gluten Free Variation: Make sure the tamari and oat flour are gluten free.

Directions:

1. Steam broccoli for 5-7 minutes until al dente, then set aside.

2. While the broccoli is steaming, heat coconut oil in a large pan over medium heat. Add minced garlic, black pepper, white pepper, and saute until fragrant 1-2 minutes.

3. Then add vegetable stock, tamari, rice wine vinegar, and maple syrup. Bring to a boil, then reduce heat to simmer for 1 min.

4. As the sauce simmers, quickly dissolve 1 tbps of oat flour in 2 tablespoons of water. Slowly add this oat flour solution to the sauce while stirring constantly. Continue simmering 3-5 minutes until sauce thickens, stirring frequently.

5. Once the sauce is done, remove pan from heat, and pour about half the sauce into a small bowl for dipping. Then mix in broccoli and cashews, coating the vegetables thoroughly with remainder of the sauce.

6. Serve with rice and sauce on the side for a delicious meal.

see recipe

Broccoli:
Supercharge and Regulate!

Broccoli is super rich in vitamin C and is also a good source of zinc. Because of this, it's a great immune system booster.

Researchers found that broccoli also regulates the immune system with a flavonoid called "kaempferol." This substance can decrease the effects of allergy related substances in the body, *and help you control unnecessary inflammation!*

Garlic:
Retaining The Benefits

Overcooking will reduce the potency of garlic's health promoting compounds. If you want to get the most out of this ingredient, add it to step 4 instead!

Cashews and Maple Syrup:
A Zinc Powerhouse Combo

Cashews and maple syrup are some of the richest sources of zinc in the vegan diet. Zinc is central to proper immune system function and even DNA repair! Yet it's quite common for people to be deficient in this dietary mineral.

So add more of these ingredients to your diet. *You can satisfy your cravings, and keep your body running strong!*

Nutrition Facts
Recipe makes 2 servings

Amount per serving	
Calories	**307**
Total Fat	**16g**
Saturated Fat	3g
Total Carbohydrates	**36g**
Carbohydrates from Fiber	6g
Sugars	**13g**
Protein	**12g**

Vegan Brazilian Stroganoff

SERVES: **6** PREP TIME: **45 MIN**
GLUTEN FREE (Option) SOY FREE

Ingredients:

- ½ tablespoon **coconut oil**
- 1 cup chopped **carrots**
- 1 cup fresh **mushrooms,** sliced
- ½ cup minced Italian **parsley**
- 1 ½ cups **seitan** cut into thin strips
- 2 cups **marinara** or **tomato sauce**
- 1 ½ cups unsweetened **coconut milk**
- ½ cup unsweetened **almond milk**
- 2 tablespoons *Vogue Cuisine* Vegetable Soup **& Seasoning Base powder**
- 1 teaspoon **real maple syrup** (optional)
- **Salt** to taste

tip Marinara/ tomato sauce can differ in acidity depending on brand and season. To balance the flavor of a more acidic sauce, add a small amount of maple syrup to the mixture. A little more Vegetable Soup powder or coconut milk can be used in the same way.

tip To avoid exposure to the chemical BPA, look for coconut milk and marinara/ tomato sauce in jars or BPA free cans.

Directions:

1. Add a ½ tablespoon coconut oil to pan and bring to med-high heat. Add 1 cup diced carrots and sauté for 5 minutes to caramelize sugars.

2. Using a 3 quart sauce pan, combine 2 cups marinara/ tomato sauce, 1 ½ cups coconut milk, ½ cup unsweetened almond milk, ½ cup minced Italian parsley, and 2 tbsp vegetable base powder. Bring to gentle boil. Add salt to taste.

3. Add the sautéd carrots, 1 ½ cups seitan, and 1 cup sliced mushrooms into the sauce mixture. Bring to boil again, then cook on medium heat for additional 10 minutes stirring frequently. Then let simmer for another 5 minutes.

4. If mixture becomes too thick, add a little more almond milk.

5. Add salt to taste.

6. Serve over a bed of rice.

Gluten Free Variation: In place of seitan, use crumbled tempeh or lentils (cooked to al dente in water).

Lower Fat Variation: Use half the recommended amount of coconut milk.

see recipe

Coconut Fat:
Beat The Bugs and The Belly Fat

The coconut oil in this recipe creates the rich and creamy flavor that we all love. *But can this oil actually benefit the immune system?* Absolutely.

Coconut oil is rich in immune supporting fats and compounds like lauric acid and monolaurin. Studies have shown their ability to help fight viruses, bacteria, and unwanted fungal infections! But there's more! Because coconut oil is a special kind of saturated fat, it can actually balance cholesterol levels, help you burn fat more efficiently, and has shown to reduce stubborn belly fat without increasing body-weight! *Now that's something you can feel good about!*

More great tips...

tip For a more authentic Brazilian experience, serve with Terra Stix on the side.

tip To make this recipe even tastier, brown the Seitan in 1 tbsp of oil before adding to the sauce. This way it will absorb more flavor while cooking.

tip Also, this recipe stores very well. In fact, the flavors become more complex the next day.

Mushrooms:
Dollar for Dollar Champion!

The common mushroom is proving to be economical in so many ways. Their immune supporting effects rival those of more exotic mushrooms, they're super rich in many nutrients, and... *they even made the Clean 15 list!*

So if you're feeling thrifty, you can go ahead and opt for conventionally grown mushrooms without worrying about pesticides. *Dollar for dollar, conventional mushrooms may be the best value around!*

Nutrition Facts
Recipe makes 6 servings

Amount per serving	
Calories	**401**
Total Fat	**18.6g**
Saturated Fat	12.8g
Total Carbohydrates	**41g**
Carbohydrates from Fiber	3.5g
Sugars	**12g**
Protein	**23g**

Lemon Garlic Kale

Ingredients:

- 8 cups **dinosaur (dino) kale,** chopped
- 1 tablespoon **lemon juice**
- 2 **cloves garlic,** crushed and exposed to air for 5-10 mins.
- 2 teaspoons **coconut oil**
- ½ teaspoon **black pepper**
- **Salt** to taste

SERVES: **4** PREP TIME: **15 MIN** **(GF)** **(SF)** **(R)**
GLUTEN FREE · SOY FREE · RAW (Option)

Directions:

1. Bring water to a boil in a medium pot. Add Kale, a pinch of salt, and cook for 5-7 minutes. Drain water.

2. In a large mixing bowl, add cooked kale, lemon juice, coconut oil, garlic, pepper, and sea salt to taste. Mix thoroughly and serve

Raw Variation: Skip step one, replace coconut oil with olive oil, and let marinate overnight.

see recipe

Kale: *Draining The Unwanted*

Many leafy green vegetables like kale and spinach are high in something called "oxalates." This substance can cause many of the problems in people suffering a wide range of disorders, including kidney stones, fibromyalgia and possibly even autism. Oxalates can be especially problematic for these people when eaten in excess. Draining your leafy green vegetables after a quick boil can do wonders to reduce oxalate levels!

And if you want to retain the maximum amount of nutrients, make sure to boil for only a minute or two instead.

Kale: *Popular and Amazing*

An immune booster that fights cancer and detoxifies the body? Absolutely!

Though kale is super rich in immune supporting vitamin C, it has many other tricks up its sleeve. Kale is rich in a variety of glucosinolates which have shown to be cancer preventative. These same compounds stimulate the body's detoxification mechanisms. *No wonder kale is so popular!*

Nutrition Facts
Recipe makes 4 servings

Amount per serving	
Calories	78
Total Fat	1.2g
Saturated Fat	1g
Total Carbohydrates	15g
Carbohydrates from Fiber	2g
Sugars	0g
Protein	4g

Wild Rice Cabbage and Mushroom Soup

SERVES: **4** PREP TIME: **1h 15 MIN** (GF) (SF)
GLUTEN FREE · SOY FREE

Ingredients:

- 1 tablespoon **coconut oil**
- 2 **garlic cloves,** pressed
- ¾ cup **leeks,** chopped
- ½ cup **shiitake mushrooms,** hydrated and sliced
- ½ cup **dry wild rice**
- 2 cups **tomatoes,** coarsely chopped
- 3 cups of **cabbage,** coarsely chopped
- 5 cups **vegetable broth**
- **Salt** to taste
- 2 ½ tablespoons **lime juice** or to taste

Directions:

1. Using a medium sized pot, bring coconut oil to medium heat. Add garlic and sauté until fragrant about 2-3 minutes. Add leeks, mushrooms, and wild rice. Sauté until leeks are soft, about 2-3 min.

2. Add tomatoes, cabbage, and sauté for another 7 minutes stirring frequently.

3. Add vegetable broth, sea salt to taste, bring to boil, cover, reduce heat, and simmer until the wild rice is tender, about 40-50 minutes.

4. Add lime juice just before serving.

see recipe

Wild Rice:
Double The Protein?

Wouldn't you love it if rice had double the protein <u>and</u> double the fiber?

Well look no further. Though wild rice is actually a grass seed, this ingredient is uniquely delicious and highly nutritious. Besides having more protein and fiber, *it is also rich in many vitamins, minerals, and has less calories per serving!*

Shiitake Mushrooms:
Immune Boosting Sugar?

Sugar is the last thing you would think of when trying to boost the immune system. Yet, it turns out that the immune boosting components of shiitake mushrooms involve exactly that... sugar! But we're not talking about the sugar you put into cookies and cupcakes. We're talking about "glucan polysaccharides." These special carbohydrates are known to activate immune cells so they can do a better job of protecting your body and removing unwanted cells.

So give your immune system the kick that it needs and add some shiitake mushrooms to your meals!

Nutrition Facts	
Recipe makes 4 servings	
Amount per serving	
Calories	**160**
Total Fat	**3.7g**
Saturated Fat	3g
Total Carbohydrates	**31g**
Carbohydrates from Fiber	4g
Sugars	**7g**
Protein	**4.5g**

Immuni-Tea

 GLUTEN FREE **SOY FREE**

Ingredients:

- ½ cup **fresh mint leaves,** chopped
- ¼ cup **fresh ginger,** chopped
- ¼ cup **maple syrup** or to taste
- 3 cups **boiling water**
- ⅓ cup **lemon juice**

Try adding the lemon juice after the tea has cooled down to help preserve vitamin C levels.

Directions:

1. Using a medium bowl or large tea press, combine mint, ginger, and boiling water. Let steep for 10 minutes.

2. When tea is done steeping, strain into cups making sure to squeeze the pulp thoroughly.

3. Add lemon juice and maple syrup before serving.

tip If you need to cut down your sugar intake try stevia, monk fruit, or yacon natural sweeteners instead of maple syrup.

see recipe

Immuni-Tea:
A Balanced Immune Booster

This Immuni-Tea recipe is a great all around immune tonic.

Because it combines the cooling properties of mint, with the warming properties of ginger, you can use it for various types of colds and flus. But if your cold makes you feel more feverish, then you can **add more mint**. If you feel like you're shivering with the chills, **add more ginger!**

Combine these with the vitamin C in lemons and the zinc in the maple syrup, and you'll be better in no time!

Peppermint:
The **Cool** Herb

Wouldn't it be awesome if your medicine actually tasted good? Well if you like the taste of mint, then reach for some next time you're feeling run down. This herb has been used against colds in Chinese herbal medicine for centuries, especially for high fevers, cough and sore throat. Modern research has also found compounds in mint that can benefit conditions like asthma and allergic rhinitis. *Medicine never tasted so good!*

VS

Ginger:
The **Hot** Herb

Ever get a rush of warm energy after drinking ginger tea? Like mint, ginger has also been used for centuries in Chinese herbal medicine for colds and flus. But unlike mint's cooling nature, ginger is known for having warming properties. Amazingly, researchers have found that ginger's immune boosting properties come from its ability to promote sweating. They found that sweat itself contains an antibiotic compound called "dermicidin." So when Chinese herbalists induce sweating to help fight off bugs, this is why it works!

Nutrition Facts
Recipe makes 2 servings

Amount per serving	
Calories	**155**
Total Fat	**0.1g**
Saturated Fat	0g
Total Carbohydrates	**38g**
Carbohydrates from Fiber	2g
Sugars	**25g**
Protein	**0.2g**

Spicy Thai Coconut Soup

SERVES: **6** PREP TIME: **30 MIN**
GLUTEN FREE **SOY FREE (Option)**

Ingredients:

- 2 cans (27 oz) **coconut milk** (lite or full-fat)
- 4 cups **vegetable broth**
- 1 piece **fresh ginger**
- 1 teaspoon **grated lime zest**
- 1 (14 oz) package of **extra firm tofu,** cubed
- 1 cup **crimini mushrooms,** sliced
- 1 cup **tomatoes,** cubed
- 4 **Thai chilies** (or any other spicy chili), chopped (optional)
- 2 tablespoons **maple syrup**
- 1 ½ tablespoons **lime juice**
- 1 teaspoon **salt** or to taste
- 2 tablespoons **fresh cilantro,** chopped

Soy Free Variation: Omit tofu.

tip The ginger and lime zest in this recipe gives it an authentic Thai flavor without the difficult to find ingredients!

Directions:

1. Grate lime zest into a small dish and set aside. Be careful not to grate into the white lime pith as this will cause your soup to be bitter.

2. Using a medium pot, combine coconut milk, vegetable broth, ginger, lime zest, and bring to a boil. Reduce heat, cover, and simmer on medium for 10 minutes stirring occasionally.

3. Add tofu, mushrooms, tomatoes, and chilies. Bring to a boil, cover, reduce heat and simmer for another 10 minutes.

4. Remove from heat, add maple syrup, lime juice, salt, and mix well.

5. Add fresh cilantro before serving.

see recipe

Lime/ Lime Peel:
Money In The Trash?

We've all juiced a lime and discarded the peel at some point in our lives. *But are we throwing away valuable substances in the trash?* Not only is this recipe super tasty, it's also a great way to use the nutrient rich skin of the lime! Researchers found citrus peels to contain substances called *"polymethoxylated flavones."* Not only can they help to reduce serum triglycerides and cholesterol, they may also help prevent diabetes! So next time you're about to throw away a lime peel, think of how you can use the zest in a recipe. *Or you can just make another coconut soup!*

The many names of the common mushroom include: white mushroom, button mushroom, table mushroom, crimini/ cremini mushroom, brown mushroom & portobello mushroom (when mature).

ON THE AIR

Mushrooms:
Cheaper and Better?

Exotic immune boosting mushrooms are all the rage these days. *But what if you could find a mushroom that was cheaper, easier to find, and better for boosting immunity than pricier mushrooms?* Well look no further than the common button mushroom! Researchers have found the common mushroom to actually surpass its more exotic cousins in its ability to balance unwanted inflammation. *So whether you want to boost or balance the immune system, the common mushroom can save the day!*

Nutrition Facts
Recipe makes 6 servings

Amount per serving

Calories	**213**
Total Fat	**14g**
Saturated Fat	0g
Total Carbohydrates	**19g**
Carbohydrates from Fiber	1g
Sugars	**8g**
Protein	**13g**

Strawberry-Kiwi Almond Butter Sandwich

Ingredients:

- 2 slices of **millet** (or your favorite) **bread**
- ⅛ cup **rolled oats**
- 2 tablespoons **almond butter** (raw is best)
- ¼ cup **strawberries,** chopped
- 1 **kiwi**, sliced
- 2 teaspoons **real maple syrup**
- pinch of **salt**

Raw Variation: Use raw vegan bread or your favorite raw crackers. Substitute maple syrup with raw agave or date paste.

tip If the mixture in step 2 gets too thick and dry, add some of your favorite vegan milk a few drops at a time, until you get the perfect consistency.

Directions:

1. Toast bread.

2. In small bowl, mix almond butter, rolled oats, strawberries, maple syrup, and a pinch of sea salt.

3. Spread onto toasted bread, layer with sliced kiwi, and serve.

A favorite with the kids... like peanut butter and jelly, but healthier!

see recipe

Kiwi: *Powerful and Economical*

Not only is kiwi a champion when it comes to vitamin C, it has also been shown to protect DNA and prevent respiratory illnesses in children! Researchers found that 6-7 year olds who ate more kiwis (or citrus fruits) were less likely to have issues like asthma, wheezing, and night coughing. This wonderful fruit is also on the Clean 15 list, *so you can save some money by buying conventional!*

IMMUNE

Vitamin C: *The Illusive Champion?*

Everybody knows about vitamin C, and its ability to boost the immune system! Most people think of lemons and oranges for vitamin C. Yet pound for pound, kiwis and strawberries are richer in vitamin C than both lemons and oranges. In fact, kiwis lead the pack by about double! *Both of these fruits are a delicious way to boost your immunity!*

Vitamin C comparison chart

100 grams	Vitamin C	Daily Value
Kiwi	92.7 mg	155%
Strawberry	58.8 mg	98%
Lemon	53 mg	88%
Orange	45 mg	75%

Nutrition Facts
Recipe makes 1 serving

Amount per serving

Calories	**433**
Total Fat	**22g**
Saturated Fat	2g
Total Carbohydrates	**54g**
Carbohydrates from Fiber	9g
Sugars	**16g**
Protein	**13g**

Mix and Match Breakfast Muesli

SERVES: **2** PREP TIME: **15 MIN**

 GLUTEN FREE **SOY FREE** **RAW (Option)**

Ingredients:

- 1 cup **rolled oats**
- ½ cup **zinc rich nuts/seeds** of your choice, chopped
- 1 ½ cups **coconut milk beverage***
- ½ tablespoon **lemon juice**
- **Maple syrup** or favorite vegan sweetener to taste
- ½ cup **apples,** grated or chopped
- 1 cup vitamin C rich **fruit of your choice,** sliced

*Unlike culinary canned coconut milk/ cream, coconut milk beverage is like soy or almond milk but made from coconut. If not available use your favorite vegan milk.

Coconut milk beverage is like soy or almond milk but with immune boosting fatty acids!

Directions:

1. In a large mixing bowl, combine oats, your choice of seeds/nuts, coconut milk beverage, lemon juice, and maple syrup/ vegan sweetener to taste. Let soak for 5-10 minutes.

2. Add apples, vitamin C rich fruit of your choice, mix thoroughly, and serve.

Gluten Free Variation: Make sure to use certified gluten free oats.

Raw Variation: Make sure to get your seeds, nuts, and coconut milk in raw form. You can also make raw coconut milk yourself with a fresh mature coconut! Just blend the coconut flesh with water and strain through cheesecloth. Adjust the water to coconut ratio until the desired level of creaminess is achieved!

see recipe

Oats: *An Immune Boosting Fiber*

Oats have long been touted for their cardiovascular benefits. But these nutrient packed grains also benefit the immune system in more ways than one!

Oats are a rich vegan source of zinc, a widely known immune booster. But oats are also packed with a special fiber called *"Beta Glucans,"* which help your immune cells respond to infections more efficiently.

So start your day off with some oats! Your immune system will thank you for it.

IMMUNE

Vitamin C and Zinc Comparison Charts:

Here's a pound for pound list of fruits, seeds and nuts rich in immune supporting vitamin C and zinc. Choose your favorites to make your Mix and Match Muesli.

The goal is to get the most vitamin C and zinc from the foods you enjoy most!

Vitamin C in Fruits:

100 grams	Vitamin C	Daily Value
Guava	228 mg	381%
Kiwi	92.7 mg	155%
Papaya	61.8 mg	103%
Strawberry	58.8 mg	98%
Pineapple	47.8 mg	80%
Orange	45 mg	75%
Cantaloupe	36.7 mg	61%

Zinc in Seeds and Nuts:

100 grams	Zinc	Daily Value
Sesame Seeds	7.8 mg	52%
Pumpkin Seeds	7.5 mg	50%
Pine Nuts	6.4 mg	43%
Cashews	5.8 mg	39%
Sunflower Seeds	5.0 mg	33%
Brazil Nuts	4.1 mg	27%
Pistachios	2.2 mg	15%

Nutrition Facts

Recipe makes 2 servings

Amount per serving

Calories	**423**
Total Fat	**22g**
Saturated Fat	2.7g
Total Carbohydrates	**54g**
Carbohydrates from Fiber	8g
Sugars	**16g**
Protein	**13g**

Spinach Garlic Bruschetta

Ingredients:

- 8 slices **French bread** or your favorite gluten free bread, toasted
- 1 tablespoon **coconut oil**
- 4 **garlic cloves,** minced and exposed to air for 5-10 minutes
- 3 cups **fresh spinach** tightly packed
- **Salt, pepper, olive oil** and **lemon juice** to taste

Gluten Free Variation: This recipe works wonderfully with gluten free bread.

Raw Variation: If you are on a raw diet, replace the sunflower oil with cold pressed olive oil, mix all ingredients together, let marinate for 5-10 minutes, and serve over your favorite raw bread!

SERVES: **4** PREP TIME: **10 MIN**

GLUTEN FREE (Option) SOY FREE RAW (Option)

Directions:

1. Preheat broiler and lightly toast bread on a cooking sheet.

2. Bring a medium pot of water to a boil, add spinach, and boil for no more than 1 minute. Strain and set aside.

3. As the bread is toasting, bring oil to medium heat in a large pan, add ½ of the total garlic and sauté for 30 seconds until fragrant.

4. Remove garlic from heat, add spinach, the rest of the garlic, salt, pepper, lemon juice to taste, and mix thoroughly.

5. Remove toasted bread from oven, top with spinach, drizzle with a little olive oil and serve!

tip To boost the garlic's immune boosting effects, add it all at the end of the recipe!

see recipe

Garlic + Lemon: *Immune Boosting Secrets*

Both garlic and lemon have powerful immune boosting properties. *But did you know?* How you handle these ingredients can actually make or break their immune boosting effects! Lemons are rich in kaempferol. Garlic is rich in allicin. Both have antibiotic effects. But if you forget to expose chopped garlic to air for at least 5 minutes, or add an acidic ingredient like lemon without waiting first, you can actually deactivate the enzymes that form the antibiotic compounds! So next time you use garlic in a recipe, chop it up, wait 5 minutes, and try to cook it for less than 15 minutes.

Spinach: *Nutrient vs. Anti-Nutrient*

Spinach is one of the richest sources of immune boosting zinc. *But can different ways of cooking determine how spinach affects your body?* Unfortunately spinach also contains high amounts of a substance called "oxalates." Not only can high levels cause health issues in some people, they can also reduce absorption of minerals including zinc. Boiling the spinach for just a minute helps to eliminate this substance, while retaining maximum nutrition. *This way you get all the good, without the bad!*

Nutrition Facts

Recipe makes 4 servings

Amount per serving

Calories	**219**
Total Fat	**8.4g**
Saturated Fat	1g
Total Carbohydrates	**28g**
Carbohydrates from Fiber	4g
Sugars	**0.2g**
Protein	**5g**

Coconut Flax Milk

SERVES: **2** PREP TIME: **Overnight + 5 MIN**

GLUTEN FREE **SOY FREE** **RAW**

Ingredients:

- ½ cup **water**
- 3 tablespoons **flax seeds**
- 1 ½ cups **coconut water,** chilled

Raw Variation:

Make sure to use fresh, or unpasteurized coconut water if you are on a raw foods diet.

Directions:

1. Soak flax seeds, covered, in luke-warm water over night.

2. Add chilled coconut water and hydrated flax (water included) to blender. Blend thoroughly.

3. Strain mixture through cheesecloth making sure to squeeze the pulp dry.

4. Enjoy promptly!

Try using the leftover flax pulp as a topping, or mixed it in a raw piecrust recipe!

see recipe

Flax:
Powerful Relief and Extra Protection

Flax oil, rich in Omega 3 fatty acids, can help you combat the inflammation involved in many chronic diseases. But if you have to take over-the-counter pain relievers (NSAIDs) on a regular basis, *researchers found that flax may also help to reduce the risk of developing ulcers!*

Cow Milk vs Flax Milk:
Healthier Options

Cow Milk:
Highly Inflammatory

Flax Milk:
Anti-Inflammatory

Coconut Water:
Nature's Sports Drink and More?

Coconut water really is nature's wonder drink! Not only is it rich in electrolytes to keep you hydrated, it has also been shown to be a powerful anti-inflammatory and pain reliever (analgesic).

In fact, Japanese researchers found its effects to be on par with the drugs they used in their study. *Amazing!*

Nutrition Facts
Recipe makes 2 servings

Amount per serving

Calories	**117**
Total Fat	**6g**
Saturated Fat	0g
Total Carbohydrates	**11.3g**
Carbohydrates from Fiber	6.8g
Sugars	**4.5g**
Protein	**4.5g**

Rosemary Berry Cooler

Ingredients:

- 4 cups **water**
- 4 **green tea bags**
- 2 sprigs of **fresh rosemary,** chopped and crushed (about 5 inches each)
- 2 tablespoons **fresh ginger,** chopped and crushed
- ½ cup **blackberries**
- ½ cup **blueberries**
- 2 tablespoons **lemon juice**
- **Real maple syrup, stevia,** or your favorite vegan sweetener to taste
- 1 pinch **salt** (optional)

SERVES: **4** PREP TIME: **20 MIN**

GLUTEN FREE   SOY FREE   RAW (Option)

Directions:

1. Boil water and pour over green tea bags, rosemary, and ginger. Let steep until cool.

2. Add both berries to a small pitcher and smash. Then strain the tea into the pitcher making sure to squeeze all the liquid out of ingredients.

3. Add lemon juice, maple syrup/ sweetener, and an optional pinch of sea salt.

4. Be sure to stir vigorously before pouring. Serve with ice.

Raw Variation: To make this recipe raw, steep everything at room temperature for a longer period of time. Strain into a cheese cloth and squeeze ingredients very dry. Use your favorite raw sweetener.

see recipe

Rosemary:
Reduce The Asthma, Increase Brain Power

Rosemary is beyond just delicious... it's an extraordinary medicinal herb! This wonderful ingredient contains anti-inflammatory substances that can reduce the severity of asthma attacks.

What's even more fascinating is that it can actually increase blood flow to the brain to increase thinking speed and accuracy. *Amazing!*

Green Tea:
Drug Like Effects?

Can it be that green tea works like a natural drug? Much like pain drugs Vioxx and Celebrex, the EGCG in green tea was actually found to inhibit a pro-inflammatory enzyme called COX-2. But unlike Vioxx and Celebrex, which were found to have some very serious side effects, green tea EGCG had none whatsoever!

So protect yourself from cancer and unwanted inflammation. *Get yourself some green tea!*

Nutrition Facts
Recipe makes 4 servings

Amount per serving

Calories	**24**
Total Fat	**0.1g**
Saturated Fat	0g
Total Carbohydrates	**5.6g**
Carbohydrates from Fiber	1.5g
Sugars	**3.5g**
Protein	**0.4g**

Spicy Ginger Cauliflower

SERVES: **4** PREP TIME: **30 MIN**
GLUTEN FREE   SOY FREE

Ingredients:

- 3 tablespoons high oleic **sunflower oil**
- 4 **garlic cloves,** minced
- 1 tablespoon **fresh ginger,** peeled and grated
- 1 ½ tablespoons **mustard seeds**
- 1 **head cauliflower,** cut into florets
- 1 teaspoon **turmeric**
- ½ teaspoon **cumin**
- ¼ teaspoon **black pepper**
- **Salt** to taste

Directions:

1. Set oven to 400 degrees F.

2. Heat oil to medium-high heat in a large pan. Sauté garlic, ginger, and mustard seeds. When seeds begin to sputter, remove from heat.

3. Place cauliflower in a large baking dish. Add garlic-ginger-mustard seed mixture, turmeric, cumin, pepper, and salt to taste. Toss to coat evenly.

5. Place in oven and roast until tender, about 20 to 25 minutes.

see recipe

Ginger:
Better Than Placebo

Ginger if often regarded for its ability to prevent nausea and boost the immune system. *But can this common ingredient actually save your joints?* Well, researchers conducted a 12 month study to evaluate ginger's effect on arthritic knees... and it passed with flying colors! After the first 6 months of adding ginger to their diets, participants reported increased function, and a nearly 50% reduction in pain from their condition. The placebo group on the other hand got worse!

So if your joints aren't feeling their best, add ginger to your daily diet and get back on the road to health.

Turmeric:
The Power Couple

Turmeric, rich in curcumin, is one of the most well studied culinary spices available. Cruciferous vegetables on the other hand, are some of the most well researched foods in your local produce section. *But could it be that they work better together than alone?* You guessed it! When researchers tested curcumin and cauliflower compounds alone, they were both able to slow down the cancer cells implanted into mice (poor mice!). But neither could do much alone for well-established tumors. Yet, when curcumin was combined with the cauliflower compounds, they significantly reduced tumor growth, and the ability for them to metastasize! But remember, there are specific ways to increase and retain the potency of these compounds in food... *This recipe shows you how!*

Nutrition Facts
Recipe makes 4 servings

Amount per serving	
Calories	**119**
Total Fat	**12g**
Saturated Fat	0.7g
Total Carbohydrates	**3g**
Carbohydrates from Fiber	0.8g
Sugars	**0.4g**
Protein	**1.2g**

French Onion (+Onion Skin) Soup

Ingredients:

- 2 tablespoons **coconut oil**
- 3 **yellow onions,** sliced
- **Onion skins** (leftover), crushed and put in steeping bag
- 1 cup **crimini mushrooms,** sliced
- 4 **garlic cloves,** crushed
- 1 teaspoon **thyme**
- ¼ cup **tomato paste**
- 1 cup **dry red wine**
- 4 cups **vegetable broth**
- ¼ cup **tamari or soy sauce**
- ⅛ cup **dark miso paste,** dissolved in 1 cup **vegetable broth**
- 4 slices of **gluten free bread**
- ½ cup (or more) **Daiya vegan mozzarella cheese** shreds

Directions:

1. Bring oil to medium heat in a large pot. Add sliced onions and sauté for 15-20 min until brown.

2. Mix in tomato paste, mushroom, garlic and thyme. Continue cooking for 5 min, or until paste is lightly browned.

3. Pour in the wine, stirring the bottom of the pan to ensure nothing is sticking. Simmer for 2-5 min uncovered, allowing the wine to evaporate.

4. Stir in the vegetable broth, miso, and tamari or soy sauce. Place onion skin in seeping bag, and add to soup. Simmer for another 15 min uncovered.

5. Preheat the broiler.

6. As the soup simmers, toast bread until golden brown, then remove from oven and set aside.

7. Using 4 oven proof serving bowls, put 1/2 piece of bread in each.

8. When the soup is done simmering, remove the seeping bag and ladel some soup into each bowl.

9. Sprinkle each bowl with 1 tbsp of Daiya vegan mozzarella cheese shreds. Then top with the remaining pieces of toast.

10. Ladle the rest of the soup into each bowls, and top with another tablespoon of vegan cheese. You can add more vegan cheese if needed, to cover top of bowl with a layer of cheese.

11. Then place the soup bowls on a baking tray and heat under broiler for about 5 min, or until the cheese is golden brown. If the cheese starts to burn around edges, move tray to a lower oven rack.

12. Remove from oven and let cool before serving.

see recipe

Onion Skin:
Don't Throw It Away!

Are you throwing away tons of immune balancing nutrients without even knowing it? Well, if you ever discard onion skins without steeping them first, you're losing out. Onion skins contain even more anti-inflammatory nutrients, like quercetin, than the onion itself! It can add great flavor to your soups too!

So next time you have leftover onion skin, save them or make yourself a French Onion (+ Onion Skin) Soup!

Wine: *Get The Good Without The Bad*

Sometimes you just need to have a little fun...
But how do you get the health benefits of red wine without the damaging effects of alcohol? Cook with it! With all of the red wine that this recipe requires, rest assured that you are getting a healthy dose of anti-inflammatory nutrients like resveratrol. Plus, resveratrol is heat stable! *So next time you have some leftover wine, use it in a recipe to keep your immune system happy.*

Nutrition Facts
Recipe makes 4 servings

Amount per serving	
Calories	**440**
Total Fat	**13g**
Saturated Fat	1.5g
Total Carbohydrates	**45g**
Carbohydrates from Fiber	9g
Sugars	**13g**
Protein	**14g**

Shiitake and Seaweed Miso Soup

SERVES: **4** PREP TIME: **35 MIN**

GLUTEN FREE **SOY FREE (Option)**

Ingredients:

- 1 large piece (7 grams) **kombu dried kelp seaweed**
- 2 tablespoons **scallions,** sliced thin
- ½ tablespoon **sesame oil**
- 4 cups **water**
- 1 ½ ounces **dried shiitake mushrooms,** rehydrated and sliced
- ¼ cup light **miso paste,** dissolved in ¼ cup **water**
- 4 ounces **extra firm tofu,** cubed

Soy Free Variation: Use light chickpea miso paste and omit tofu.

Directions:

1. Rinse kombu kelp and set aside.

2. Bring sesame oil to medium heat in a large pot. Sauté scallions for 1 minute then add 4 cups of water.

3. Add the kombu kelp, mushrooms, and bring a boil. Then cover, reduce heat, and let simmer for 10 min.

4. Remove kombu from pot and set aside. Add tofu, bring to a boil, cover, reduce heat, and let simmer for another 5 minutes.

5. Then remove from heat and add dissolved miso paste, stirring gently until evenly mixed.

6. (Optional) To get the most out of seaweed's health benefits, slice the kombu kelp thin, and add it back to the miso soup.

7. Serve as an appetizer or side dish for a wonderful meal!

see recipe

Shiitake Mushrooms:
A Tasty Balance

What if there was an ingredient that boosted AND balanced the immune system?

That's exactly what the delicious shiitake mushroom can do. Being one of the most well studied food ingredients available, researchers have found these mushrooms to boost a weak immune system.

Yet, they've also found it to reduce overactive immune responses! Balance is the key to a healthy body, and shiitake mushrooms can show you the way.

Seaweed:
Cold Sores, Inflammation, and more?

Why take pills if your food can meet your needs? Ever had a cold sore? Unwanted inflammation? Gas from eating beans? What simple flavor-enhancing ingredient can help you avoid all of these things?

It's seaweed! Sea vegetables like kombu can add a richness and depth of flavor to your recipes. But researchers also found that seaweed compounds like *"fucoidan"* can reduce unwanted inflammation. Amazingly, they can also block binding sites for the herpes viruses which can cause cold sores and other types of infections (HSV-1&2). And if that's not enough, kombu also contains enzymes that can help break down the gas producing sugar in beans! It's also one of the richest sources of iodine for immune and thyroid health. With all of these amazing benefits, it's only a matter of time before seaweed is all the rage.

Nutrition Facts
Recipe makes 4 servings

Amount per serving

Calories	**107**
Total Fat	**5g**
Saturated Fat	0.4g
Total Carbohydrates	**13g**
Carbohydrates from Fiber	2g
Sugars	**1.4g**
Protein	**6g**

Pomegranate Millet Tabouli

SERVES: **4** PREP TIME: **25 MIN** **GLUTEN FREE** **SOY FREE**

Ingredients:

- ½ cup **millet,** dry
- 1 cup **water**
- 1 cup **parsley,** minced
- ¼ cup **fresh peppermint,** minced
- ¼ cup **cucumber,** diced
- ¼ cup **sweet onion,** diced
- ¾ cup **pomegranates arils**
- ¼ cup **pine nuts**
- 1 tablespoon **olive oil**
- 1 tablespoon **lemon juice**
- **Salt & pepper** to taste

Raw Variation: Replace cooked millet with sprouted millet or even quinoa!

tip To avoid mushy millet, be careful not to overcook.

tip Add just enough salt to highlight the richness of the pine-nuts and sweetness of the pomegranate.

Directions:

1. Combine ½ cup of millet with 1 cup water in a medium saucepan, bring to a boil, then cover and let simmer for 20-25 min. When the millet is soft, fluff with a fork, cover, and let rest for 5 min.

2. Meanwhile, using a large bowl, combine lemon juice, olive oil, onions, cucumber, parsley, peppermint, pomegranates, and pine nuts. Stir in cooled millet, and add salt and pepper to taste.

Serve as the perfect side dish to compliment any meal!

see recipe

Peppermint:
Soothe your upset stomach with peppermint!

Peppermint's volatile oils have demonstrated many digestion-regulating properties.

Peppermint also has anti-inflammatory properties, especially for the digestive system. If you suffer from chronic inflammatory disorders like irritable bowel syndrome, Crohn's disease, ulcerative colitis, or even general upset stomach, this is the herb for you. *Its antispasmodic properties will also help alleviate cramping, bloating, and gas!*

Pomagranate:
Nature's wonder fruit!

Pomegranate has shown to help the body in so many ways! Research shows that it's able to boost the immune system, reduce pain from rheumatoid arthritis, fight cancer, and prevent cardio-vascular disease.

Also, pomegranate seeds are one of the few vegan sources of conjugated linoleic acid (CLA), a healthy anti-inflammatory fat mostly found in animal products.

Reduce gluten
to reduce inflammation

Reducing or eliminating gluten in your diet can help to reduce chronic inflammation and regulate the immune system. *Because of this, millet is a tasty and gluten free substitute for wheat in many recipes!*

But be careful, millet in large quantities can mildly inhibit an enzyme related to thyroid function. So if you suffer from hypothyroidism, include millet in your diet only in small quantities.

Nutrition Facts
Recipe makes 4 servings

Amount per serving

Calories	**153**
Total Fat	**10g**
Saturated Fat	1g
Total Carbohydrates	**15g**
Carbohydrates from Fiber	2.5g
Sugars	**6g**
Protein	**3g**

Raw Spicy Walnut Burrito

PREP TIME: **25 MIN** (GF) GLUTEN FREE (SF) SOY FREE (R) RAW

Ingredients:

- 4 medium to large **collard leaves**
- 1 cup **raw walnuts**
- 1 ½ teaspoon **lime juice**
- ½ teaspoon **chili powder**
- ¼ teaspoon **garlic powder**
- ¼ teaspoon **onion powder**
- ¼ teaspoon **crushed red pepper flakes**
- ¼ teaspoon **dried oregano**
- ¼ teaspoon **smoked paprika**
- ¼ teaspoon **ground cumin**
- ½ teaspoon **black pepper**
- **Salt** to taste

Directions:

1. Add walnuts and all dry spices into food processor and grind untily coarsely chopped. Add all ingredients to a mixing bowl with lime juice, salt to taste, and mix thoroughly.

2. Add walnut mix to a collard leaf and serve.

tip We topped our burrito with pico de gallo salsa and guacamole for a tasty and satisfying meal.

see recipe

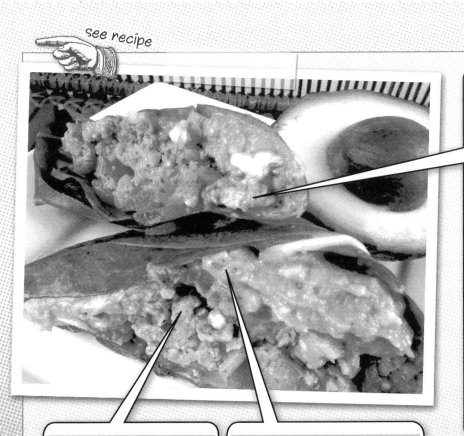

Topping Recipe 1:
Pico De Gallo Salsa (4 servings)

Ingredients:
- 1 cup **tomato**, deseeded and chopped
- ¼ cup **onion**, chopped
- 2 teaspoons **cilantro**, chopped
- 1 teaspoon **lime juice**
- **Sea salt** to taste

Directions:
Mix all ingredients thoroughly in a mixing bowl and set aside for 5 minutes for flavors to meld.

Raw Walnuts:
Omega 3 Powerhouse

Walnuts, rich in Omega 3 ALA fatty acids, are a great way to regulate the immune system by combating chronic inflammation. But remember, Omega 3 fats are very delicate, so it's bet to get your walnuts raw.

Topping Recipe 2:
Guacamole (4 servings)

Ingredients:
- 2 ripe **avocados**
- 2 teaspoons **lime juice**
- 2 tablespoons **pico de gallo salsa**
- **Sea salt** to taste

Directions:
Smash avocado in a mixing bowl. Add the rest of the ingredients, mix thoroughly, and salt to taste.

Nutrition Facts
Recipe makes 4 servings

Amount per serving	
Calories	**200**
Total Fat	**19g**
Saturated Fat	2g
Total Carbohydrates	**6g**
Carbohydrates from Fiber	3g
Sugars	**1g**
Protein	**5g**

VEGAN SURVIVAL: BODY

Feed Your Body!

Mind and body are
two sides of the same coin.
Whether you're a athlete or an
office warrior, a well designed
vegan diet can help your body
perform at its best.

We'll show you how to maximize
your meals so you can look,
feel, and perform at your
maximum potential!

VSG: Body

The body is the vehicle for the soul, and a healthy body is a beautiful body.

Whether you are active and athletic, or just want to trim a few inches off your waistline, there are some simple adjustments that you can make for even better results.

The athlete's body is like a finely tuned machine. To perform at its best, it must be optimally supported by the foods that you eat. Being vegan can create some challenges for the high performance individual, but it's nothing that can't be overcome. Making sure that each meal has the highest amounts of certain minerals, vitamins, and protein will help you perform at your fullest.

But why should athletes be the only ones with slim and healthy looking bodies? Even those of us who are minimally active can enjoy a beautiful and balanced body. There are so many ways to optimize your diet, and best of all, slimming your waistline can be tasty!

So whether you are a competitive athlete, or just want to look your best, we'll show you how. *There are so many wonderful and delicious combinations! You'll love it.*

Top Athlete Supporting Nutrients + Foods

Examples of some top foods in this category:

Overall Best: Spinach, Swiss Chard, Granola, Beet Greens, Chickpeas, Wheat Germ, Tempeh, Pumpkin Seeds

Calcium: Tofu, Collard Greens, Okra, Sesame Seeds, Kale, Cabbage, Coriander

Magnesium: Brazil Nuts, Quinoa, Sunflower Seeds, Almonds, Cashews, Buckwheat

Iron: Pumpkin Seeds, Granola, Spelt, Lentils, Asparagus, Parsley, Collard Greens

Potassium: Pistachios, Sweet Potato, Yams, Brussels Sprouts, Guava, Coconut Water

Vitamin C: Guava, Broccoli, Bell Pepper, Brussels Sprouts, Strawberries, Papaya, Pineapple

Zinc: Spelt, Pistachios, Pine Nuts, Quinoa, Cashews, Tofu, Sunflower Seeds, Millet

Selenium: Pine Nuts, Spelt, Blackstrap Molasses, Hazelnuts, Brown Rice, Pineapple

Top Weight Loss Ingredients

Weight Loss Promoting Ingredients:

Versatile Weight Loss Ingredients: Spaghetti Squash, Cauliflower, Cannellini Beans, Parsely, Grapefruit, Cinnamon, Mustard

Low and No Calorie Sweeteners: Stevia, Monkfruit (Lo Han), Yacon Syrup

We Can Do It!

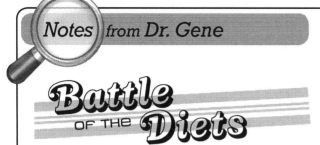

Battle OF THE Diets

As you will see, many of our weight reducing recipes aim to substitute carbohydrates with vegetables in a satisfying way. You may also notice that many of these recipes are not super low in fat. The low fat vs. low carb debate is one of the most heated amongst health practitioners. The calorie quantity vs. calorie quality debate is just as furious.

As with many debates, *there is truth to both sides of the story.* Researchers have shown lower carb diets to reduce weight more quickly... But they often end up in a tie with low fat diets in the long run. And the amount of calories is important, but the kinds of calories you eat can affect how your body burns calories overall.

People Are Unique

If there's one thing I've learned working with long term vegans struggling with their weight, it's that people respond to dietary changes in different ways. I've had patients respond well to low fat diets, while others do better by decreasing carbohydrates and increasing healthy fats. Many do well by alternating the two. Also, sticking with a particular diet may be the most important factor. Because of this, I always start with a diet that's closest to the way they already eat, then move to another if necessary.

Because inflammation itself can cause unwanted weight gain, some people can even lose weight just by eliminating foods to which they are sensitive (usually gluten, soy, corn, citrus, nightshades). Dairy also tends to be a huge offender that vegans don't have to worry about. And last but not least, many just need to increase their exercise levels a bit to jumpstart their metabolism.

Covering The Bases

A diet that worked great for someone else, may or may not work as well for you. And a diet that you can't stick to, won't work at all. But we decided to focus more on decreasing carbohydrates because most vegan recipes can readily be made ultra low fat by omitting cooking oil, seeds, and nuts. Fats aren't usually the biggest offenders in a vegan diet.

But for vegans who would respond better to a reduction in carbohydrates, it's not quite as simple. So we decided to focus on exactly that. We show you how to replace starches with vegetables in a way that is still satisfying. And a satisfying diet is one that you can stick with. Using some of our carbohydrate substitute recipes at dinner time is especially helpful. Combine these with a protein like tempeh, or use them to reduce part of your starch intake.

For those who have weight issues because of sugar, refined carbohydrates, and lack of blood sugar control, incorporating some natural, no and low calorie sweeteners like stevia, monkfruit (lo han), and yacon syrup takes care of half the battle. Choose only whole grain, unrefined carbohydrates for your meals and you'll be good to go.

Fats Aren't All Bad

Though they can easily be adjusted, many of our recipes are not ultra low in fat. To be clear, many people will do well on very low fat diets. But for others, especially those who have difficulty controlling their appetites, very low fat diets can sometimes lead to overeating and carbohydrate binging. If you are trying to reduce calories on a diet that leaves you unsatisfied, depending on will power alone rarely works in the long run. In this case, adding some extra calories via healthy fats, can also reduce some of the weight gain that can come with carbohydrate binging.

Fats in general have gotten a bad reputation amongst many healthy foodists. And unhealthy, highly processed fats should definitely be eliminated from the diet if you are looking to lose weight. *But not all fats are the same... not even close.* For example, research has shown that diets including common amounts of trans fats can induce more weight gain and belly fat, even when the calories and the amount of fats are the same. Even *non-hydrogenated,* mass market vegetable oils can contain trans fats just from the way they are processed. So just switching to naturally produced oils can easily eliminate this hurdle. There are so many different types of fat, and many levels of quality. Grouping them all in one category doesn't do them justice. Moderation is still important, but adding some healthy fats to the diet can be beneficial for many.

Finding Your Way

Ultimately, if you reduce your overall calorie intake, choose the right kinds of calories, and increase the quality of your food, you're likely to lose weight. Eating foods that are "closer to natural" is another good rule to follow. You are unique, so the most important thing is to try different ways of eating, and see what works best for you. Try a certain style of eating for few months, keep track of your results, and switch to another if you're not satisfied. You will quickly find out what works best for you! ■

Don't Forget The Lifestyle Factors...

☑ Eat slower and chew more.
☑ Eat the most at breakfast and lunch, and the least at dinner.
☑ Include healthy snacks between meals.
☑ Drink more water.
☑ Make time to relax and de-stress.
☑ Go to sleep earlier, and get enough sleep.
☑ Make more time for exercise.

Hemp Seed Quinoa with Beet Greens and Eggplant

SERVES: **4** PREP TIME: **40 MIN** **GLUTEN FREE** **SOY FREE**

Ingredients:

- 2 tablespoons high oleic **sunflower oil**
- 1 teaspoon **olive oil**
- 3 cups **eggplant,** cubed
- ½ cup uncooked **quinoa**
- 1 cup **vegetable broth**
- 1 cup **onion,** chopped
- 2 cloves **garlic,** chopped
- 1 ½ cup **tomatoes,** chopped
- 1 cup **beet greens,** chopped
- ¼ cup **shelled hemp seeds**
- **Salt** and **black pepper** to taste

Delicious, hearty and full of protein... One of my favorites!

Directions:

1. Preheat oven to 425 degrees F.

2. Using a large mixing bowl, add eggplants, drizzle with 1 tbsp of sunflower oil, add salt and pepper to taste, and toss to coat eggplant evenly. Arrange eggplant on a baking sheet and bake for 10-15 min or until tender. Then remove from oven and set aside.

3. Rinse quinoa thoroughly through a strainer. Using a medium sized pot, combine quinoa with vegetable broth, bring to a boil, then reduce to low heat, cover, and simmer until broth is absorbed, about 10-12 min. When quinoa is done, drizzle with 1 teaspoon of olive oil, fluff with a fork, and set aside.

4. Using a large pan, bring 1 tablespoon of sunflower oil to medium high heat. Add garlic, onions, and sauté until translucent, about 1-2 min. Then add tomatoes, beet greens, and sauté until the beet greens are tender, about 3-5 min.

5. When the beet greens are tender, add the baked eggplant, quinoa, and continue cooking for another 1-2 min or until heated through. Then remove from heat, add hemp seeds, salt and pepper to taste, and mix thoroughly to combine.

6. Serve as a delicious and hearty main course.

see recipe

Beet Greens:
No Way!

One day my friend was about to throw away some beet greens, and I almost grabbed straight it out of her hands! Though beets are great for eating and juicing, beet *greens* are no slouches when it comes to nutrition. In reality, beet greens are near the top of the list in many of the athlete supporting minerals. And as if we haven't picked on bananas enough... one cup of cooked beet greens provides 3 times more potassium than a medium banana! It's literally the #1 ingredient on our potassium list!

So next time you have some beet greens on hand, think of them like any other leafy vegetable! *They're super tasty too!*

Hemp Seeds:
Super-Super Food

Hemp seeds are an unrivaled source of vegan nutrition in many ways. These power packed seeds are a great source of omega 3 fatty acids, they have a great 3:1 omega 3 to 6 ratio, and they contain a special form of omega 6 called "gamma-linolenic acid." They are also rich in protein, *making them a perfect food that's fit for any athlete!*

Quinoa:
Athlete Fuel

Researchers have shown quinoa to provide more flavonoids than some flavonoid rich berries. Most people know of quinoa for being a complete plant protein which is so important for athletes. But quinoa has another trick up its sleeve and it comes in the form of omega 3 alpha linolenic acid. Though not as rich of a source as foods like flaxseeds and walnuts, quinoa can still provide the body with omega 3's to lower unwanted inflammation, and support optimal cell function.

Nutrition Facts	
Recipe makes 4 servings	
Amount per serving	
Calories	**261**
Total Fat	**13g**
Saturated Fat	1g
Total Carbohydrates	**26g**
Carbohydrates from Fiber	6.5g
Sugars	**6.2g**
Protein	**9g**

BODY

High Performance Piña Colada

SERVES: **4** PREP TIME: **5 MIN** (GF) GLUTEN FREE (SF) SOY FREE

Ingredients:

- 1 ½ cups **fresh pineapple**
- ½ cup **almond milk**
- ½ cup **coconut milk,** light or full fat
- ⅛ cup **cashews**
- ⅛ cup **flax seeds**
- 1 tablespoon **dates** or to taste
- 1/16 teaspoon **salt**
- 1 cup **ice**

Directions:

1. Combine all ingredients in a blender and blend until smooth.

tip If available, replace ½ of the pineapple with fresh guava for even more vitamin C!

The sea salt not only balances the taste of this smoothie, it also provides sodium, which is especially important for vegan athletes.

see recipe

Minerals:
Nature's Mineral Pods

Nuts and seeds give this smoothie its rich and creamy flavor. *Can something so tasty actually be useful to an athlete's performance?* Well between cashews and flax seeds, you have a huge variety of performance supporting effects. Magnesium for muscle and cellular health, iron for oxygen metabolism and endurance, zinc for hormone production and immune support, *the list is endless!*

So give your smoothie an extra boost with some nuts and seeds... *your body will love it!*

BODY

Almond Milk:
Gentle Non-Dairy Calcium

Cow's milk gets so much publicity as a good source of calcium, you would think that it's better than the alternatives. *Wrong...* In fact, many brands of almond milk provide much more calcium per serving than cow's milk. Plus, whether you are clearly dairy intolerant, or just mildly sensitive, you won't have these types of issues with almond milk. So rest assured, you're getting the good stuff. *It's tastes great too!*

Dates: *Lost In Publicity*

What's the first thing you think of when you get a muscle cramp? Bananas for potassium, right? Did you know that you can get even more potassium by sweetening your smoothie with some dates? In fact, just 3 dates can give you 25% more potassium than a medium banana! And you'll get yourself a healthy dose of calcium, magnesium, and zinc in the process. So next time you need to sweeten a smoothie, give your body what it wants and reach for the dates!

Nutrition Facts
Recipe makes 4 servings

Amount per serving	
Calories	**183**
Total Fat	**13g**
Saturated Fat	0.2g
Total Carbohydrates	**17g**
Carbohydrates from Fiber	3.3g
Sugars	**10g**
Protein	**3.5g**

Super Charged Yogurt Parfait

SERVES: **4** PREP TIME: **5 MIN** **GF** GLUTEN FREE **SF** SOY FREE

Ingredients:

- 1 cup **granola**
- 2 teaspoons **blackstrap molasses**
- 4 **Brazil nuts,** chopped
- 2 tablespoons **pistachios,** chopped
- 1 tablespoon **flax seeds**
- ½ cup **strawberries,** sliced
- 1 cup of your favorite **vegan yogurt**

Directions:

1. Using 2 bowls or cups, layer granola, molasses, seeds/ nuts, strawberries, yogurt. Repeat to create 2 layers in each cup.

2. Serve as a snack, breakfast side, or even a quick meal.

see recipe

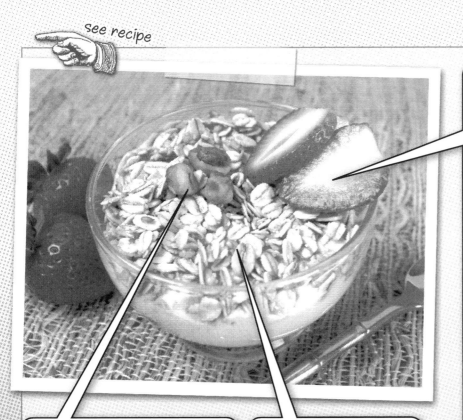

Strawberries:
Filthy Rich

As one of the richest common sources of vitamin C, strawberries are definitely something to keep in your arsenal of health boosting foods. But conventionally grown strawberries are #2 on the Dirty Dozen list, beating out everything except conventional apples.

So get all the benefits of strawberries without the toxins; make sure to buy them organic.

BODY

Pistachios:
A Vegan's Best Friend

If you could only have one kind of nut in your diet, which one would it be? Well, with so many benefits from so many types of nuts, I'm thankful we don't actually have to make that kind of decision! But if you chose pistachios, that would be a great choice! Pistachios are one of the richest vegan sources of lysine, making it an important nut for optimizing protein intake. Pistachios are also one of the top providers of potassium and zinc. In fact, a quarter cup of pistachios provides three times more potassium than a medium banana! *Now that's bananas!*

Granola:
Granola Muncher?

Ever start your day with a healthy portion of granola? If so, great choice! From calcium, magnesium, and iron, to potassium, selenium, and zinc, granola is one of the richest sources of all the trace minerals an athlete could ever want. And if that wasn't enough, the beta glucans in oats will also support your immune system and stabilize blood sugar levels! When in doubt, reach for the granola.

Nutrition Facts
Recipe makes 2 servings

Amount per serving	
Calories	**504**
Total Fat	**21g**
Saturated Fat	1.2g
Total Carbohydrates	**59g**
Carbohydrates from Fiber	15g
Sugars	**16.5g**
Protein	**13.5g**

Spicy Omega 3 Greens

Ingredients:

Walnut Crumbles:
- ½ cup **raw walnuts pieces**
- ¼ teaspoon **olive oil**
- 1/8 teaspoon **garlic powder**
- 1/8 teaspoon **smoked paprika**
- 1/16 teaspoon **black pepper**
- **Salt** to taste

Greens:
- ½ tablespoon **coconut oil**
- 2 **garlic cloves,** minced
- 2 cups **kale,** coarsely chopped
- 2 tablespoons **vegetable broth**
- 2 cups **Swiss chard,** coarsely chopped
- 1/8 teaspoon **crushed red pepper**
- 1 teaspoon **smoked paprika**
- ½ teaspoon **fresh lemon juice**
- **Salt** and **cayenne pepper** to taste

tip Adding *lemon juice* to this recipe will help your body absorb the iron in these ingredients, so you can perform at your best!

SERVES: **4** PREP TIME: **20 MIN**
GLUTEN FREE SOY FREE RAW (Option)

Directions:

1. Using a medium size mixing bowl, toss walnuts pieces in olive oil (olive oils pump sprayer is ideal). Then sprinkle with garlic powder, smoked paprika, black pepper, and sea salt to taste. Set aside.

2. In a large cooking pan, heat coconut oil to medium high heat. Add minced garlic and sauté until fragrant, about 1 min.

3. Add kale, 2 tbsp of vegetable broth, lower to medium heat, and cook covered for 5-7 min.

4. When the kale has softened, add Swiss chard and smoked paprika. Cover and let cook on medium-low heat for 5-7 min until tender. Stir occasionally.

5. Remove cover and let cook for another 2-3 min, or until most of the liquid evaporates.

6. Stir in lemon juice, sea salt to taste, and sprinkle with seasoned walnut crumbles.

7. Serve as a delicious side dish to complete any meal.

Raw Variation: Make recipe as a marinated salad instead of cooking. Omit vegetable broth and sunflower oil. Add 3 tbsp of olive oil and 2 tbsp of lemon juice and let the greens marinate in the refrigerator for 1-2 hours. Then add the rest of the ingredients, toss, and top with seasoned walnut crumbles.

see recipe

Kale + Walnuts:
Omega 3 Power Team

Though kale may not be top dog in this recipe, it still has much to offer. When we think of this green leafy veggie, we mostly think of cancer preventing phytonutrients and detox promoting sulfur compounds. *But omega 3s? What?*

Amazingly, one cup of kale provides over 30% of the recommended daily intake of omega 3 alpha linolenic acid! *Add that to the walnuts in this recipe and you'll have all the omega 3s that you need!*

BODY

Swiss Chard:
Kale Dethroned?

Kale seems to be the king of notoriety when it comes to healthy foods. And while kale brings so many benefits to this recipe, *is it possible that another vegetable is top dog in this dish?*

Well, kale better watch out! Take a look next to see how they stack up. ▶

Swiss Chard vs Kale
Let's compare...

100 grams	Swiss Chard	Kale
Ca	6%	**7%**
Mg	**21%**	5%
K	**16%**	7%
Fe	**13%**	5%
Vita C	30%	**68%**
Zinc	2%	2%
Se	1%	1%

(100 grams of cooked swiss chard versus cooked kale.)

Nutrition Facts
Recipe makes 4 servings

Amount per serving

Calories	**138**
Total Fat	**12g**
Saturated Fat	1g
Total Carbohydrates	**7g**
Carbohydrates from Fiber	2.g
Sugars	**3.7g**
Protein	**3.7g**

South-Western Millet Stew

SERVES: **5** PREP TIME: **55 MIN**

GLUTEN FREE   SOY FREE (Option)

Ingredients:

- 1 cup **dry millet**
- 2 cups **water**
- 8 ounces **tempeh,** cubed
- 1 tablespoon **coconut oil**
- 1 cup chopped **onions**
- 1 cup chopped **red bell peppers**
- 1 cup **brussels sprouts**
- 2 **plum tomatoes,** chopped
- 2 teaspoons **ground cumin**
- 1 tablespoon **smoked paprika**
- ¾ teaspoon **chili powder**
- ¼ teaspoon **black pepper**
- 2 tablespoons **tamari or soy sauce**
- 3 cups **vegetable stock**
- **Salt** to taste

Gluten Free Variation: Make sure to use gluten free tamari and that your tempeh does not have added gluten containing grains.

Soy Free Variation: Replace tempeh with brown or green lentils. Cook until al dente in water with a pinch of salt. Replace soy sauce with add'l salt.

Directions:

1. Combine 1 cup of millet with 2 cups of water in a medium saucepan, bring to a boil, then cover and let simmer for 20-25 min. When the millet is soft, fluff with a fork, cover, and let rest for 5 min.

2. As the millet is cooking, use a separate steamer to steam tempeh cubes and set aside.

3. Using a large pot, bring coconut oil to medium-high heat. Add onions, bell peppers, Brussels sprouts, and cook until vegetables are soft, about 5 min.

4. Add the steamed tempeh, tomatoes, cumin, smoked paprika, chili powder, black pepper, tamari/ soy sauce, and cook for another 5 min on medium heat. Stir regularly.

5. Then add veg stock, bring to boil, cover, reduce heat, and let simmer for another 10-15 min. Salt to taste.

6. When the stew is done, ladle over bowls of millet and serve as a super-hearty main course!

see recipe

Tempeh:
Mold For Health?

Moldy food is not what most think of as "healthy." But in the case of tempeh, a type of fermented soy, the fungi used in the fermentation process is actually our friend! The Rhizopus fungi used to create tempeh produce an enzyme that actually increases mineral bioavailability in the soybeans. This way our bodies can absorb these nutrients more effectively!

Tempeh also provides all the athlete supporting minerals, *so if you're not sensitive to soy, make sure to get lots of tempeh in your diet!*

BODY

tip Millet also soaks up water very easily. So if you are planning to store this recipe, *make sure to store the stew and millet separately.*

tip Also try adding some of your favorite vegan cheese for an even tastier meal!

Millet:
Money In The Bank

Millet is a wonderful gluten free grain that can be used in so many ways. *But what's that have to do with money in the bank?* Beside the performance supporting benefits of magnesium, iron, zinc, and selenium, millet is also a great source of phosphorus. This important trace mineral is essential for your cells to produce ATP, which is the energy currency of the body.

Posphorous is also important for fat metabolism, optimal bone formation, and tissue formation. *Now those are things that you can take to the bank!*

Nutrition Facts
Recipe makes 5 servings

Amount per serving	
Calories	**235**
Total Fat	**8.5g**
Saturated Fat	2g
Total Carbohydrates	**34g**
Carbohydrates from Fiber	4.5g
Sugars	**9g**
Protein	**13.5g**

Spinach and Collard Lentils

SERVES: **4** PREP TIME: **45 MIN**
GLUTEN FREE **SOY FREE**

Ingredients:

- 3 tablespoons **coconut oil**
- 3 cups **onion,** chopped
- 1 cup **dry red lentils,** rinsed and drained
- 6 cups **broth**
- 4 cups **collard greens,** thinly sliced
- 1 ½ cups **spinach**
- 2 tablespoons **garlic,** minced
- 1 tablespoon **ground cumin**
- ¼ teaspoon **ground cinnamon**
- 2 tablespoons **lemon juice**
- **Salt** to taste

Directions:

1. Bring 1 tablespoon coconut oil to medium-high heat in a large pot. Add onions and sauté until transluscent, about 2-3 minutes.

2. Add lentils, continue sautéing for another 1-2 minutes, then add vegetable broth. Bring to a boil, lower to medium-low heat, cover, and let simmer for 15 minutes or until the lentils are tender.

3. As the lentils are simmering, bring 2 tablespoons of coconut oil to medium-high heat in a large pan. Add collard greens and sauté until soft, about 10 min.

4. Then combine the sautéd collard greens, spinach, garlic, cumin, and cinnamon, with the pot of lentils. Let simmer for 10 minutes.

5. Remove from heat and stir in the lemon juice.

6. Serve over a bed of rice or your favorite grain!

see recipe

Pumping Iron:
Lentils, Collards and Spinach

Iron is important for vegans in general, but especially for athletes and the physically active. Fortunately, there are many great sources of iron in the plant kingdom, and this recipe combines some of the best. Lentils, collard greens, and spinach are all some of the best sources of plant based iron available. *They also make for a delicious recipe!*

Combine these with the vitamin C in lemon juice, and your body will have a better time absorbing the iron it needs to succeed!

BODY

Spinach:
Strong Foundations

Spinach is a top source of all the major athlete supporting minerals. But spinach goes the extra mile when it comes to bone health. Just 1 cup of boiled spinach gives you over 1000% of the Daily Value of vitamin K. This important vitamin prevents the excessive breakdown of bone and helps to anchor calcium in the bone itself. Spinach is literally top of the list when it comes to vitamin K with only kale ranking a bit higher.

So keep you bones strong and eat more spinach!

Nutrition Facts
Recipe makes 4 servings

Amount per serving	
Calories	**327**
Total Fat	**5.8g**
Saturated Fat	0g
Total Carbohydrates	**57g**
Carbohydrates from Fiber	13g
Sugars	**7g**
Protein	**6g**

Spicy Chickpea and Spinach Soup

SERVES: **6** PREP TIME: **40 MIN**
GLUTEN FREE   SOY FREE

Ingredients:

- 1 tablespoon **coconut oil**
- 3 cups **onion,** chopped
- 1 **bell pepper,** seeded and chopped
- 8 **cloves garlic,** minced
- 2 teaspoons **cumin powder**
- 1 teaspoon **paprika**
- ¼ teaspoon **cinnamon**
- ⅛ teaspoon **cayenne pepper** or to taste
- ⅛ teaspoon **black pepper**
- 2 cups **chickpeas,** drained
- 1 ½ cups **tomatoes,** chopped
- 4 cups **vegetable broth**
- 1 tablespoon **tamari or soy sauce**
- 4 cups **baby spinach**
- 2 teaspoons **lime juice**
- **Salt** to taste

tip *Bell Peppers Quick Tip:* The vitamin C in bell peppers is very sensitive to heat. If you want to optimize the vitamin C in this recipe, try adding the bell peppers just before serving!

Directions:

1. Bring oil to medium-high heat in in a large pot. Add onion, bell pepper and garlic and sauté until the onions become translucent, about 2-3 min.

2. Add cumin, paprika, cinnamon, cayenne, black pepper, and continue cooking for 1-2 minutes. Then add chickpeas, tomatoes, vegetable broth, tamari/ soy sauce, bring to a boil, reduce to low heat, cover, and let simmer for 25 minutes.

3. Using a wooden spatula or potato masher, mash some of the chickpeas while simmering. Stir regularly. Add more vegetable broth if needed.

4. Add spinach and let cook for another 2-3 min. Then remove from heat, add lemon juice, and salt to taste.

5. Serve as a delicious side dish to complement any meal.

see recipe

Tomatoes:
Tomatoes Are Bananas!

Bananas can be a tasty way to boost your body's potassium. But if you feel like eating something different, even something as simple as tomatoes can give you what your body needs. In fact, 1 cup of cooked tomatoes gives you 25% more potassium than a medium banana! So next time you include some tomatoes in a dish, know that you are getting the potassium that your active body needs.

BODY

Chickpeas:
Sustained Energy

For an endurance athlete, sustained energy is crucial for optimal performance. Though carbohydrates are an important part of the equation, how quickly they are processed by the body can make a huge difference. Simple carbohydrates that are absorbed too quickly can cause your blood sugar to spike, then crash. On the other hand, ingredients like chickpeas can provide your body with slower burning, complex carbohydrates for long term energy. It can also improve your blood sugar regulation in general! Research has shown that even a 1/2 cup with meals can change how your body controls blood sugar, in as little as a week.

So get the endurance that you always wanted and load up on the chickpeas!

Nutrition Facts	
Recipe makes 6 servings	
Amount per serving	
Calories	**832**
Total Fat	**6g**
Saturated Fat	0.5g
Total Carbohydrates	**56g**
Carbohydrates from Fiber	15g
Sugars	**14g**
Protein	**16g**

Mashed Rosemary Garlic Cauliflower

SERVES: **3** PREP TIME: **20 MIN** **GF** GLUTEN FREE **SF** SOY FREE

Ingredients:

- 1 medium **head of cauliflower,** cut into small pieces
- 1 tablespoon **crushed garlic**
- 1 tablespoon **coconut oil**
- ¼ cup **vegetable stock**
- ¼ cup **almond milk**
- ¼ teaspoon **vegetable soup base powder***
- ½ teaspoon **rosemary**
- 1 teaspoon **oat flour** (mixed in 1 tbsp water before adding)
- **Salt** and **pepper** to taste

*In this recipe, we used *"Vogue Cuisine Vegetable Soup & Seasoning Base."* This is one of the best tasting and healthiest soup bases we could find.

Directions:

1. Boil cauliflower in large pot of water for 8-10 min or until very soft.

2. As the cauliflower is cooking, sauté garlic in 1 tbsp of cocout oil over medium-high heat until fragrant. Then add almond milk, vegetable stock, vegetable soup base powder, and rosemary. Bring to a boil, then let simmer for 2-3 min. As the sauce simmers, add the oat flour to water, mix thoroughly, and slowly add it to the sauce while stirring constantly. Let simmer for another 2-3 min until sauce thickens. Set aside for step 4.

3. When the cauliflower is soft, drain thoroughly and pat dry with a few sheets of paper towels (carefully) while still hot. Cauliflower should be patted very dry.

4. Using a potato masher or fork, smash the cauliflower while adding the sauce from step 2. Mix until smooth. If the mixture becomes too thick, add almond milk a little at a time while mixing until the desired texture is achieved.

5. Salt and pepper to taste.

6. Serve this healthy side dish to compliment any meal.

see recipe

Cauliflower: *Trim and Healthy*

Mashed cauliflower, instead of mashed potatoes, is one of best ways to slim down without depriving yourself. This lets you decrease carbohydrate consumption, and increase nutrient intake at the same time!

BODY

Rosemary: *Delicious and Satisfying*

According to Swiss researchers, rosemary extracts can actually induce weight loss by inhibiting fat digestion! But while this herb can make your dishes taste great, try taking a rosemary extract supplement to get the slimming effect.

Carbohydrate Comparison Chart

100 grams	Carbs	Calories
Cauliflower	5 g	25
Potato	21 g	95

Nutrition Facts
Recipe makes 3 servings

Amount per serving	
Calories	**96**
Total Fat	**5g**
Saturated Fat	4g
Total Carbohydrates	**12g**
Carbohydrates from Fiber	5g
Sugars	**6g**
Protein	**4g**

Garden Herb Spaghetti Squash

SERVES: **4** PREP TIME: **1h** **GF** GLUTEN FREE **SF** SOY FREE

Ingredients:

- 1 **spaghetti squash,** about 2 pounds
- ½ tablespoon **coconut oil**
- 3 **cloves garlic,** minced.
- 1 **plum tomato,** deseeded and chopped
- 1 tablespoon **basil,** chopped
- 1 tablespoon **flat leaf parsley,** chopped
- ⅛ cup **pine nuts** (optional)
- ⅛ teaspoon **freshly ground black pepper**
- ½ teaspoon **salt** or to taste
- 1 tablespoon **olive oil**

Directions:

1. Set oven to 357 degrees F.

2. Cut squash in half lengthwise. Lay the squash face down on a baking tray. Add water to the tray until it is about ¼ to ½ inch deep with water. Cover with aluminum foil and bake for 45 minutes.

3. When the squash is done, remove from oven and uncover. After squash has cooled for a few minutes, remove seeds, scoop the squash out of the peel, and discard peel. Set aside.

4. Bring coconut oil to medium-high heat in large pan. Add garlic and sauté until fragrant about 1 min. Mix in spaghetti squash, tomatoes, basil, parsley, optional pine nuts, black pepper, and salt to taste. Sauté over medium heat until warm, 2-3 min.

5. Remove from heat and toss with the olive oil before serving.

6. Serve as a main course or a delicious side dish to complement any meal.

see recipe

BODY

Weight Loss Confusion?

Low fat, low calorie, low carb... there are so many schools of thought when it comes to weight-loss. *So what's the deal?* The reality is, everyone is different, and what brings excellent results for one person, may or may not be the best for you. Weight loss can depend on so many factors. Calorie intake, fat intake, healthy fats vs. unhealthy fats, carbohydrate intake, complex carbohydrates vs. simple carbohydrates, hormone levels, inflammation levels, food sensitivities, exercise, sleep... there are too many variables to narrow weight loss into a single catch phrase. So *be sure to experiment with different approaches, methods, and variables that interest you.*

Some of them are sure to bring you great results!

Small Change, **Big** Results

One little adjustment can create huge changes over time. If losing some inches off your waistline is your goal, then spaghetti squash should definitely be part of your arsenal. *One cup of regular pasta has 4 times more carbohydrates and 5 times more calories than a cup of spaghetti squash!* Even choosing spaghetti squash for every other meal could make a huge difference in your body composition. And beyond just calories and carbohydrates, inflammation levels may also play a role in weight loss for many people. Fortunately spaghetti squash also contains anti-inflammatory plant compounds that could help reduce this unwanted inflammation. So give it a try. *Making this small change could bring you some great results!*

Nutrition Facts
Recipe makes 4 servings

Amount per serving

Calories	**369**
Total Fat	**9g**
Saturated Fat	1g
Total Carbohydrates	**11g**
Carbohydrates from Fiber	0.5g
Sugars	**1.5g**
Protein	**2g**

Indian Cauliflower Rice

SERVES: **2** PREP TIME: **5 MIN** **(GF)** GLUTEN FREE **(SF)** SOY FREE

Ingredients:

- ½ head **cauliflower**
- 1 tablespoon **coconut oil**
- ½ teaspoon **cumin seeds**
- **Salt** to taste

Raw Variation: Add ⅛ teaspoon cumin powder, replace coconut oil with olive oil, and mix ingredients thoroughly.

Directions:

1. Process cauliflower in food processor or chop to a rice like consistency.

2. Heat coconut oil to medium-high heat in a medium size skillet. Add cumin seeds and cook 1-2 minutes until fragrant. Then add cauliflower and cook for about 2-3 minutes.

3. Salt to taste. Be careful not to overcook.

see recipe

Coconut Oil: *Nature, Misunderstood*

Did you know? Coconut oil was poorly represented in the past by its highly processed and hydrogenated cousin. But in its natural form, this oil has many health benefits ranging from immune support to blood sugar control.

Researchers also found that coconut oil's medium chain triglycerides (MCT's) can even help to burn and reduce abdominal fat!

Cumin: *Versatile and Flavorful*

Cumin is a great way to enhance your recipes without the unnecessary calories. And not only does it benefit digestion by stimulating enzyme production, it has also shown to protect against stomach tumors.

Cauliflower: *Less Is More*

As you can see, cauliflower is super versatile for losing those unnecessary inches! But if you miss the taste of real rice, try this recipe with half rice and half cauliflower. You'll get all the taste, and only half the carbohydrates!

Nutrition Facts
Recipe makes 2 servings

Amount per serving

Calories	89
Total Fat	7g
Saturated Fat	6g
Total Carbohydrates	5.2g
Carbohydrates from Fiber	2.5g
Sugars	2.5g
Protein	2.5g

BODY

Super Parsley Pesto

SERVES: **10** PREP TIME: **10 MIN** (GF) **GLUTEN FREE** (SF) **SOY FREE (Option)** (R) **RAW (Option)**

Ingredients:

- 2 cups tightly packed, **flat leaf parsley,** without stems
- 2 cloves **garlic,** chopped
- ¼ cup **olive oil**
- ¼ cup **vegetable stock**
- ¼ cup **walnuts**
- ¼ cup **pine nuts**
- 2 teaspoons **miso paste**
- 2 teaspoons **lemon juice**
- ¼ teaspoon **black pepper**
- ⅛ teaspoon **salt,** or to taste

Directions:

1. Combine parsley, garlic, and olive oil into a strong blender, pushing all ingredients into the oil. Cover with lid and pulse the blender 6-7 times or until all ingredients are roughly chopped.

2. Then add all remaining ingredients and pulse the blender until all ingredients are rendered into a course puree.

Soy Free Variation: Using chickpea instead of soy miso paste makes this a great recipe for those who want to avoid soy.

Raw Variation: Replace vegetable stock with water, and make sure that your miso paste is unpasteurized.

see recipe

Pine Nuts & Parsley: *The One Two Punch!*

This pesto combines two of the best ingredients for promoting weight loss. For a quick and temporary trim-down, we've included fresh parsley, a natural diuretic. Whether it's to fit in that dress, or just to look your best, parsley can help you release water through the urine, to reduce bloating and unwanted water retention.

But to help you with more than just water weight, we've added pine nuts which contain a special fat called *"pinolenic acid."* This fatty acid has actually been shown to stimulate the release of a hunger-suppressing hormone called cholecystokinin (CCK). For some people, the hunger suppressing effect of CCK can even last for 2 hours! *Keeping trim has never tasted so good!*

Pine Nuts & Walnuts: *Fats Can Make You Thin?*

There are many approaches to weight loss, and some are even contradictory. *But what's at the root of the issue?* Hunger and fat metabolism! We all know about rollercoaster dieting. Well according to researchers, there's more to overeating than just "lack of self-discipline." For some, overeating may be due to an imbalance of the hormone *"leptin,"* which controls appetite, fat burning, and fat storage through the brain. If someone is constantly spiking their blood sugar (i.e. simple carbohydrates), their fat cells will grow and produce lots of leptin. Too much of this can lead to "leptin resistance," which promotes overeating and increased fat storage! One of the keys to reducing this is to control your blood sugar. For the vegan diet, eating more healthy fats, avoiding excess carbohydrates, and choosing complex carbohydrates can all help to balance blood sugar and restore leptin sensitivity. Seeds and nuts are a critical part of your weight loss arsenal because they are full of the beneficial fats that keep your blood sugar in balance. And don't worry about the extra calories from healthy fats. This new understanding about leptin shows us that calories are only part of the equation.

Nutrition Facts
Recipe makes 10 servings

Amount per serving	
Calories	**71**
Total Fat	**7g**
Saturated Fat	0.4g
Total Carbohydrates	**2.2g**
Carbohydrates from Fiber	0.6g
Sugars	**0.5g**
Protein	**1.4g**

Spicy White Bean Chili

SERVES: **4** PREP TIME: **55 MIN** **GF** GLUTEN FREE **SF** SOY FREE

Ingredients:

- 1 tablespoon **coconut oil**
- ½ tablespoon **garlic,** minced
- 1 cup **onion,** finely chopped
- 3/4 cup **bell pepper,** chopped
- ¼ cup **celery,** chopped
- 1 cup **carrots,** chopped
- 1 cup **mushrooms,** sliced
- ½ tablespoon **cumin**
- ½ tablespoon **chili powder**
- ½ teaspoon **black pepper**
- ½ teaspoon **dried oregano**
- ½ teaspoon **dried basil**
- 1 ½ cups **diced tomatoes with juice** (from jar)
- 1 cup **white kidney beans,** boiled
- ¼ cup **bean water**
- 1 cup **vegetable broth**
- 3 tablespoons **tomato paste**
- ⅛ cup **red wine**
- ½ teaspoon **hot sauce or tabasco**
- 1 ½ teaspoons **cocoa powder**
- 1 ⅛ teaspoons **salt** or to taste

Directions:

1. Using a large pot, bring oil to medium heat. Add garlic, onions, bell pepper, celery, carrots, mushrooms, cumin, chili powder, black pepper, oregano, basil, and sauté for 3-5 minutes.

2. Add in diced tomatoes, white beans, bean water, vegetable broth, tomato paste, red wine, hot sauce, cacao powder, and salt to taste.

3. Mix thoroughly, bring to a boil, reduce heat to low heat, cover and let simmer for 20-25 minutes.

4. Serve with rice, pasta or your favorite grain for a delicious and hearty meal.

see recipe

Hot Sauce:
Double Fat Burner

Hot sauces like Tabasco are rich in fat burning capsaicin... *But can it help to reduce fat in more ways than one?* In addition to capsaicin, hot sauces that contain vinegar are also rich in acetic acid. Researchers found that acetic acid actually stimulates genes that burn fat and reduce hunger! But don't worry, if you're not a fan of hot sauce, you can get this same effect from things like balsamic and apple cider vinegar! But before you buy, make sure to look on the label. Many sauces are full of sugar and things like high fructose corn syrup which should be avoided.

BODY

Cayenne:
Burn That Fat Away

Some people love it... others can't take the heat. But spicy ingredients like cayenne pepper can actually help the body burn fat. Spicy ingredients contain capsaicin, which give peppers the heat that many love. Capsaicin has also been found to shrink fat tissue, reduce fat buildup, increase metabolism and even suppress appetite. So spice up your dishes to spice up your life! And if you're not used to eating spicy foods, start with just a little. It's only a matter of time until you start to love it!

White Bean:
Block Starch, Regulate Sugar

White kidney beans, also known as cannellini beans, are a great food to include in your weight conscious pantry. These beans rich in protein and fiber, can help to keep your blood sugar nice and stable. And it's not just the fiber that keeps your blood sugar stable, white kidney beans actually contain compounds that can help block carbohydrate digestion!

Nutrition Facts
Recipe makes 4 servings

Amount per serving

Calories	**191**
Total Fat	**4.2g**
Saturated Fat	0.2g
Total Carbohydrates	**30g**
Carbohydrates from Fiber	8g
Sugars	**10g**
Protein	**8g**

Mustard Rosemary Tempeh

SERVES: **4** PREP TIME: **30 MIN** **GF** GLUTEN FREE

Ingredients:

- 1 (8 ounce) **pack tempeh,** cut into ¼ inch slices
- 1 tablespoon **sunflower oil** (optional)
- 2 cloves **garlic,** crushed
- 6 tablespoons **dijon mustard**
- ½ tablespoon **dry white wine**
- ½ tablespoon **dry rosemary**
- ½ teaspoon **black pepper**
- ½ teaspoon **salt** or to taste

Gluten Free: Make sure your tempeh does not have any added gluten containing grain.

Directions:

1. Set oven to 400 degrees F.

2. Poke each slice of tempeh a few times with fork. Set aside.

3. Using a large mixing bowl, combine oil (optional), garlic, Dijon mustard, wine, rosemary, black pepper, and salt. Mix thoroughly.

4. Add tempeh to mixing bowl and toss to coat evenly. Make sure to rub the sauce into the tempeh slices to maximize flavor.

5. Spread tempeh in a single layer over large baking sheet. Bake for about 20 minutes.

6. Serve as a delicious side dish to complement any meal.

see recipe

Tempeh:
Lean And Mean

On a vegan diet, adjusting carbohydrates to just what your body needs is not always an easy task. But with ingredients like tempeh, it's not as difficult as one may think. Tempeh is one of the most natural and least processed sources of complete vegan protein available. With most of its carbohydrates coming from fiber, it is also low in net carbohydrates. As if that's not enough, tempeh is also full of easily absorbed nutrients making it a great addition to your culinary repertoire! But be careful, many brands of tempeh are made with other types of carbohydrate rich grains. So be sure to look at the label before you buy.

BODY

Mustard:
The Underdog

Ketchup's little brother actually packs a huge punch! Mustard doesn't get as much attention as it should considering the effects that it can have on metabolism. Mustard seeds themselves have shown the ability to boost metabolism by 25%! This will help you burn more fat, all the time. And since mustard is made from ground up mustard seeds, you'll be getting all the goodness that you need. Plus, the turmeric and vinegar in mustard can also help to reduce fat formation! *That's a win, win, win, situation!*

Nutrition Facts
Recipe makes 4 servings

Amount per serving	
Calories	**171**
Total Fat	**12g**
Saturated Fat	0.7g
Total Carbohydrates	**15g**
Carbohydrates from Fiber	9g
Sugars	**1.5g**
Protein	**16g**

Baked Grapefruit with Cinnamon and Pistachio

SERVES: **2** PREP TIME: **20 MIN**

GF GLUTEN FREE **SF** SOY FREE **R** RAW (Option)

Ingredients:

- 1 **grapefruit**
- ⅛ teaspoon **coconut oil**
- 1 packet (½ teaspoon) **stevia**
- ¼ teaspoon **ground cinnamon**
- 1 tablespoon **pistachios,** chopped

Raw Variation: If you are on a raw foods diet, skip the baking, and just mix the ingredients together. But make sure your stevia and pistachios are both raw.

tip To make these baked grapefruits even more delicious, mash and mix the pulp with a spoon right before eating! You can also try adding double or triple the pistachios to get even more health benefits. Adding more cinnamon can also give you an extra boost.

Directions:

1. Set oven to 375 degrees F.

2. Cut the grapefruit in half and cut around the grapefruit sections to loosen.

3. Brush with a thin layer of coconut oil.

4. Sprinkle with stevia and cinnamon.

5. Bake grapefruit at 375 for 15 minutes.

6. Sprinkle with chopped pistachios before serving.

see recipe

Cinnamon:
Skinny Spice

Cinnamon's unique flavor can bring warmth and richness to so many foods... *but how does it help you lose weight?* Well cinnamon contains a compound that can help your stomach empty at a slower pace, increase glucose metabolism, and ultimately improve your blood sugar levels. When less sugar is stored as fat, you can maintain your waistline and have more energy throughout the day! *So keep that blood sugar under control and spice up your meals with cinnamon!*

Grapefruit:
Clean and Mean

Grapefruits are awesome in more ways than one. For starters, grapefruit made the Clean 15 list, meaning that you can safely buy non organic grapefruit to save money. But grapefruit has another trick up its sleeve. This citrus powerhouse can actually help stabilize blood sugar to increase weight loss! Researchers studied the effects of adding grapefruit before meals, both in the form of juice (8 oz.) and whole grapefruit (½). Not only did they find a reduction of blood sugar after meals, but participants also lost an average of over 3 lbs after just 12 weeks! Those who did not get grapefruit in their diet on the other hand lost only a ½ lb.

So add grapefruits to your weight busting arsenal, it's sure to pack a punch!

Nutrition Facts
Recipe makes 2 servings

Amount per serving	
Calories	**80**
Total Fat	**3.3g**
Saturated Fat	0.5g
Total Carbohydrates	**11g**
Carbohydrates from Fiber	2g
Sugars	**0.5g**
Protein	**2g**

White Bean Dip

SERVES: **4** PREP TIME: **1h**

GLUTEN FREE **SOY FREE**

Ingredients:

- 2 heads of **garlic**
- 2 teaspoons **olive oil**
- 2 cups **white kidney beans,** cooked and drained
- 2 tablespoons **fresh lemon juice**
- ½ teaspoon **cumin**
- ½ teaspoon **salt** or to taste
- 1/8 cup **pine nuts**
- ½ tablespoon **olive oil** (optional, to drizzle on top)

Directions:

1. Set oven at 350 degrees F.

2. Cut the tops from garlic heads to expose cloves. Drizzle garlic tops with olive oil, wrap with foil, place on a baking pan, and bake for 40 minutes or until soft.

3. Once the roasted garlic has cooled, squeeze into a food processor bowl, add beans, lemon juice, and blend until smooth. Add cumin, salt to taste, and blend again. Top with pine nuts and drizzle with olive oil (optional).

4. Serve as a dip for your favorite vegetable, chips, or spread onto a sandwich!

see recipe

Garlic:
Even More Benefits?

Garlic is a super food known for so many health benefiting properties. From protecting against high blood pressure and diabetes, to its anti-bacterial and anti-cancer properties, there are just too many things that garlic can do. *But who would have thought that garlic would have another trick up its sleeve?* Researchers have shown that it may also help prevent weight gain for people eating high sugar diets, and could even promote weight loss! So keep yourself healthy in every way, and make sure to add more garlic to your meals!

BODY

White Beans:
Super Bean Dip

Instead of a standard bean dip, this bean dip utilizes the power of white kidney beans to keep blood sugar and body fat under control! White kidney beans contain compounds that can actually block starches from being digested. Though extracts of white bean will create the strongest carb blocking effects, these compounds make white bean the better choice when it comes to stabilizing blood sugar. *So why have regular bean dip when you can have super bean dip?* These beans are also rich in metabolism boosting "resistant starches" making them a weight loss no brainer!

Nutrition Facts	
Recipe makes 4 servings	
Amount per serving	
Calories	**211**
Total Fat	**6g**
Saturated Fat	0.7g
Total Carbohydrates	**27g**
Carbohydrates from Fiber	6g
Sugars	**1g**
Protein	**10.5g**

VEGAN SURVIVAL:
DETOX

Let's Detox!

The modern world is full of toxins
that our bodies have to fight on
an everyday basis.

We'll show you how to reduce
this toxic burden with the foods
that you eat!

VSG: Detox

Our bodies are constantly working to keep us healthy!

Modern living didn't come without some costs. Though industry and technology have helped our lives in so many ways, the presence of industrial toxins has been one of the unfortunate side effects. Until the planet shifts to mostly green and eco-friendly industries, we have to protect ourselves from the burden of environmental toxicity.

Fortunately our bodies have their own detoxification mechanisms that are working around the clock.

But the foods that you eat will affect how well your detoxification pathways are working. Fortunately, most of these foods come from the plant kingdom! Sulphur compounds in garlic and cruciferous vegetables, polyphenols in fruits and berries, selenium in spinach and pineapples... plant foods are full of these detox supporting nutrients!

Knowing what these foods are, and eating them on a daily basis will help your body stay clean, healthy, and strong!

Detoxification Supporting Nutrients + Foods

Hmmm... Should I have some raspberries or strawberries today?

With so many delicious options, chosing your favorite detox supporting foods for the day *will be easier than ever!* ■

Examples of some top foods in this category:

Sulphur Compounds: Broccoli, Cabbage, Kale, Garlic, Onions, Horseradish, Wasabi

Polyphenols: Green Tea, Raspberries, Blackberries, Tart Cherries, Strawberries

Zinc: Granola, Pumpkin Seeds, Pistachios, Pine Nuts, Quinoa, Cashews, Sunflower Seeds

Selenium: Granola, Pine Nuts, Blackstrap Molasses, Hazelnuts, Pumpkin Seeds, Spinach, Pineapple

Crushed Broccoli Coleslaw

SERVES: **4** PREP TIME: **15 MIN**

 GLUTEN FREE **SOY FREE** **RAW**

Ingredients:

Salad:
- 1 cup **raw broccoli,** finely chopped and smashed
- 1 cup **raw cabbage,** finely chopped and smashed
- ¼ cup **dried cherries** (unsweetened is best)
- ¼ cup crushed **pecan pieces** (raw is best)

Dressing:
- ½ very **ripe avocado,** smashed
- 1 ½ teaspoon **apple cider vinegar**
- 1 tablespoon **spicy mustard**
- 2 teaspoons **garlic,** crushed and exposed to air
- ¼ teaspoon **salt**
- 1/8 teaspoon **black pepper**
- 2 teaspoons **maple syrup**

Grinding these vegetables maximizes their nutritional potential!

Directions:

1. Mix salad ingredients together in a large bowl.

2. Mix dressing ingredients thoroughly in a small bowl.

3. Combine dressing with salad, toss, and serve. Serve as a healthy and delicious appetizer or side dish to brighten up any meal!

tip To save time, throw all ingredients into a food processor to make this a super quick, one dish recipe!

tip Using broccoli and cabbage stems in this recipe is a great way to use every part of the plant. Give it a try!

tip To make this recipe completely raw, make sure to use raw mustard, unpasteurized apple cider vinegar, and replace maple syrup with date paste or raw agave.

see recipe

Broccoli + Mustard:
A Spicy Power Combo

Broccoli is rich in sulforaphane, an anti-cancer compound that also increases the body's phase II detoxification enzymes.

Spicy mustards contain the enzyme myrosinase, which activates the sulforaphane. In fact, the spicier the better!

Combine these two ingredients for a powerful detoxifying and anti-cancer combo.

Cherries:
Sweet And Healthy

Polyphenols are antioxidants that also increase your body's detoxification mechanisms. Cherries are a rich source of polyphenols, and are a great way to sweeten up any recipe!

Garlic:
Repel The Bugs And Toxins

Garlic is widely known for its immune supporting properties. But this tasty ingredient is also rich in sulfur compounds that supercharge your internal detoxification enzymes!

Garlic also contains "allicin" which has anti-microbial and anti-parasitic properties! But make sure to chop and expose the garlic to air. Doing this greatly increases its allicin content.

Nutrition Facts
Recipe makes 4 servings

Amount per serving	
Calories	**115**
Total Fat	**8.3g**
Saturated Fat	0.8g
Total Carbohydrates	**9.2g**
Carbohydrates from Fiber	3g
Sugars	**3.8g**
Protein	**6g**

DETOX

Garlic Cabbage with Capers

SERVES: **4** PREP TIME: **15 MIN** **GF** GLUTEN FREE **SF** SOY FREE

Ingredients:

- 1 tablespoon **coconut oil**
- 2 **cloves garlic,** minced
- 1 tablespoon **capers**
- 4 cups **cabbage,** sliced
- ¼ cup **klamata olives,** chopped
- 1 tablespoon **lemon juice**
- ¼ teaspoon **black pepper**
- **Salt** to taste

Directions:

1. Bring oil to medium-high heat in large sauce pan.

2. Add garlic, capers, and sauté until fragrant, about 1-2 minutes.

3. Add cabbage, continue sautéing for 3-5 minutes or until soft.

4. Stir in the olives, lemon juice, cover, reduce to low heat, and cook until heated through, 2-3 minutes. Season with black pepper, and salt to taste.

5. Serve as a side dish to complement any meal.

see recipe

Garlic:
Bad For Health?

Garlic is well known for its antibiotic and detox promoting substances. With all of its beneficial effects, garlic is something that people should include in their diet on a regular basis. *But can this tasty ingredient be bad for your health?*

If you suffer from the autoimmune disease "lupus," the answer is maybe. In fact, The Johns Hopkins Lupus Center advises its patients to avoid garlic in their diet. Though adding the occasional garlic while cooking is probably ok for many lupus patients, some may experience flare-ups of their symptoms. So if this applies to you, try avoiding garlic in your cooking. And if you're a garlic lover, you can always reintroduce it back into your diet to see if it affects your condition.

Capers:
Tiny, But Mighty

Most people think of capers as just a garnish, or a flavor enhancing addition to a recipe. *But could it be that this little flower bud is doing much of the heavy lifting?*

From reducing inflammation to balancing allergy responses, researchers have found quercetin to be beneficial in many ways... and capers are absolutely packed with this health promoting phytonutrient! Even with the small amounts that are added to recipes, capers can pack a big punch. In fact, 1 tbsp of capers can have almost double the quercetin of a medium sized onion. And onions are widely touted for providing this nutrient! So next time you are preparing a meal, *give your immune system a break and find a way to add some capers!*

Nutrition Facts
Recipe makes 4 servings

Amount per serving	
Calories	**59**
Total Fat	**4.5g**
Saturated Fat	0.2g
Total Carbohydrates	**6g**
Carbohydrates from Fiber	2g
Sugars	**0g**
Protein	**0g**

DETOX

Grilled Tempeh Sandwich with Wasabi Aoli

GF
GLUTEN FREE

Ingredients:

Wasabi Aoli Sauce:
- ¼ cup **reduced fat vegenaise w/ flax oil**
  by *Follow You Heart*
- ½ teaspoon **wasabi paste,** or powder mixed
  with 2 teaspoons **water**
- ½ teaspoon **lemon juice**
- **Salt** to taste

Sandwich:
- ½ tablespoon **coconut oil**
- 1 (8 ounce) pack of **tempeh,** cut in half
- 1 cup **sliced cabbage,** exposed to air for 5-10 min
- 2 slices **tomato**
- 2 slices **onion**
- **Salt and pepper** to taste
- 2 of your favorite **gluten free bread/ buns**

tip To add even more flavor to the tempeh, slice each half into 2 thinner sheets of tempeh and season both sides before cooking.

Directions:

1. Mix all sauce ingredients together in a small bowl and set aside.

2. Bring oil to medium-high heat in a medium pan. Pepper the tempeh generously on both sides and pan-fry for 3-5 minutes on each side. Salt to taste.

3. In a small bowl, toss cabbage with ½ of the sauce and set aside.

4. Toast your favorite gluten free bun and smear it with some of the sauce on each side. Then layer the tempeh, tomatoes, onions, and cabbage.

5. Serve with your favorite side dish or as a meal of its own!

tip The vegenaise really helps to soften the wasabi's bite. But if the wasabi aioli is too spicy for you, try replacing the wasabi with of a ½ tbsp of crushed garlic. Be sure to expose it to air for 5-10 min to maximize its detox properties. You can also give the garlic a quick sauté to reduce the spiciness!

see recipe

Wasabi + Cabbage:
Detox Condiments

Can condiments and toppings be designed with detoxification in mind? Certainly!

A few simple adjustments and replacements can take your sandwich toppers from insignificant to amazingly beneficial. Rather than the normal lettuce and mayonnaise, we topped our sandwich with sliced cabbage and wasabi (or garlic) aoli. Rich in anti-cancer and detox promoting compounds, you can jazz up your sandwich and protect your well-being. Plus, using a gluten free bun will also decrease inflammation for many people. This helps the body maintain efficient detoxification in its day to day activities. *It's amazing what a modified sandwich can do!*

Omega 3 Vegenaise:
Out With The Normal

A good sandwich needs a good dressing. *But what is the healthiest alternative to mayonnaise?*

Well, *Reduced Fat Vegenaise* made by *Follow Your Heart* can be a great option! This particular mayonnaise substitute is great because it is rich in the omega 3 fatty acids found in cold-pressed flax seed oil. And reducing inflammation is one of the foundations for keeping your detoxification pathways working efficiently. Mix it with another detox promoting ingredient like wasabi or garlic, and you have a really powerful combination! *Yum...*

Nutrition Facts
Recipe makes 2 servings

Amount per serving	
Calories	**332**
Total Fat	**28g**
Saturated Fat	1.5g
Total Carbohydrates	**33g**
Carbohydrates from Fiber	14.5g
Sugars	**1g**
Protein	**24g**

DETOX

Steamed Bok Choy Tofu

SERVES: **4** PREP TIME: **15 MIN** **GF**
GLUTEN
FREE

Ingredients:

- 2 teaspoons **garlic,** minced and exposed
  to air 5-10 mins
- 2 tablespoons **rice wine vinegar**
- 3 tablespoons **tamari or soy sauce**
- 8 cups **bok choy,** chopped
- 1 block **extra firm tofu,** cubed (14 oz.)

Gluten Free Variation: Make sure to use gluten
free tamari instead of soy sauce

Directions:

1. In a small bowl, mix all sauce ingredients, and
set aside to let flavors meld.

2. Using a large sized steamer, steam bok choy and
tofu for 5-7 minutes.

3. Mix bok choy and tofu with sauce.

4. Serve with rice, or as a delicious side dish.

see recipe

Sesame Oil: *Don't Just Eat It?*

Sesame oil gives recipes a distinct flavor that we often get in Asian style foods. With its anti-inflammatory and pain reducing properties, it's more than just a way to flavor our foods. But sesame oil in particular is also great outside of the kitchen. This wonderful oil, often used on the skin in the practice of Ayurveda, was actually found to inhibit melanoma cancer cells in their tests. Researchers believe that the omega 6 linoleic acid was responsible for this effect. *Here's another tip: If the smell of sesame oil bothers you, you can try safflower oil which was just as effective!*

Bok Choy: Less Common, *But More Nutritious?*

Cabbage comes in a few different varieties. Though they all have their unique strengths, *are we ignoring one of the most nutritious varieties?*

Though the Bok Choy cabbage is one of the most popular vegetables used in Chinese cuisine, it is not as popular in other parts of the world. *But did you know?* Bok Choy has more vitamin A and beta-carotene than any other variety of cabbage! Best of all, it still comes with all the detox promoting and anti-cancer nutrients found in other types of cabbage.

Nutrition Facts	
Recipe makes 4 servings	
Amount per serving	
Calories	**137**
Total Fat	**7g**
Saturated Fat	0g
Total Carbohydrates	**10g**
Carbohydrates from Fiber	4g
Sugars	**2g**
Protein	**18g**

DETOX

Green Tea Cold Noodles

Ingredients:

- 8 ounces **dried buckwheat soba noodles**
- 4 bags **green tea**
- 1 teaspoon **sesame oil**
- 2 tablespoons **rice wine vinegar**
- 2 ½ tablespoons **tamari or soy sauce** (or to taste)
- 1 teaspoon **lime juice**
- 2 cloves **garlic,** minced
- ½ cup **carrots,** finely grated
- ¼ cup **walnuts,** crushed
- 2 tablespoons **fresh cilantro,** chopped
- ½ cup **bok choy,** chopped
- ½ cup **edamame**
- 1 pinch **salt**

tip: Don't have the extra hour to spare before dinner? These noodles can also be served warm, *making it a quick and delicious 25 min recipe!*

SERVES: **4** PREP TIME: **1h 25 MIN**

GLUTEN FREE   SOY FREE (Option)   RAW (Option)

Directions:

1. Bring water to boil with a pinch of salt in a large pot. Add soba noodles, edamame, 4 bags of green tea, and cook according to directions on noodle package. Then drain and rinse the noodles and edamame in cold water.

2. Using a large mixing bowl, combine the tamari/soy sauce, rice wine vinegar, sesame oil, garlic, lime juice, walnuts, carrots and cilantro.

3. Gently fold in noodles and edamame with all other ingredients to distribute evenly. Cover and refrigerate until chilled.

4. Serve as a main course or delicious side dish.

Gluten Free Variation: Be sure that your buckwheat soba noodles are 100% buckwheat and gluten free. Use gluten free tamari instead of soy sauce.

Soy Free Variation: Replace edamame with lentils boiled to al-dente texture. Use coconut aminos or sea salt in place of soy sauce.

Raw Variation: Replace soba with raw grated zucchini, replace rice wine vinegar with raw apple cider vinegar, and use coconut aminos (raw) or "nama shoyu" which is an unpasteurized raw soy sauce.

see recipe

Garlic: *Does It Have To Stink?*

Next to its antibiotic and detox promoting substances, garlic is notorious for its odorous properties. *But can the stink actually be part of its benefit?* Researchers have shown part of garlic's healing abilities come from its (stinky) sulfur containing molecules. Our red blood cells actually use these to form hydrogen sulfide gas (which also smells really bad) to widen blood vessels and balance blood pressure! And if you think you can get around the smell with garlic extract pills, research shows that it's not so effective for this particular function.

So try some real garlic... and if bad breath is your main concern, try chewing on some parsley after you eat.

Cilantro: *Toxic Urine?*

Some people love it, others can't stand the taste, but cilantro definitely brings a unique flavor to the dishes that incorporate it. *But can cilantro actually make your urine toxic?*

Cilantro contains compounds known to be natural chelators of heavy metals. This means that they bind to toxic metals like mercury for your body to remove. Amazingly, this effect occurred at dosages that we get from food! But don't forget the other aspects of detoxification. From sulfur compounds and polyphenols, to fiber and anti-inflammatory oils, all of these factors work as a system to strengthen your body's detoxification pathways.

Nutrition Facts
Recipe makes 4 servings

Amount per serving

Calories	**193**
Total Fat	**9.5g**
Saturated Fat	1g
Total Carbohydrates	**19g**
Carbohydrates from Fiber	4g
Sugars	**2.5g**
Protein	**10.5g**

DETOX

Detox Smoothie

SERVES: **4** PREP TIME: **5 MIN**
GLUTEN FREE · SOY FREE · RAW (Option)

Ingredients:

- 1 cup **green tea,** chilled
- ½ cup **kale,** frozen
- ½ cup **broccoli,** frozen
- ½ **banana,** frozen
- 1 cup **raspberries, blackberries or strawberries,** frozen
- 1 scoop of **rice protein powder**
- ½ cup **ice**
- **Stevia,** maple syrup, or your favorite sweetener to taste

Directions:

1. Combine all ingredients in a blender and blend until smooth.

Raw Variation: Replace maple syrup with raw agave or dates. Use an unheated/ raw protein powder. Brew tea without heat by soaking tea leaves in water and leaving in the refrigerator for 8-12 hours.

tip Try using stevia instead of maple syrup to reduce sugar intake!

see recipe

Kale:
Can Kale Affect Your Genes?

When people think of genetics, they usually think of the traits they inherit from their mother and father. But researchers are finding that many things in our environment constantly interact with our genes, for better and for worse. Luckily, things like *"isothiocyanates"* found in kale can actually increase the expression of genes involved in detoxification. *Who would have thought that something so simple can have such a profound effect!*

Green Tea and Berries:
National Cancer Institute Loves Green Tea

The idea that green tea detoxifies the body isn't just something that the internet conjured up. In fact, research supported by the *National Cancer Institute* found that green tea's *polyphenols* can actually help the body generate and stimulate its own detoxification enzymes! Combine these with the compounds in berries and cruciferous vegetables, and you'll have yourself a triple threat against toxins.

Nutrition Facts
Recipe makes 4 servings

Amount per serving	
Calories	**107**
Total Fat	**0.4g**
Saturated Fat	0g
Total Carbohydrates	**11g**
Carbohydrates from Fiber	2g
Sugars	**5.6g**
Protein	**16.6g**

DETOX

VEGAN SURVIVAL:
For the Soul

Feed your Soul!

What good is a healthy
mind and body if you don't
feed the soul?

Sometimes you just need
a tasty dessert to put a smile
on your face! Plus, make these
treats in a healthier way and you
have a win-win situation!

VSG: For the Soul

Let's get started with treats and desserts! :)

We all need a little pick-me-up from time to time. With all of this focus on healthy minds and bodies, it's easy to forget about the most important part of ourselves, the soul! A little fun and excitement is often necessary to balance the discipline it takes to maintain a healthy diet, right?

Thankfully, nature has given us a huge variety of ingredients that are delicious and nutritious. *Why eat a normal dessert when you can make one that tastes just as good, and supports your health?*

DELICIOUS & HEALTHY?

From the decadence of cacao and coconut cream, to the natural sweetness of dates and stevia, nature provides us with everything that we could ever want. Tasty treats that feed the soul and benefit the body! *What more can we ask for?*

Delicious and Healthy Dessert Ingredients

Did You Know?

Though it has gotten much attention lately, agave nectar is much less nutritious than many other natural sweeteners. Maple syrup, dates, coconut sugar, and molasses are all much richer in beneficial trace minerals. And though the fructose in agave nectar puts it low on the glycemic index, it can still have a wide range of unhealthy effects when eaten in excess. Because of this, sweeteners in general should be taken in moderation. ■

Examples of versatile ingredients in this category:

Natural No / Low Calorie Sweeteners: Monk Fruit Sweetener (Lo Han Fruit), Stevia, Yacon Syrup, Xylitol

---

Natural Nutrient Rich Sweeteners: Brown Rice Syrup, Brown Sugar (Certified Vegan), Coconut Sugar/ Nectar, Dates, Fruit Juices, Maple Syrup, Molasses

---

Gluten Free Flours: Almond Meal, Amaranth Flour, Bean Flours, Brown Rice Flour, Buckwheat Flour, Oat Flour (Certified Gluten Free), Coconut Flour, Potato Flour, Quinoa Flour, Teff Flour, Sorghum Flour, Tapioca Flour

Make these treats in a healthier way and you have a win-win situation!

Honeydew Omega Ice Cream

SERVES: **8** PREP TIME: **1-3h**

GF GLUTEN FREE **SF** SOY FREE **R** RAW (Option)

Ingredients:

- 1 cup **hemp milk,** or your favorite vegan milk
- 1 can **coconut milk,** full fat
- ½ cup **raw walnuts**
- 2 cups **cantaloupe**
- ¼ cup **raw pistachios,** chopped
- 1 pinch **salt**
- 4 teaspoons **lemon juice**
- **Stevia,** maple syrup, or your favorite vegan sweetener to taste

Directions:

In a powerful blender, combine coconut milk, hemp milk, cantaloupe, walnuts, and blend until completely smooth. Then add salt, lemon juice, sweetener to taste, and blend thoroughly.

With Ice Cream Maker:
Make in ice cream maker as directed, adding pistachios when the ice cream begins to solidify.

With a Hand Held Stick Blender:
Pour mixture into the stick blender's mixing cup.

(cont.) Put in freezer, remove it after 45 min, blend it thoroughly, making sure to get all the frozen bits on the side. Then put it back in freezer and re-blend thoroughly every 25-30 min (about 5x total), until a semi-solid ice cream is formed. Then mix in pistachios, mix thoroughly, and leave in freezer until desired texture is achieved. Smash and mix with a wooden spatula if ice chunks appear.

Without any tools: Put mixture in sturdy bowl and place in the freezer. After about 45 min, or when it starts freezing around the sides, use a wooden spatula to smash and mix, making sure to break up any chunks of ice thoroughly. Repeat the process every 25-30 min (about 5x total) until a semi-solid ice cream is formed. Then mix in pistachios, mix thoroughly, and leave in the freezer until desired texture is achieved. Smash and mix with a wooden spatula if ice chunks appear.

If serving after prolonged freezing, let thaw until slightly soft, then smash and mix with a wooden spatula before serving.

see recipe

Cantaloupe + Pistachios: *Functional Flavors*

Cantaloupe and pistachios bring just as much function as they do flavor to this ice cream recipe. Cantaloupe is one of the richest sources of inositol available in the produce section. Beyond its role in GABA synthesis to promote calmness in the mind, inositol is also known to promote healthy hair growth. Pistachios on the other hand are super rich in vitamin B6, which is important for brain health. It's is also an exceptional source of the amino lysine, which is very important for vegans to obtain complete proteins in their diet. *In fact, pistachios have more lysine per serving than any other nut!*

Raw Variation: Use raw nut and coconut milks if available. If not, you can make them yourself by blending fresh raw nuts of your choice with water, and filtering through cheesecloth. Adjust the water to nut ratio until desired level of creaminess is achieved! Use the same process with fresh mature coconut flesh for coconut milk.

Hemp + Coconut Milk: *Super Creamy Blend*

Hemp milk and coconut milk create a super balanced and nutritious base for this delicious ice cream recipe. Hemp milk has more than just anti-inflammatory omega 3's, it's also rich in a special type of omega 6 fatty acid called gama linolenic acid (GLA). GLA has shown to benefit a variety of illnesses ranging from eczema and asthma to rheumatoid and even cancer! Researchers have also found GLA to help maintain body weight after weight loss has already been achieved. *Combine this with the anti-inflammatory, immune boosting, and fat burning effects of coconut milk and you have yourself an awesome base for some delicious ice cream!*

Nutrition Facts
Recipe makes 8 servings

Amount per serving

Calories	**187**
Total Fat	**16g**
Saturated Fat	8g
Total Carbohydrates	**9.3g**
Carbohydrates from Fiber	1.5g
Sugars	**6g**
Protein	**3.2g**

Brazilian "Pão de Queijo" Cheese Puffs

SERVES: **4 (16 pieces total)** PREP TIME: **1h** GF GLUTEN FREE SF SOY FREE

Ingredients:

- 3/4 cups of **tapioca flour**
- ½ teaspoon **salt,** or to taste
- ½ tablespoon of **baking powder**
- ¼ cup **water**
- 2 tablespoons high oleic **sunflower oil**
- ½ cup **Daiya vegan mozzarella cheese shreds**
- 1 cup **potatoes,** boiled and mashed

A gluten-free cheesy roll with a soft chewy center... A favorite with the kids!

Directions:

1. Set your oven to 350 degrees F.

2. Using a large mixing bowl, combine tapioca flour, salt, baking powder, mix thoroughly, and set aside. Sift if necessary.

3. In a small pan, mix sunflower oil, water, and bring to a gentle boil.

4. Combine dry ingredients with Daiya vegan cheese, mashed potatoes, hot oil and water mixture, and mix together to form dough.

5. To form the dough balls, rub a little oil onto your hands, and grab enough dough to form balls of 1 ½ in diameter. There should be a total of about 16 dough balls. (You can also make them any size you like.)

6. Space the dough balls apart on a large baking sheet, and bake at 350 degrees F for about 40-45 min or until golden brown. Let cool before serving.

7. These Brazilian cheese puffs are a delicious complement to any meal!

tip These cheese puffs store very well in the fridge or freezer. Just pop them in the toaster for a quick and easy treat!

see recipe

Potato:
Why The Bad Rap?

Though potatoes are high in blood sugar spiking carbohydrates, these popular spuds aren't as bad as many people think! In fact, researchers have found potatoes to contain a huge variety of health benefiting phytonutrients. Even more surprising, is that their phytonutrient concentrations can rival those of nutrient dense vegetables like broccoli and Brussels sprouts! So as you eat these awesome cheese balls, remember that you're also getting lots of nutrients in the process. But remember, potato skins contain a huge amount of nutrients. *So no need to peel the potatoes...*

just boil and mash them with the skin on, before adding it to the recipe!

Tapioca:
Chewy Goodness

Tapioca starch brings a uniquely chewy texture to these tasty vegan cheese puffs. This unique ingredient isn't the most powerful for boosting the body's nutrition stores. *But... it does bring some chewy goodness to these wonderful cheese puffs! And it's gluten free!* Sometimes you just have to feed your soul.

Once you get a bite, you will see... this chewy cheesy vegan goodness really hits the spot!

...on Facts
makes 4 servings

Amount per serving	
Calories	**243**
Total Fat	**10g**
Saturated Fat	1.5g
Total Carbohydrates	**37g**
Carbohydrates from Fiber	1.2g
Sugars	**1.4g**
Protein	**1g**

For the Soul

Apple Cinnamon Millet Pudding

SERVES: **6** PREP TIME: **35 MIN** **GF** GLUTEN FREE **SF** SOY FREE

Ingredients:

- 1 cup **lite coconut milk**
- 4 ¼ cups of your **favorite vegan milk** (almond, hemp, soy, etc)
- ¾ cup **dry millet**
- 1 cup **apples,** chopped
- ¼ cup **maple syrup** or sweetener of choice to taste
- ½ teaspoon **vanilla extract**
- 1 teaspoon **cinnamon**
- ¼ teaspoon **salt**

Directions:

1. Combine all ingredients in a large pot. Bring to a boil while stirring, reduce to low heat, cover and let simmer for 20-25 minutes. Stir regularly.

2. Serve warm or cold. Both are delicious!

see recipe

Millet:
Miracle Mineral

Besides its rich fiber content, millet also beats out white rice when it comes to magnesium. From the brain and nervous system, to bones and muscles, this super important mineral supports health in so many ways. Just like its fiber content, millet also has nearly 4 times the magnesium of white rice! *So next time you have a craving for some good old rice pudding, try millet pudding instead!*

Rice Pudding:
A Classic Reinvented

Rice pudding is a classic dessert that has been eaten all around the world for centuries. *But this timeless dessert is getting a facelift!*

Though rice itself is a great gluten free grain, millet can offer advantages to this recipe with its higher fiber content. In fact, millet has 4 times the fiber of white rice! And because millet is just as soft and delicious, millet makes a great substitute for this recipe.

Nutrition Facts
Recipe makes 6 servings

Amount per serving	
Calories	**198**
Total Fat	**7g**
Saturated Fat	1.5g
Total Carbohydrates	**30g**
Carbohydrates from Fiber	2.3g
Sugars	**8g**
Protein	**3.7g**

For the Soul

Peaches and Cream Chia

SERVES: **6** PREP TIME: **1h 30 MIN** **GF** GLUTEN FREE **SF** SOY FREE **R** RAW (Option)

Ingredients:

- 1 can **full fat coconut milk,** refrigerated overnight
- 3 - 3 ½ cups of your **favorite vegan milk** (almond, hemp, soy, etc)
- ¾ cups **whole chia seeds**
- 3 teaspoons **vanilla extract**
- **Maple syrup** or your favorite sweetener to taste
- 2 **peaches,** sliced or chopped
- 1 tablespoon **vegan powdered sugar,** or sweetener to taste

Raw Variation: Make sure to get your seed, nut, and coconut milks in raw form. You can also make these yourself with the raw nuts, seeds, and fresh mature coconut flesh! Just blend them with water and strain through cheesecloth. Adjust the amount of water until the desired level of creaminess is achieved!

Directions:

1. Pre-refrigerate the can of coconut milk overnight, making sure not to shake it so the cream can settle on top. When ready, skim the thick cream from top (cont.) of the can with a fork, put into a large mixing bowl, and set aside.

2. Add your favorite vegan milk (3 - 3 ½ cups) to the remainder of the coconut milk until they equal 4 cups total.

3. Using a large jar, or sealed container, combine chia seeds, the 4 cup vegan milk mixture, 2 tsp of vanilla extract, and, your choice of vegan sweetener to taste. Shake vigorously to mix, and leave in refrigerator for 1-2 hrs.

4. As the chia seeds are refrigerating, prepare the coconut whipped cream. Put the metal whisks from electric hand mixer into the bowl with the coconut cream, cover, and put the coconut cream with the whisks in the refrigerator for 20 min to cool.

5. Then remove from refrigerator, add the vegan powdered sugar or sweetener of your choice, 1 tsp vanilla extract, and beat with hand mixer until fluffy. If the cream becomes too thin, put back into refrigerator for 20 min with whisks, and beat again. Leave it in the refrigerator to store, and whip before serving.

6. When the chia pudding is done, ladle into a dessert cup, top with a side of peaches and a dollop of whipped cream. And most importantly... enjoy!

see recipe

Peaches:
Kill'em with Sweetness!

Who can resist the taste of a juicy peach on a hot summer day? The peach is such a unique and delicious fruit. But this wonderful ingredient does more than just delight your taste buds. Researchers studying a common commercial variety called "Rich Lady" peaches, found it to contain high levels of something called chlorogenic acid. In their experiments, this compound killed even the most aggressive breast cancer cells, without harming normal healthy cells! So next time you bite into a juicy peach, enjoy it in every way. *It might just protect you when you need it most.*

Chia:
New Kid On The Block?

Chia seeds are getting really popular in the world of natural foods. *But are they really the new kid on the block?* As an integral part of Mayan and Aztec diet, these nutrient packed seeds have actually been eaten for centuries! They were also fed to their warriors, and for a good reason. Chia seeds are even richer in omega 3's than their flaxseed counterpart! They also resist spoiling because of their super high anti-oxidant contents. So enjoy this chia pudding recipe... *Your body is going to love it!*

Nutrition Facts
Recipe makes 6 servings

Amount per serving

Calories	259
Total Fat	9g
Saturated Fat	10g
Total Carbohydrates	11g
Carbohydrates from Fiber	8g
Sugars	1g
Protein	5g

Double Cherry Pie

SERVES: **8** PREP TIME: **1h 30 MIN**

 GF GLUTEN FREE **SF** SOY FREE **R** RAW (Option)

Ingredients:

Pie Crust:
- 1 cup **raw walnuts**
- ½ cup **raw pecans**
- ½ cup **raw pistachios**
- 1 cup **dates,** pitted
- ¼ teaspoon **salt** (optional)

Fruit Filling:
- 2 cups **tart cherries,** chopped into quarters.
- 1 cup **sweet cherries,** chopped into quarters

Sauce:
- 3/4 cup **tart cherries**
- 6 tablespoons **dates,** pitted and soaked for 15 min

Coconut Whipped Cream:
- 2 cans **full fat coconut milk,** refrigerated overnight
- 2 tablespoons **vegan powdered sugar**
  or stevia to taste
- 2 teaspoons **vanilla extract**

Pie Crust:
1. Combine nuts in food processor and pulse until coarsely chopped. Add dates, sea salt, and continue pulsing until thoroughly mixed. The resulting mixture should holds together when compressed.

2. Compress the date and nut mixture evenly around a 9-inch pie tin to form a piecrust. Place in the freezer for about 15 min.

Pie Filling: 1. Put 3/4 cup of tart cherries with the soaked, drained, and pitted dates into the blender. Blend until smooth and gently mix in large bowl with remaining cherries.

2. Pour fruit filling into your piecrust. Spread filling around until smooth. Cover and refrigerate for 1 hr.

Coconut Whipped Cream: 1. Make sure the coconut milk has not been shaken so the cream can settle on top. Leave in refrigerator overnight before opening.

2. As the pie is settling in the refrigerator, prepare the whipped cream. Skim the top layer of thick cream with a fork and place into a large mixing bowl. Put the metal whisks from an electric hand mixer into the bowl with the coconut cream, cover, and let cool in the refridgerator for 20 min.

3. Remove from refrigerator, add vegan powdered sugar or sweetener, 2 tsp vanilla extract, and beat with hand mixer until fluffy. If the cream becomes too thin, put back into refrigerator for 20 min with whisks, and beat again. When the pie is ready, remove from refrigerator, slice, and serve with a dollop of coconut whipped cream.

see recipe

Tart Cherries:
The Dark Horse

Tart cherries do more than just make a delicious cherry pie. This awesome super fruit has become popular for its endless list of health boosting properties. Two of the most notable abilities of tart cherries include their ability to benefit migraine headaches and gout in the joints. Both of these effects come from the ability of tart cherries to slow down the activity of inflammatory enzymes called COX 1&2.

And since cherries can increase melatonin levels in the blood, it may also help you sleep better too!

tip You can use fresh or frozen cherries in this recipe. But if you can't find fresh or frozen tart cherries at your local market, try using dried unsweetened tart cherries, reconstituted in tart cherry juice over night!

Raw Variation: If you can't find raw powdered sugar, you can make it yourself by grinding raw sugar into a powder. Make sure to get your coconut milk in raw form. You can also make this yourself with fresh mature coconut flesh! Just blend it with water and strain through cheesecloth. Adjust the amount of water until the desired level of creaminess is achieved!

Pie Crust:
Super Pie Crust

Normal pie crusts can be full of inflammation promoting flour and oils. Well this pie crust is just the opposite. With a blend of raw walnuts, pecans, and pistachios, this piecrust has all of your bases covered. From a healthy ratio of unheated omega 3's and 6's, to lysine rich pistachios, there's nothing more you could ever ask for from a pie crust. *Combine these with mineral rich dates, and you have yourself a real sweet winner!*

Nutrition Facts
Recipe makes 8 servings

Amount per serving	
Calories	**472**
Total Fat	**35.6g**
Saturated Fat	16.5g
Total Carbohydrates	**37.5g**
Carbohydrates from Fiber	5.6g
Sugars	**25g**
Protein	**7.5g**

For the Soul

Strawberry Pistachio Bon-Bons

Ingredients:

- ¼ cup **oat flour**
- 6 tablespoons **dates,** pitted
- ½ cup **pistachios**
- 1 cup **fresh strawberries**
- 2 pinches of **salt**
- 1 ½ cups **vegan chocolate chips**

Gluten Free Variation: Make sure to use certified gluten free oat flour.

Directions:

1. In a food processor, add pistachios and pulse into roughly shopped pieces. Add strawberries, dates, and pulse until smooth. Add oat powder and continue pulsing until all ingredients are distributed evenly in a paste like mixture.

2. Scoop mixture into a bowl, cover and put into the freezer for 1-2 hours, or until solid enough to roll into balls

3. When mixture solidifies, roll into one-inch balls, place on a wax paper lined plate, and freeze overnight or until solid.

4. When the bon-bon fillings are frozen, melt chocolate chips in a double boiler. You can also melt the chocolate in a bowl simmering in a pan of water. Using a toothpick or fork, dip and coat each bon-bon filling with melted chocolate, and place on wax paper lined plate.

5. Place in freezer for the shell to harden, then store them in the freezer.

6. Allow bon-bons to thaw before eating, or eat them straight from the freezer for a delicious frozen treat!

see recipe

Strawberries and Dates: *Nice and Sweet*

Sweets don't always have to be devoid of nutrition. *With a few simple adjustments, you can make a delicious treat that's packed with nutrients too!* Unlike heated strawberry jellies, using fresh strawberries ensures that your kids get the vitamin C they need to support a strong immune system. And instead of the high fructose corn syrup so often found in sweets, using dates means that they're getting more of the minerals that their bodies need to grow big and strong. So when it's time to have a tasty treat, make it yourself and give these bon-bons a try... *Your kids will love them!*

Sneaking In The Nutrition

Getting kids to eat nutritious foods isn't always an easy task. *So what better way to get them in their diet, than to hide them in a delicious treat?* These aren't your average bon-bons after all! Using whole oat flour not only helps to control blood sugar, it's also full of beta glucans to enhance the immune system. Combine this with the B vitamin rich pistachios, and you have yourself a winning combo! Who would have thought! *A bon-bon with so many nutritious ingredients!*

Nutrition Facts
Recipe makes 16 servings

Amount per serving	
Calories	**166**
Total Fat	**9g**
Saturated Fat	5g
Total Carbohydrates	**21g**
Carbohydrates from Fiber	1g
Sugars	**15g**
Protein	**3g**

For the Soul

Avocado Chocolate Torte with Raspberry Purée

SERVES: **8** PREP TIME: **1h 30 MIN**

 GLUTEN FREE **SOY FREE** **RAW**

Ingredients:

Crust:
- ²/₃ cup **raw walnuts**
- ²/₃ cup **raw pistachios**
- ²/₃ cup **raw pumpkin seeds**
- 1 cup **dates,** pitted
- ¼ teaspoon **salt**

Mousse:
- 2 cups **ripe avocado**
- 2 tablespoons of **vegan sugar** or your favorite dry sweetener to taste
- 1 ½ tablespoons **vanilla extract**
- ¼ teaspoon **salt**
- ½ cup **cacao powder**
- 2 tablespoons **coconut oil**

Raspberry Puree:
- 1 cup **fresh or frozen raspberries**
- ½ cup **water**
- **Vegan sugar** or your favorite sweetener to taste

Directions:

Crust:
1. Combine all nuts and seeds in a food processor and pulse until coarsely chopped. Then break up the dates, spread them evenly in the food processor, and continue pulsing until thoroughly mixed. Add salt a little at a time as the ingredients are being processed. The result should be a semi-fine nut meal that holds together when compressed.

2. Compress the date and nut mixture evenly around a 9-inch pie tin to form a piecrust. Place in the freezer for about 15 min.

Mousse Filling:
1. Combine all mousse ingredients in a food processor and blend until smooth.

2. When the piecrust is ready, add the mousse to the pie tin and spread evenly. Place in the refrigerator for about 1 hour.

Raspberry Puree:
1. Add all raspberry puree ingredients in a powerful blender and blend until smooth.

2. When the pie is ready, slice and serve with raspberry puree.

see recipe

Avocado:
A Sweet Ingredient

Using avocado in desserts is a great way to get this ingredient into our diets. In fact, avocados are generally used as a sweet ingredient in Brazil, where they are often blended into smoothies. But avocados are versatile in more ways than one.

What's most interesting is avocados' versatility in its anti-oxidant capabilities. Avocados' unique antioxidants protect normal healthy cells, and can actually promote oxidative stress to fight cancer cells! *So avocados are more than just a treat in this recipe, they're like smart bombs against cancer!*

tip This recipe is also amazing when topped with coconut whipped cream and a side of sliced strawberries. *It's absolutely delicious!*

Raw Variation: If you are on a raw foods diet, make sure that your coconut oil, cacao powder, vanilla extract, and sugar are purchased in raw form.

Cacao:
Bliss In Every Bite

Sometimes we just need a little treat to feed our souls. *But who would have known that a food ingredient could actually release happy chemicals in our brains?* Well cacao can do exactly that. Rich in a compound called *"anadamide,"* cacao has almost drug like effects for increasing mood, alertness, and excitement! It's also rich in anti-oxidants and can benefit blood pressure too. *So when you need a little "pick me up," sit back, relax, and have yourself some cacao!*

Nutrition Facts
Recipe makes 8 servings

Amount per serving

Calories	**408**
Total Fat	**30.5g**
Saturated Fat	6.7g
Total Carbohydrates	**29.5g**
Carbohydrates from Fiber	9.6g
Sugars	**14g**
Protein	**13.2g**

Complete Protein Red Velvet Cupcake

SERVES: **12 Cupcakes** PREP TIME: **45 MIN**
GLUTEN FREE   SOY FREE

Ingredients:

Red Velvet Cupcake:
- 1 cup **coconut milk beverage** or almond milk
- 1 teaspoon **apple cider vinegar**
- 1/3 cup high oleic **sunflower oil**
- 3/4 cup **vegan sugar**
- 1 tablespoon **vanilla extract**
- 1 teaspoon **apple cider vinegar**
- 2 tablespoons **beet juice** or 1 tablespoon natural food coloring in 1 tablespoon water
- 1 1/2 cups **oat flour**
- 1 cup **chickpea flour**
- 2 tablespoons **cocoa powder**
- 1/2 teaspoon **baking soda**
- 1/2 teaspoon **baking powder**
- 1/2 teaspoon **sea salt**

Vegan Cream Cheese Icing:
- 1 cup **Daiya vegan cream cheese,** plain
- 3/4 cup **non-hydrogenated vegan butter,** margarine, or shortening, softened
- 1 cup **vegan powdered sugar** or your favorite dry sweetener to taste
- 1 teaspoon **vanilla extract**

Directions:

1. Set oven to 350 degrees F.

2. In a large mixing bowl, combine your choice of vegan milk with 1 teaspoon of apple cider vinegar. Stir and let curdle for 5-10 min.

3. When the vegan milk is finished curdling, add oil, sugar, vanilla extract, another teaspoon of apple cider vinegar, and beet juice or natural food coloring. If you are using natural food coloring, add another tablespoon of water. Mix thoroughly.

4. In another mixing bowl, sift together and mix oat flour, chickpea flour, cocoa powder, baking soda, baking powder, and sea salt.

5. Combine the wet and dry ingredients, mix thoroughly, divide evenly amongst 12 cupcake tins, and quickly put into the oven.

6. Bake for 20-22 min. Test with a toothpick to see if cupcakes are done.

7. To make the frosting, combine Daiya vegan cream cheese, vegan butter, vanilla, and blend thoroughly with electric hand mixer. Then mix in powdered sugar, and blend until fluffy.

8. When cupcakes are done, remove from tin and let cool on a wire rack for 5 min before frosting!

see recipe

Doing the impossible?

What's better than a red velvet cupcake? How about one that is gluten free, soy free, dairy free, with no artificial colors? Combine that with the protein of chickpea flour, the health supporting effects of oat flour, and we have ourselves a real winner! We tried making this cupcake over a dozen times. It was a huge challenge but we finally got it!

You're going to love the vegan cream cheese icing too! Red velvet deliciousness at its best!

tip If you use vegan powdered sugar in the frosting, make sure to get it organic. Then you can be sure that the cornstarch does not come from genetically modified corn.

Gluten Free Variation:
Make sure to use gluten free certified oat flour.

Everyone loves frosting!

For the perfect frosting, try some different types of shortenings that do not contain any hydrogenated oils. Between the *Spectrum* and the *Earth Balance* brands (in the US) we had many options to work with. But be extra careful because shortenings and margarines are the most common sources of hydrogenated oils in general.

Nutrition Facts
Recipe makes 12 servings

Amount per serving	
Calories	**293**
Total Fat	**21g**
Saturated Fat	1.5g
Total Carbohydrates	**23.5g**
Carbohydrates from Fiber	3g
Sugars	**2g**
Protein	**6g**

VSG Food for Function

4

Food for Function

Maximizing Nutrients for Optimal Health.

Before we could design any of the recipes, I worked closely with Dr. Gene to create a list of ingredients to fulfill each of the VSG functions, including Brain, Body, Immune and Detox. Based on his guidance I then spent weeks sorting through nutritional data and cataloguing hundreds of ingredients, all vegan of course!

We looked at all common vegan ingredients and ranked them by single nutrient levels based on typical serving amounts for each one. Based on the unique function boosting formulas we picked ingredients that were the highest in each of the necessary nutrients for a function. We then designed our recipes around that.

So, in this chapter, we wanted to give you a simplified version of the top foods on each category.

Here are some things that you can try:

1. *Use the VSG ingredient lists to create your own delicious functional recipes!*
2. *Add additional ingredients to your favorite recipes to promote a VSG function.*
3. *Have fun and look at recipes your family already enjoys and see if it excels in any particular function.*

VSG Recipe Example

Making a Brain Boosting Dopamine Recipe:

Dopamine (energy, alertness, focus, motivation) =
Tyrosine + B6 + Folate + Vitamin C + Iron + Zinc

> Use the dopamine charts to find the richest ingredients in each of these 6 nutrient categories.
>
> Combine them to create a delicious dopamine supporting recipe. And don't forget, many ingredients will excel in multiple nutrients!

Behind the Scenes of the VSG

Our recipe charts were a little more nerdy and detailed... but it basically looked like this. As you can see below, ingredients have multiple strengths, so we could have used fewer ingredients. But we wanted our recipes to be super tasty, and *who doesn't want a double boost, right?* As long as all of your nutritional bases are covered you've got yourself a functional recipe.

Recipe: Chickpea Pumpkin Seed Stir-fry

Dopamine	Tyrosine	B6	Folate	Vitamin C	Iron	Zinc
Pumpkin Seed	●				●	●
Garbanzo	●		●		●	●
Tomato		●		●	●	
Spinach	●	●	●	●	●	●
Lemon Juice				●		

(Dopamine = Energy, Alertness, Focus, Motivation)

As you can see, if tomatoes and spinach weren't included, this recipe would not have been optimal for dopamine support due to lack of vitamin B6.

Food can be a science, but it doesn't have to be. If you eat a lot of healthy whole foods, and vary your diet on a regular basis, you will more or less get everything you need.

These charts just give you a detailed view of the nutrients you are putting in your body. *So if you want to maximize your diet, we show you how!* ■

| Dopamine | Serotonin | Acetylcholine | GABA |

| Tyrosine | B6 | Folate | Vitamin C | Iron | Zinc |

Ingred / Portions / Tyrosine in mg			Ingred / Portions / Tyrosine in mg			Ingred / Portions / Tyrosine in mg		
Pumpkin Seeds (C)	1/4 cup	776.2	Garbanzo Beans (C)	1/2 cup	180.5	Mustard Greens (R)	1 cup	80.1
Tofu	4 oz	592	Navy Beans (C)	1/2 cup	179	Kale (R)	1 cup	78.4
Tempeh	1/2 cup	551	Pine Nuts (D)	1/4 cup	171.7	Cacao	2 tbsp	77.2
Granola, homemade	1 cup	532	Macadamia Nuts (R)	1/4 cup	171.2	Pumpkin (C)	1 cup	73.5
Green Garbanzo Beans (R)	1/2 cup	479	Cashew Nuts (R)	1/4 cup	168.2	Asparagus (R)	1 cup	69.7
Peanuts	1/4 cup	383	Mustard Greens (C)	1 cup	167	Coconut Cream/Milk (R)	1/4 cup	67.2
Wheat (D)	1/2 cup	371.5	Oat Bran (R)	1/4 cup	157	Turnip Greens (C)	1 cup	63.4
Spelt (D)	1/2 cup	328	Quinoa (C)	1 cup	154	Wheat Bran	1/4 cup	63.2
Soy Beans, Edamame	1/2 cup	260.5	White Rice (C)	1 cup	142	Oat Bran (C)	1/4 cup	62.5
Adzuki Beans (C)	1/2 cup	257.5	Brazilnuts (D)	1/4 cup	139.7	Winter Squash (C)	1 cup	61.5
Wheat Germ (C)	1/4 cup	250	Okra (C)	1 cup	129.6	Broccoli Raab (C)	1 cup	61.2
Lentils (C)	1/2 cup	238.5	Pistachio Nuts	1/4 cup	127.5	Miso	1 tbsp	60.5
Split Peas (C)	1/2 cup	237	Walnuts (R)	1/4 cup	115	Pecans	1/4 cup	58.5
Oatmeal (C)	1 cup	236	Collard Greens (C)	1 cup	106	Carambola/ Starfruit (R)	1 cup	58.1
Sunflower Seed Kernels (D)	1/4 cup	233	Buckwheat Groats (C)	1 cup	104	Winter Squash (R)	1 cup	56.8
Sesame Seeds	2 tbsp	224	Hazelnuts or Filberts	1/4 cup	104	Green Beans (C)	1 cup	55
Oats (D)	1/4 cup	223.5	Yellow Sweet Corn (C)	1/2 cup	103.5	Yam (C)	1 cup	53
Black Beans (C)	1/2 cup	215	Asparagus (C)	1 cup	102.6	Coconut Water	1 cup	52.8
Mung Beans (C)	1/2 cup	212	Barley (C)	1 cup	102	Guavas (R)	1 cup	51.2
Great Northern Beans (C)	1/2 cup	208	Flaxseed	2 tbsp	101	Cauliflower (C)	1 cup	49.6
Fava Beans (C)	1/2 cup	205	Lentils, sprouted (R)	1/2 cup	97	Avocados	1/2 ea	49.2
Spinach (C)	1 cup	203	Yellow Corn (R)	1/2 cup	94.5	Pumpkin (R)	1 cup	48.7
Wheat Germ (R)	1/4 cup	202.5	Broccoli (C)	1 cup	93.6	Mung Beans (C)	1 cup	47.1
Almonds, blanched	1/4 cup	198.2	Green Peas (C)	1/2 cup	89.5	Green Beans (R)	1 cup	46.2
Rye	1/3 cup	191	Potatoes (C)	1 cup	89	Broccoli (R)	1 cup	45.5
Brown Rice (C)	1 cup	189	Sweet Potato with Skin (C)	1 cup	88	Summer Squash (C)	1 cup	43.2
Millet (C)	1 cup	188	Beet Greens (C)	1 cup	87.8	Red Tomatoes (C)	1 cup	43.2
Lima Beans (C)	1/2 cup	186	Kale (C)	1 cup	87.1	Cauliflower (R)	1 cup	43
Pinto Beans (C)	1/2 cup	182	Okra (R)	1 cup	87	Crimni Mushrooms (C)	1/2 cup	42.9
Kidney Beans (C)	1/2 cup	181.5	Green Peas (R)	1/2 cup	82.5	Rutabagas (C)	1 cup	42.5

(C) Cooked | (R) = Raw | (D) = Dried

VSG Brain

Dopamine | Serotonin | Acetylcholine | GABA

Tyrosine | B6 | Folate | Vitamin C | Iron | Zinc

Ingred / Portions / B6 %		
Sweet Potato with Skin (C)	1 cup	29
Green Garbanzo Beans (R)	1/2 cup	27
Pistachio Nuts	1/4 cup	26.2
Sunflower Seed Kernels (D)	1/4 cup	23.5
Bananas (R)	1 med	22
Spinach (C)	1 cup	22
Taro (C)	1 cup	22
Wheat Germ (R)	1/4 cup	18.7
Granola, homemade	1 cup	18
Potatoes (C)	1 cup	18
Winter Squash (C)	1 cup	17
Cherimoya (R)	1/2 each	16.5
Sweet Green Bell Pepper (C)	1 cup	16
Broccoli (C)	1 cup	16
Yam (C)	1 cup	16
Sugar-Apples (R)	1 ea	15
Wheat, hard red (D)	1/2 cup	14.5
Brussels Sprouts (C)	1 cup	14
Okra (C)	1 cup	14
Brown Rice (C)	1 cup	14
Zucchini (R)	1 cup	14
Wheat Germ (C)	1/4 cup	13.7
Avocados	1/2 ea	13
Kohlrabi (C)	1 cup	13
Turnip Greens (C)	1 cup	13
Carrots (C)	1 cup	12
Collard Greens (C)	1 cup	12
Summer Squash (R)	1 cup	12
Cauliflower (R)	1 cup	11
Mangos (R)	1 cup	11

Ingred / Portions / B6 %		
Okra (R)	1 cup	11
Quinoa (C)	1 cup	11
Beet Greens (C)	1 cup	10
Green Bell Pepper (R)	1 cup	10
Brussels Sprouts (R)	1 cup	10
Cauliflower (C)	1 cup	10
Kohlrabi (R)	1 cup	10
Lychee (R)	1 cup	10
Pinto Beans (C)	1/2 cup	10
Spelt (D)	1/2 cup	10
Wheat Bran	1/4 cup	9.5
Barley (C)	1 cup	9
Carrots (R)	1 cup	9
Chayote Fruit (C)	1 cup	9
Chestnuts (C)	1/4 cup	9
Dates, Medjool	3 pieces	9
Guavas (R)	1 cup	9
Kale (C)	1 cup	9
Kale (R)	1 cup	9
Lentils (C)	1/2 cup	9
Millet (C)	1 cup	9
Pineapple (R)	1 cup	9
Rutabagas (C)	1 cup	9
Tempeh	1/2 cup	9
Red Tomatoes (C)	1 cup	9
Winter Squash (R)	1 cup	9
Green Peas (C)	1/2 cup	8.5
Rye	1/3 cup	8.3
Asparagus (C)	1 cup	8
Broccoli (R)	1 cup	8

Ingred / Portions / B6 %		
Cabbage (C)	1 cup	8
Coriander (cilantro)	2 tbsp	8
Dandelion Greens (C)	1 cup	8
Hazelnuts or Filberts	1/4 cup	8
Lima Beans (C)	1/2 cup	8
Parsnips (C)	1 cup	8
Walnuts (R)	1/4 cup	8
Broccoli Raab (C)	1 cup	7.4
Artichokes (R)	1 med	7
Blackstrap Molasses	1 tbsp	7
Bok Choy (R)	1 cup	7
Dandelion Greens (R)	1 cup	7
Honeydew Melon (R)	1 cup	7
Mustard Greens (C)	1 cup	7
Onions (C)	1/2 cup	7
White Rice (C)	1 cup	7
Rutabagas (R)	1 cup	7
Swiss Chard (C)	1 cup	7
Red Tomatoes (R)	1 cup	7
Turnip Greens (R)	1 cup	7
Zucchini with skin (C)	1 cup	7
Navy Beans (C)	1/2 cup	6.5
Peanuts	1/4 cup	6.2
Asparagus (R)	1 cup	6
Buckwheat Groats (C)	1 cup	6
Cabbage (R)	1 cup	6
Cantaloupe (R)	1 cup	6
Celery (C)	1 cup	6
Figs (R) (fresh)	2 med	6
Garlic (R)	3 cloves	6

(C) Cooked | (R) = Raw | (D) = Dried

VSG Brain

| Dopamine | Serotonin | Acetylcholine | GABA |

| Tyrosine | B6 | Folate | Vitamin C | Iron | Zinc |

Ingred / Portions / Folate %			Ingred / Portions / Folate %			Ingred / Portions / Folate %		
Green Garbanzo Beans (R)	1/2 cup	139.5	Peanuts	1/4 cup	22	Oranges (R)	1 med	10
Asparagus (C)	1 cup	68	Avocados	1/2 ea	20.5	Spelt (D)	1/2 cup	10
Spinach (C)	1 cup	66	Wheat Germ (R)	1/4 cup	20.2	Winter Squash (C)	1 cup	10
Soy Beans, Edadame	1/2 cup	60.5	Guavas (R)	1 cup	20	Yellow Sweet Corn (C)	1/2 cup	9.5
Lentils (C)	1/2 cup	45	Sunflower Seed Kernels (D)	1/4 cup	19.7	Lentils, sprouted (R)	1/2 cup	9.5
Collard Greens (C)	1 cup	44	Quinoa (C)	1 cup	19	Blackberries (R)	1 cup	9
Broccoli (C)	1 cup	42	Beets (R)	1/2 cup	18.5	Celery (R)	1 cup	9
Turnip Greens (C)	1 cup	42	Endive (R)	1 cup	18	Yellow Corn (R)	1/2 cup	9
Mung Beans (C)	1/2 cup	40	Okra (C)	1 cup	18	Mung Beans (C)	1 cup	9
Pinto Beans (C)	1/2 cup	37	Asparagus (R)	1 cup	17	Strawberries (R)	1 cup	9
Garbanzo Beans (C)	1/2 cup	35.5	Beets (C)	1/2 cup	17	Summer Squash (C)	1 cup	9
Adzuki Beans (C)	1/2 cup	35	Coriander (cilantro)	2 tbsp	16	Wheat (D)	1/2 cup	9
Black Beans (C)	1/2 cup	32	Romaine Lettuce (R)	1 cup	16	Zucchini (R)	1 cup	9
Navy Beans (C)	1/2 cup	32	Split Peas (C)	1/2 cup	16	Daikon Radish (R)	1 cup	8.7
Chayote Fruit (R)	1 cup	31	Collards (R)	1 cup	15	Rye	1/3 cup	8.3
Kidney Beans (C)	1/2 cup	29	Spinach (R)	1 cup	15	Broccoli Raab (R)	1 cup	8
Artichokes (C)	1 med	27	Broccoli (R)	1 cup	14	Cantaloupe (R)	1 cup	8
Turnip Greens (R)	1 cup	27	Cauliflower (C)	1 cup	14	Celery (C)	1 cup	8
Mustard Greens (C)	1 cup	26	Cauliflower (R)	1 cup	14	Hazelnuts or Filberts	1/4 cup	8
Mustard Greens (R)	1 cup	26	Pomegranates (R)	1 cup	14	Honeydew Melon (R)	1 cup	8
Granola, homemade	1 cup	25	Brussels Sprouts (R)	1 cup	13	Millet (C)	1 cup	8
Wheat Germ (C)	1/4 cup	24.75	Papaya (R)	1 cup	13	Pumpkin Seeds, (C)	1/4 cup	8
Brussels Sprouts (C)	1 cup	24	Green Peas (C)	1/2 cup	12.5	Sesame Seeds	2 tbsp	8
White Rice (C)	1 cup	23	Broccoli Raab (C)	1 cup	12.2	Summer Squash (R)	1 cup	8
Great Northern Beans (C)	1/2 cup	22.5	Bok Choy (R)	1 cup	12	Tofu	4 oz	8
Artichokes (R)	1 med	22	Cabbage (C)	1 cup	12	Red Tomatoes (C)	1 cup	8
Fava Beans (C)	1/2 cup	22	Green Peas (R)	1/2 cup	12	Zucchini with skin (C)	1 cup	8
Okra (R)	1 cup	22	Napa Cabbage (C)	1 cup	12	Chayote Fruit (C)	1 cup	7
Parsnips (C)	1 cup	22	Cabbage (R)	1 cup	10	Cherimoy (R)	1/2 each	7
Parsnips (R)	1 cup	22	Green Beans (C) & (R)	1 cup	10	Leeks (R)	1/2 cup	7

(C) Cooked | (R) = Raw | (D) = Dried

VSG·Brain

| Dopamine | Serotonin | Acetylcholine | GABA |

| Tyrosine | B6 | Folate | Vitamin C | Iron | Zinc |

Ingred / Portions / Vita C %		
Guavas (R)	1 cup	628
Lychee (R)	1 cup	226
Pummelo (R)	1 cup	193
Broccoli (C)	1 cup	168
Sweet Green Bell Pepper (C)	1 cup	167
Brussels Sprouts (C)	1 cup	162
Kohlrabi (C)	1 cup	149
Strawberries (R)	1 cup	149
Papaya (R)	1 cup	144
Kohlrabi (R)	1 cup	140
Broccoli (R)	1 cup	135
Kale (R)	1 cup	134
Pineapple (R)	1 cup	131
Brussels Sprouts (R)	1 cup	125
Green Bell Pepper (R)	1 cup	123
Kumquats (R)	1 cup	120.4
Kiwi Fruit	1 med	117
Oranges (R)	1 med	116
Cantaloupe (R)	1 cup	98
Cauliflower (C)	1 cup	96
Cabbage (C)	1 cup	94
Sugar-Apples (R)	1 ea	94
Red Tomatoes (C)	1 cup	91
Kale (C)	1 cup	89
Cauliflower (R)	1 cup	77
Carambola/ Starfruit (R)	1 cup	76
Mangos (R)	1 cup	76
Grapefruit, pink red white (R)	1/2 med	73
Gooseberries (R)	1 cup	69
Turnip Greens (C)	1 cup	66

Ingred / Portions / Vita C %		
Mustard Greens (R)	1 cup	65
Sweet Potato with Skin (C)	1 cup	65
Beet Greens (C)	1 cup	60
Mustard Greens (C)	1 cup	59
Collard Greens (C)	1 cup	58
Rutabagas (R)	1 cup	58
Turnip Greens (R)	1 cup	55
Cabbage (R)	1 cup	54
Raspberries (R)	1 cup	54
Rutabagas (C)	1 cup	53
Swiss Chard (C)	1 cup	53
Tangerines (R)	1 large	53
Bok Choy (R)	1 cup	52
Coriander (cilantro)	2 tbsp	52
Honeydew Melon (R)	1 cup	51
Blackberries (R)	1 cup	50
Green Peas (R)	1/2 cup	48.5
Lemon Juice (R)	1/4 cup	46.7
Daikon Radish (R)	1 cup	46.2
Turnips (R)	1 cup	46
Okra (C)	1 cup	44
Broccoli Raab (C)	1 cup	42.1
Jicama (R)	1 cup	40
Parsnips (R)	1 cup	38
Red Tomatoes (R)	1 cup	38
Daikon Radishes (C)	1 cup	37
Okra (R)	1 cup	35
Zucchini (R)	1 cup	35
Parsnips (C)	1 cup	34
Winter Squash (C)	1 cup	33

Ingred / Portions / Vita C %		
Dandelion Greens (R)	1 cup	32
Summer Squash (R)	1 cup	32
Lime Juice (R)	1/4 cup	30.5
Cherimoya (R)	1/2 each	30
Green Beans (R)	1 cup	30
Pomegranates (R)	1 cup	30
Turnips (C)	1 cup	30
Radishes (R)	1 cup	29
Spinach (C)	1 cup	29
Grapes, red or green (R)	1 cup	27
Persimmons, native (R)	1 each	27
Yam (C)	1 cup	27
Potatoes (C)	1 cup	26
Tomatillos (R)	1 cup	26
Artichokes (R)	1 med	25
Asparagus (C)	1 cup	24
Blueberries (R)	1 cup	24
Mung Beans (C)	1 cup	24
Watercress (R)	1 cup	24
Winter Squash (R)	1 cup	24
Dill Weed, fresh	1 tsp	21.3
Chayote Fruit (C)	1 cup	21
Collards (R)	1 cup	21
Watermelon (R)	1 cup	21
Green Beans (C)	1 cup	20
Beet Greens (R)	1 cup	19
Green Peas (C)	1/2 cup	19
Pumpkin (C)	1 cup	19
Romaine Lettuce (R)	1 cup	19
Swiss Chard (R)	1 cup	18

(C) Cooked | (R) = Raw | (D) = Dried

VSG Brain

Dopamine	Serotonin	Acetylcholine	GABA

Tyrosine	B6	Folate	Vitamin C	Iron	Zinc

Ingred / Portions / Iron %			Ingred / Portions / Iron %			Ingred / Portions / Iron %		
Pumpkin Seeds (C)	1/4 cup	47	Black Beans (C)	1/2 cup	10	Split Peas (C)	1/2 cup	7
Spinach (C)	1 cup	36	Black Pepper	1 tsp	10	Thyme (D)	1 tsp	7
Green Garbanzo Beans (R)	1/2 cup	34.5	Brussels Sprouts (C)	1 cup	10	Macadamia Nuts (R)	1/4 cup	6.7
Granola, homemade	1 cup	29	Dandelion Greens (C)	1 cup	10	Broccoli (C)	1 cup	6
Swiss Chard (C)	1 cup	22	Pinto Beans (C)	1/2 cup	10	Flaxseed	2 tbsp	6
Spelt (D)	1/2 cup	21.5	Soy Beans, Edadame	1/2 cup	10	Green Beans (R)	1 cup	6
Lentils (C)	1/2 cup	18.5	Wheat Germ (R)	1/4 cup	10	Green Peas (R)	1/2 cup	6
Wheat (D)	1/2 cup	17	Peanuts	1/4 cup	9.2	Kale (C) & (R)	1 cup	6
Asparagus (R)	1 cup	16	Artichokes (R)	1 med	9	Millet (C)	1 cup	6
Tofu	4 oz	16	Dandelion Greens (R)	1 cup	9	Parsnips (C)	1 cup	6
Beet Greens (C)	1 cup	15	Red Tomatoes (C)	1 cup	9	Turnip Greens (C)	1 cup	6
Quinoa (C)	1 cup	15	Wheat Bran	1/4 cup	8.5	Dill Weed, fresh	1 tsp	5.5
Wheat Germ (C)	1/4 cup	14.2	Rye	1/3 cup	8.3	Beet Greens (R)	1 cup	5
Adzuki Beans (C)	1/2 cup	13	Kumquats (R)	1 cup	8.2	Blackberries (R)	1 cup	5
Garbanzo Beans (C)	1/2 cup	13	Cacao	2 tbsp	8	Blackstrap Molasses	1 tbsp	5
Tempeh	1/2 cup	12.5	Mung Beans (C)	1/2 cup	8	Broccoli Raab (R)	1 cup	5
Barley (C)	1 cup	12	Olives	4 tbsp	8	Green Beans (C)	1 cup	5
Collard Greens (C)	1 cup	12	Pumpkin (C)	1 cup	8	Leeks (R)	1/2 cup	5
Coriander (cilantro)	2 tbsp	12	Sweet Potato with Skin (C)	1 cup	8	Mustard Greens (C) & (R)	1 cup	5
Navy Beans (C)	1/2 cup	12	Almonds, blanched	1/4 cup	7.5	Pumpkin (R)	1 cup	5
Oatmeal (C)	1 cup	12	Coconut Cream/Milk (R)	1/4 cup	7.5	Raspberries (R)	1 cup	5
Cashew Nuts (R)	1/4 cup	11.5	Hazelnuts or Filberts	1/4 cup	7.5	Brown Rice (C)	1 cup	5
Lima Beans (C)	1/2 cup	11.5	Brussels Sprouts (R)	1 cup	7	Rutabagas (C)	1 cup	5
Kidney Beans (C)	1/2 cup	11	Buckwheat Groats (C)	1 cup	7	Spinach (R)	1 cup	5
White Rice (C)	1 cup	11	Cumin seed	1 tsp	7	Sugar-Apples (R)	1 ea	5
Great Northern Beans (C)	1/2 cup	10.5	Fava Beans (C)	1/2 cup	7	Taro (C)	1 cup	5
Oats (D)	1/4 cup	10.2	Green Peas (C)	1/2 cup	7	Turmeric, ground	1 tsp	5
Pine Nuts (D)	1/4 cup	10.2	Lentils, sprouted (R)	1/2 cup	7	Walnuts (R)	1/4 cup	5
Sunflower Seed Kernels (D)	1/4 cup	10.2	Oat Bran (R)	1/4 cup	7	Winter Squash (C)	1 cup	5
Asparagus (C)	1 cup	10	Pistachio Nuts	1/4 cup	7	Broccoli Raab (C)	1 cup	4.7

(C) Cooked | (R) = Raw | (D) = Dried

VSG Brain

| Dopamine | Serotonin | Acetylcholine | GABA |

| Tyrosine | B6 | Folate | Vitamin C | Iron | Zinc |

Ingred / Portions / Zinc %			Ingred / Portions / Zinc %			Ingred / Portions / Zinc %		
Granola, homemade	1 cup	33	Buckwheat Groats (C)	1 cup	7	Brussels Sprouts (C)	1 cup	4
Wheat Germ (C)	1/4 cup	31.5	Chayote Fruit (R)	1 cup	7	Cacao	2 tbsp	4
Pumpkin Seeds (C)	1/4 cup	28.2	Soy Beans, Edadame	1/2 cup	7	Lentils, sprouted (R)	1/2 cup	4
Wheat Germ (R)	1/4 cup	23.5	Wheat Bran	1/4 cup	7	Mung Beans (C)	1 cup	4
Green Garbanzo Beans (R)	1/2 cup	23	Black Beans (C)	1/2 cup	6.5	Okra (C)	1 cup	4
Spelt (D)	1/2 cup	19	Green Peas (C)	1/2 cup	6.5	Okra (R)	1 cup	4
Pistachio Nuts	1/4 cup	18	Shiitake Mushroms (C)	1/2 cup	6.5	Pomegranates (R)	1 cup	4
Wheat (D)	1/2 cup	17	Split Peas (C)	1/2 cup	6.5	Pumpkin (C)	1 cup	4
Oatmeal (C)	1 cup	16	Tempeh	1/2 cup	6.5	Rutabagas (C)	1 cup	4
Pine Nuts (D)	1/4 cup	14.5	Flaxseed	2 tbsp	6	Sweet Potato with Skin (C)	1 cup	4
Rye	1/3 cup	14	Green Peas (R)	1/2 cup	6	Swiss Chard (C)	1 cup	4
Adzuki Beans (C)	1/2 cup	13.5	Maple Syrup	1 tbsp	6	Coconut Cream/Milk (R)	1/4 cup	3.7
Quinoa (C)	1 cup	13	Navy Beans (C)	1/2 cup	6	Yellow Sweet Corn (C)	1 cup	3.5
Cashew Nuts (R)	1/4 cup	12.7	Walnuts (R)	1/4 cup	6	Chayote Fruit (C)	1 cup	3
Tofu	4 oz	12	Fava Beans (C)	1/2 cup	5.5	Collard Greens (C)	1/2 cup	3
Sunflower Seed Kernels (D)	1/4 cup	11.7	Mung Beans (C)	1/2 cup	5.5	Crimni Mushrooms (C)	1/2 cup	3
Millet (C)	1 cup	11	Pinto Beans (C)	1/2 cup	5.5	Dates, Medjool	3 pieces	3
Oats (D)	1/4 cup	10.2	Asparagus (R)	1 cup	5	Guavas (R)	1 cup	3
Sesame Seeds	2 tbsp	10	Beet Greens (C)	1 cup	5	Kohlrabi (C)	1 cup	3
Kidney Beans (C)	1/2 cup	9.5	Blackberries (R)	1 cup	5	Macadamia Nuts (R)	1 cup	3
Barley (C)	1 cup	9	Great Northern Beans (C)	1/2 cup	5	Raspberries (R)	1 cup	3
Brazilnuts (D)	1/4 cup	9	Parsnips (R)	1 cup	5	Rutabagas (R)	1 cup	3
Spinach (C)	1 cup	9	White Rice (C)	1 cup	5	Winter Squash (C)	1 cup	3
Garbanzo Beans (C)	1/2 cup	8.5	Summer Squash (C)	1 cup	5	Miso	1 tbsp	2.9
Lentils (C)	1/2 cup	8.5	Hazelnuts or Filberts	1/4 cup	4.7	Broccoli Raab (C)	1 cup	2.7
Pecans	1/4 cup	8.2	Oat Bran (R)	1/4 cup	4.7	Yellow Corn (R)	1/2 cup	2.5
Asparagus (C)	1 cup	8	Avocados	1/2 ea	4.5	Alfalfa Seeds, sprouted (R)	1 cup	2
Peanuts	1/4 cup	8	Lima Beans (C)	1/2 cup	4.5	Beets (C)	1/2 cup	2
Brown Rice (C)	1 cup	8	Artichokes (R)	1 med	4	Blueberries (R)	1 cup	2
Almonds, blanched	1/4 cup	7.5	Broccoli (C)	1 cup	4	Broccoli (R)	1 cup	2

(C) Cooked | (R) = Raw | (D) = Dried

VSG Brain

| Dopamine | Serotonin | Acetylcholine | GABA |

| Tryptophan | B6 | Magnesium | Zinc | Calcium |

Ingred / Portions / Tryptophan mg			Ingred / Portions / Tryptophan mg			Ingred / Portions / Tryptophan mg		
Pumpkin Seeds (C)	1/4 cup	328	Mung Beans (C)	1/2 cup	76.5	Oat Bran (C)	1/4 cup	31.2
Tofu	4 oz	275.6	Lima Beans (C)	1/2 cup	75.5	Cacao	2 tbsp	30.8
Granola, homemade	1 cup	239	Spinach (C)	1 cup	72	Crimini Mushrooms (C)	1/2 cup	30.2
Green Garbanzo Beans (R)	1/2 cup	185	Almonds, blanched	1/4 cup	71.7	Broccoli (R)	1 cup	30
Tempeh	1/2 cup	161	Garbanzo Beans (C)	1/2 cup	69.5	Kale (C)	1 cup	29.9
Wheat (D)	1/2 cup	153.5	Millet (C)	1 cup	66.1	Cauliflower (C)	1 cup	29.8
Sunflower Seed Kernels (D)	1/4 cup	121.7	Brown Rice (C)	1 cup	64.4	Green Peas (C)	1/2 cup	29.6
Sesame Seeds	2 tbsp	117	Fava Beans (C)	1/2 cup	61	Turnip Greens (C)	1 cup	28.8
Spelt (D)	1/2 cup	115	Flaxseed	2 tbsp	60.8	Green Peas (R)	1/2 cup	26.8
Wheat Germ (C)	1/4 cup	112.5	Barley (C)	1 cup	59.7	Kale (R)	1 cup	26.8
Soy Beans, Edadame	1/2 cup	97.5	Beet Greens (C)	1 cup	57.6	Winter Squash (C)	1 cup	26.7
Quinoa (C)	1 cup	96.2	Hazelnuts or Filberts	1/4 cup	55.5	Miso	1 tbsp	26.6
Oatmeal (C)	1 cup	93.6	Broccoli (C)	1 cup	53	Cauliflower (R)	1 cup	26
Pinto Beans (C)	1/2 cup	92.5	Asparagus (C)	1 cup	52.2	Okra (C)	1 cup	25.6
Kidney Beans (C)	1/2 cup	92	Collard Greens (C)	1 cup	51.3	Coconut Cream/Milk (R)	1/4 cup	25.2
Oats (D)	1/4 cup	91.2	White Rice (C)	1 cup	49	Pecans	1/4 cup	25.2
Peanuts	1/4 cup	91.2	Walnuts (R)	1/4 cup	48	Avocados	1/2 ea	25.1
Wheat Germ (R)	1/4 cup	91.2	Brazilnuts (D)	1/4 cup	47	Green Beans (C)	1 cup	25
Navy Beans (C)	1/2 cup	91	Brussels Sprouts (C)	1 cup	43.6	Winter Squash (R)	1 cup	24.4
Split Peas (C)	1/2 cup	91	Wheat Bran	1/4 cup	41	Rutabagas (C)	1 cup	23.8
Black Beans (C)	1/2 cup	90.5	Mung Beans (R)	1 cup	38.5	Macadamia Nuts (R)	1/4 cup	22.4
Great Northern Beans (C)	1/2 cup	87.5	Potatoes (C)	1 cup	36.6	Pumpkin (C)	1 cup	22
Rye	1/3 cup	86.6	Guavas (R)	1 cup	36.3	Onions (C)	1/2 cup	21
Pistachio Nuts	1/4 cup	84	Asparagus (R)	1 cup	36.2	Green Beans (R)	1 cup	20.9
Adzuki Beans (C)	1/2 cup	83	Pine Nuts (D)	1/4 cup	36	White Mushrooms (C)	1/2 cup	20
Buckwheat Groats (C)	1 cup	82.3	Broccoli Raab (C)	1 cup	35.3	Coconut Water	1 cup	19.2
Cashew Nuts	1/4 cup	81.2	Mustard Greens (C)	1 cup	35	Red Tomatoes (C)	1 cup	19.2
Lentils (C)	1/2 cup	80	Mung Beans (C)	1 cup	34.7	Sweet Yellow Corn (C)	1/2 cup	18.8
Sweet Potato (C)	1 cup	80	Brussels Sprouts (R)	1 cup	32.6	Kohlrabi (C)	1 cup	18.2
Oat Bran (R)	1/4 cup	78.7	Swiss Chard (C)	1 cup	31.5	Rutabagas (R)	1 cup	18.2

(C) Cooked | (R) = Raw | (D) = Dried

VSG Brain

| Dopamine | Serotonin | Acetylcholine | GABA |

| Tryptophan | B6 | Magnesium | Zinc | Calcium |

Ingred / Portions / B6 %		
Sweet Potato with Skin (C)	1 cup	29
Green Garbanzo Beans (R)	1/2 cup	27
Pistachio Nuts	1/4 cup	26.2
Sunflower Seed Kernels (D)	1/4 cup	23.5
Bananas (R)	1 med	22
Spinach (C)	1 cup	22
Taro (C)	1 cup	22
Wheat Germ (R)	1/4 cup	18.7
Granola, homemade	1 cup	18
Potatoes (C)	1 cup	18
Winter Squash (C)	1 cup	17
Cherimoya (R)	1/2 each	16.5
Sweet Green Bell Pepper (C)	1 cup	16
Broccoli (C)	1 cup	16
Yam (C)	1 cup	16
Sugar-Apples (R)	1 ea	15
Wheat, hard red (D)	1/2 cup	14.5
Brussels Sprouts (C)	1 cup	14
Okra (C)	1 cup	14
Brown Rice (C)	1 cup	14
Zucchini (R)	1 cup	14
Wheat Germ (C)	1/4 cup	13.7
Avocados	1/2 ea	13
Kohlrabi (C)	1 cup	13
Turnip Greens (C)	1 cup	13
Carrots (C)	1 cup	12
Collard Greens (C)	1 cup	12
Summer Squash (R)	1 cup	12
Cauliflower (R)	1 cup	11
Mangos (R)	1 cup	11

Ingred / Portions / B6 %		
Okra (R)	1 cup	11
Quinoa (C)	1 cup	11
Beet Greens (C)	1 cup	10
Green Bell Pepper (R)	1 cup	10
Brussels Sprouts (R)	1 cup	10
Cauliflower (C)	1 cup	10
Kohlrabi (R)	1 cup	10
Lychee (R)	1 cup	10
Pinto Beans (C)	1/2 cup	10
Spelt (D)	1/2 cup	10
Wheat Bran	1/4 cup	9.5
Barley (C)	1 cup	9
Carrots (R)	1 cup	9
Chayote Fruit (C)	1 cup	9
Chestnuts (C)	1/4 cup	9
Dates, Medjool	3 pieces	9
Guavas (R)	1 cup	9
Kale (C)	1 cup	9
Kale (R)	1 cup	9
Lentils (C)	1/2 cup	9
Millet (C)	1 cup	9
Pineapple (R)	1 cup	9
Rutabagas (C)	1 cup	9
Tempeh	1/2 cup	9
Red Tomatoes (C)	1 cup	9
Winter Squash (R)	1 cup	9
Green Peas (C)	1/2 cup	8.5
Rye	1/3 cup	8.3
Asparagus (C)	1 cup	8
Broccoli (R)	1 cup	8

Ingred / Portions / B6 %		
Cabbage (C)	1 cup	8
Coriander (cilantro)	2 tbsp	8
Dandelion Greens (C)	1 cup	8
Hazelnuts or Filberts	1/4 cup	8
Lima Beans (C)	1/2 cup	8
Parsnips (C)	1 cup	8
Walnuts (R)	1/4 cup	8
Broccoli Raab (C)	1 cup	7.4
Artichokes (R)	1 med	7
Blackstrap Molasses	1 tbsp	7
Bok Choy (R)	1 cup	7
Dandelion Greens (R)	1 cup	7
Honeydew Melon (R)	1 cup	7
Mustard Greens (C)	1 cup	7
Onions (C)	1/2 cup	7
White Rice (C)	1 cup	7
Rutabagas (R)	1 cup	7
Swiss Chard (C)	1 cup	7
Red Tomatoes (R)	1 cup	7
Turnip Greens (R)	1 cup	7
Zucchini with skin (C)	1 cup	7
Navy Beans (C)	1/2 cup	6.5
Peanuts	1/4 cup	6.2
Asparagus (R)	1 cup	6
Buckwheat Groats (C)	1 cup	6
Cabbage (R)	1 cup	6
Cantaloupe (R)	1 cup	6
Celery (C)	1 cup	6
Figs (R)	2 med	6
Garlic (R)	3 cloves	6

(C) Cooked | (R) = Raw | (D) = Dried

| Dopamine | Serotonin | Acetylcholine | GABA |

| Tryptophan | B6 | Magnesium | Zinc | Calcium |

Ingred / Portions / Magnesium %	Ingred / Portions / Magnesium %	Ingred / Portions / Magnesium %
Pumpkin Seeds (C) 1/4 cup 75.7	Black Beans (C) 1/2 cup 15	Guavas (R) 1 cup 9
Granola, homemade 1 cup 53	Coconut Water 1 cup 15	Lentils (C) 1/2 cup 9
Spinach (C) 1 cup 39	Cacao 2 tbsp 14	Split Peas (C) 1/2 cup 9
Swiss Chard (C) 1 cup 38	Okra (C) 1 cup 14	Kumquats (R) 1 cup 8.2
Brazilnuts (D) 1/4 cup 31.2	Okra (R) 1 cup 14	Pecans 1/4 cup 8.2
Quinoa (C) 1 cup 30	Sweet Potato w/ Skin (C) 1 cup 14	Bananas (R) 1 med 8
Wheat (D) 1/2 cup 30	Oat Bran (R) 1/4 cup 13.7	Broccoli (C) 1 cup 8
Spelt (D) 1/2 cup 29.5	Artichokes (C) 1 med 13	Brussels Sprouts (C) 1 cup 8
Green Garbanzo Beans (R) 1/2 cup 29	Soy Beans, Edadame 1/2 cup 12.5	Coriander (cilantro) 2 tbsp 8
Sunflower Seed Kernels (D) 1/4 cup 28.5	Blackstrap Molasses 1 tbsp 12	Green Peas (C) 1/2 cup 8
Almonds, blanched 1/4 cup 25	Mung Beans (C) 1/2 cup 12	Kohlrabi (C) 1 cup 8
Beet Greens (C) 1 cup 24	Navy Beans (C) 1/2 cup 12	Potatoes (C) 1 cup 8
Wheat Germ (C) 1/4 cup 22.5	Parsnips (C) 1 cup 12	Rutabagas (R) 1 cup 8
Cashew Nuts (R) 1/4 cup 22.2	Hazelnuts or Filberts 1/4 cup 11.75	Sesame Seeds 2 tbsp 8
Wheat Bran 1/4 cup 22.2	Great Northern Beans (C) 1/2 cup 11	Sugar-Apples (R) 1 ea 8
Pine Nuts (D) 1/4 cup 21.2	Macadamia Nuts (R) 1/4 cup 11	Turnip Greens (C) 1 cup 8
Buckwheat Groats (C) 1 cup 21	Summer Squash (C) 1 cup 11	Avocados 1/2 ea 7.5
Brown Rice (C) 1 cup 21	Walnuts (R) 1/4 cup 11	Beet Greens (R) 1 cup 7
Flaxseed 2 tbsp 20	Pinto Beans (C) 1/2 cup 10.5	Blackberries (R) 1 cup 7
Artichokes (R) 1 med 19	Collard Greens (C) 1 cup 10	Yellow Corn (R) 1/2 cup 7
Millet, cooked 1 cup 19	Garbanzo Beans (C) 1/2 cup 10	Green Beans (C) 1 cup 7
Oats (D) 1/4 cup 17.2	Parsnips (R) 1 cup 10	Raspberries (R) 1 cup 7
Wheat Germ (R) 1/4 cup 17.2	Rutabagas (C) 1 cup 10	Swiss Chard (R) 1 cup 7
Rye 1/3 cup 17	Taro (C) 1 cup 10	Tamarinds (R) 1/4 cup 7
Tempeh 1/2 cup 17	Zucchini with skin (C) 1 cup 10	Winter Squash (C) 1 cup 7
Oatmeal (C) 1 cup 16	Kidney Beans (C) 1/2 cup 9.5	Figs (D) 1/4 cup 6.2
Tofu 4 oz 16	Pistachio Nuts 1/4 cup 9.2	Asian Pears (R) 1 med 6
Lima Beans (C) 1/2 cup 15.5	Barley (C) 1 cup 9	Asparagus (C) 1 cup 6
Peanuts 1/4 cup 15.2	Dates, Medjool 3 pieces 9	Cabbage (C) 1 cup 6
Adzuki Beans (C) 1/2 cup 15	Fava Beans (C) 1/2 cup 9	Cherimoya (R) 1/2 each 6

(C) Cooked | (R) = Raw | (D) = Dried

VSG·Brain

Dopamine | **Serotonin** | Acetylcholine | GABA

ᵥ

Tryptophan | B6 | Magnesium | **Zinc** | Calcium

Ingred / Portions / Zinc %			Ingred / Portions / Zinc %			Ingred / Portions / Zinc %		
Granola, homemade	1 cup	33	Buckwheat Groats (C)	1 cup	7	Brussels Sprouts (C)	1 cup	4
Wheat Germ (C)	1/4 cup	31.5	Chayote Fruit (R)	1 cup	7	Cacao	2 tbsp	4
Pumpkin Seeds (C)	1/4 cup	28.2	Soy Beans, Edadame	1/2 cup	7	Lentils, sprouted (R)	1/2 cup	4
Wheat Germ (R)	1/4 cup	23.5	Wheat Bran	1/4 cup	7	Mung Beans (C)	1 cup	4
Green Garbanzo Beans (R)	1/2 cup	23	Black Beans (C)	1/2 cup	6.5	Okra (C) & (R)	1 cup	4
Spelt (D)	1/2 cup	19	Green Peas (C)	1/2 cup	6.5	Pomegranates (R)	1 cup	4
Pistachio Nuts	1/4 cup	18	Shiitake Mushroms (C)	1/2 cup	6.5	Pumpkin (C)	1 cup	4
Wheat (D)	1/2 cup	17	Split Peas (C)	1/2 cup	6.5	Rutabagas (C)	1 cup	4
Oatmeal (C)	1 cup	16	Tempeh	1/2 cup	6.5	Sweet Potato with Skin (C)	1 cup	4
Pine Nuts (D)	1/4 cup	14.5	Flaxseed	2 tbsp	6	Swiss Chard (C)	1 cup	4
Rye	1/3 cup	14	Green Peas (R)	1/2 cup	6	Coconut Cream/Milk (R)	1/4 cup	3.7
Adzuki Beans (C)	1/2 cup	13.5	Maple Syrup	1 tbsp	6	Yellow Sweet Corn (C)	1 cup	3.5
Quinoa (C)	1 cup	13	Navy Beans (C)	1/2 cup	6	Chayote Fruit (C)	1 cup	3
Cashew Nuts (R)	1/4 cup	12.7	Walnuts (R)	1/4 cup	6	Collard Greens (C)	1/2 cup	3
Tofu	4 oz	12	Fava Beans (C)	1/2 cup	5.5	Crimni Mushrooms (C)	1/2 cup	3
Sunflower Seed Kernels (D)	1/4 cup	11.7	Mung Beans (C)	1/2 cup	5.5	Dates, Medjool	3 pieces	3
Millet (C)	1 cup	11	Pinto Beans (C)	1/2 cup	5.5	Guavas (R)	1 cup	3
Oats (D)	1/4 cup	10.2	Asparagus (R)	1 cup	5	Kohlrabi (C)	1 cup	3
Sesame Seeds	2 tbsp	10	Beet Greens (C)	1 cup	5	Macadamia Nuts (R)	1 cup	3
Kidney Beans (C)	1/2 cup	9.5	Blackberries (R)	1 cup	5	Raspberries (R)	1 cup	3
Barley (C)	1 cup	9	Great Northern Beans (C)	1/2 cup	5	Rutabagas (R)	1 cup	3
Brazilnuts (D)	1/4 cup	9	Parsnips (R)	1 cup	5	Winter Squash (C)	1 cup	3
Spinach (C)	1 cup	9	White Rice (C)	1 cup	5	Miso	1 tbsp	2.9
Garbanzo Beans (C)	1/2 cup	8.5	Summer Squash (C)	1 cup	5	Broccoli Raab (C)	1 cup	2.7
Lentils (C)	1/2 cup	8.5	Hazelnuts or Filberts	1/4 cup	4.7	Yellow Corn (R)	1/2 cup	2.5
Pecans	1/4 cup	8.2	Oat Bran (R)	1/4 cup	4.7	Alfalfa Seeds, sprouted (R)	1 cup	2
Asparagus (C)	1 cup	8	Avocados	1/2 ea	4.5	Beets (C)	1/2 cup	2
Peanuts	1/4 cup	8	Lima Beans (C)	1/2 cup	4.5	Blueberries (R)	1 cup	2
Brown Rice (C)	1 cup	8	Artichokes (R)	1 med	4	Broccoli (R)	1 cup	2
Almonds, blanched	1/4 cup	7.5	Broccoli (C)	1 cup	4	Brussels Sprouts (R)	1 cup	2

(C) Cooked | (R) = Raw | (D) = Dried

| Dopamine | Serotonin | Acetylcholine | GABA |

| Tryptophan | B6 | Magnesium | Zinc | Calcium |

Ingred / Portions / Calcium %			Ingred / Portions / Calcium %			Ingred / Portions / Calcium %		
Tofu	4 oz	76	Brussels Sprouts (C)	1 cup	6	Papaya (R)	1 cup	3
Collard Greens (C)	1 cup	27	Celery (C)	1 cup	6	Quinoa (C)	1 cup	3
Spinach (C)	1 cup	24	Coconut Water	1 cup	6	Radishes (R)	1 cup	3
Turnip Greens (C)	1 cup	20	Dates, Medjool	3 pieces	6	Raspberries (R)	1 cup	3
Beet Greens (C)	1 cup	16	Figs (D)	1/4 cup	6	Spinach (R)	1 cup	3
Dandelion Greens (C)	1 cup	15	Flaxseed	2 tbsp	6	Red Tomatoes (C)	1 cup	3
Okra (C)	1 cup	12	Great Northern Beans (C)	1/2 cup	6	Walnuts (R)	1/4 cup	3
Sesame Seeds	2 tbsp	12	Mustard Greens (R)	1 cup	6	Wheat (D)	1/2 cup	3
Green Garbanzo Beans (R)	1/2 cup	10.5	Parsnips (C)	1 cup	6	Winter Squash (R)	1 cup	3
Dandelion Greens (R)	1 cup	10	Brazilnuts (D)	1/4 cup	5.2	Macadamia Nuts (R)	1/4 cup	2.7
Granola, homemade	1 cup	10	Collards (R)	1 cup	5	Sunflower Seed Kernels (D)	1/4 cup	2.7
Mustard Greens (C)	1 cup	10	Green Beans (C)	1 cup	5	Black Beans (C)	1/2 cup	2.5
Rhubarb (R)	1 cup	10	Oranges (R)	1 med	5	Leeks (R)	1/2 cup	2.5
Swiss Chard (C)	1 cup	10	Parsnips (R)	1 cup	5	Lima Beans (C)	1/2 cup	2.5
Turnip Greens (R)	1 cup	10	Soy Beans, Edadame	1/2 cup	5	Mung Beans (C)	1/2 cup	2.5
Kumquats (R)	1 cup	9.9	Summer Squash (C)	1 cup	5	Onions (C)	1/2 cup	2.5
Kale (C) & (R)	1 cup	9	Turnips (C)	1 cup	5	Pumpkin Seeds (C)	1/4 cup	2.5
Tempeh	1/2 cup	9	Winter Squash (C)	1 cup	5	Spelt (D)	1/2 cup	2.5
Broccoli Raab (C)	1 cup	8.1	Adzuki Beans (C)	1/2 cup	3	Tamarinds (R)	1/4 cup	2.2
Cabbage (C)	1 cup	8	Artichokes (C)	1 med	3	Barley (C)	1 cup	2
Coriander (cilantro)	2 tbsp	8	Asparagus (R)	1 cup	3	Cauliflower (C) & (R)	1 cup	2
Okra (R)	1 cup	8	Black Pepper	1 tsp	3	Chayote Fruit (C) & (R)	1 cup	2
Rutabagas (C)	1 cup	8	Cinnamon, ground	1 tsp	3	Sweet Cherries (R)	1 cup	2
Sweet Potato with Skin (C)	1 cup	8	Fava Beans (C)	1/2 cup	3	Cacao	2 tbsp	2
Almonds, blanched	1/4 cup	7.7	Garlic (R)	3 cloves	3	Cucumber (R)	1 cup	2
Bok Choy (R)	1 cup	7	Guavas (R)	1 cup	3	Cumin Seed	1 tsp	2
Rutabagas (R)	1 cup	7	Kidney Beans (C)	1/2 cup	3	Daikon Radishes (C)	1 cup	2
Navy Beans (C)	1/2 cup	6.5	Kiwi Fruit	1 med	3	Endive (R)	1 cup	2
Artichokes (R)	1 med	6	Kohlrabi (R)	1 cup	3	Grapefruit (R)	1/2 med	2
Broccoli (C)	1 cup	6	Napa Cabbage (C)	1 cup	3	Grapes (R)	1 cup	2

(C) Cooked | (R) = Raw | (D) = Dried

VSG·Brain

Dopamine | Serotonin | Acetylcholine | GABA

Choline | B1 | B5 | Manganese

Ingred / Portions / Choline in mg		
Green Garbanzo Beans (R)	1/2 cup	95
Brussels Sprouts (C)	1 cup	63.4
Broccoli (C)	1 cup	62.6
Collard Greens (C)	1 cup	60.4
Granola, homemade	1 cup	59.9
Wheat Germ (C)	1/4 cup	50.2
Swiss Chard (C)	1 cup	50.2
Cauliflower (C)	1 cup	48.4
Asparagus (C)	1 cup	47
Cauliflower (R)	1 cup	45.2
Artichokes (R)	1 med	44
Soy Beans, Edadame	1/2 cup	43.6
Parsnips (C)	1 cup	42.2
Artichokes (C)	1 med	41.3
Navy Beans (C)	1/2 cup	40.6
Lima beans (C)	1/2 cup	37.5
Pumpkin Seeds (C)	1/4 cup	35.7
Spinach (C)	1 cup	35.5
Garbanzo Beans (C)	1/2 cup	35.1
Buckwheat Groats (C)	1 cup	33.8
Lentils (C)	1/2 cup	32.3
Split Peas (C)	1/2 cup	32.1
Cabbage (C)	1 cup	30.4
Pinto Beans (C)	1/2 cup	30.2
Wheat (D)	1/2 cup	29.9
Mung Beans (C)	1/2 cup	29.7
Taro (C)	1 cup	28.1
Kidney Beans (C)	1/2 cup	27
Shiitake Mushrooms (C)	1/2 cup	26.7
Dandelion Greens (C)	1 cup	26.2

Ingred / Portions / Choline in mg		
Sweet Potato (C)	1 cup	26.2
Fava Beans (C)	1/2 cup	26
Rutabagas (C)	1 cup	25.8
Sweet Yellow Corn (C)	1/2 cup	23.8
Green Peas (C)	1/2 cup	23.7
Broccoli Raab (C)	1 cup	22.8
Yam (C)	1 cup	22
Kohlrabi (C)	1 cup	21.8
Winter Squash (C)	1 cup	21.7
Asparagus (R)	1 cup	21.4
Green Beans (C)	1 cup	21.1
Barley (C)	1 cup	21
Cashew Nuts	1/4 cup	20.9
Green Peas (R)	1/2 cup	20.6
Crimni Mushrooms (C)	1/2 cup	19.8
Rutabagas (R)	1 cup	19.7
Millet (C)	1 cup	19.5
Dandelion Greens (R)	1 cup	19.4
Sunflower Seed Kernels (D)	1/4 cup	19.2
Peanuts	1/4 cup	19.1
Almonds, blanched	1/4 cup	18.8
Pine Nuts (D)	1/4 cup	18.8
Brown Rice (C)	1 cup	17.9
Yellow Corn (R)	1/2 cup	17.7
Potatoes (C)	1 cup	17.6
Oatmeal (C)	1 cup	17.3
Rye	1/3 cup	17.13
Broccoli (R)	1 cup	17
Zucchini (C)	1 cup	16.9
Brussels Sprouts (R)	1 cup	16.8

Ingred / Portions / Choline in mg		
Green Beans (R)	1 cup	16.8
Kohlrabi (R)	1 cup	16.6
Red Tomatoes (C)	1 cup	16.6
Jicama (R)	1 cup	16.3
Flaxseed	2 tbsp	16.2
Pumpkin (C)	1 cup	15.2
Raspberries (R)	1 cup	15.1
Okra (C)	1 cup	14.8
Coriander (cilantro)	2 tbsp	14.4
Turnips (R)	1 cup	14.4
Avocados	1/2 ea	14.2
Summer Squash (C)	1 cup	14.2
Asian Pears (R)	1 med	14
Kumquat (R)	1 cup	13.8
Carrots (C)	1 cup	13.8
Turnips (C)	1 cup	13.6
Lychee (R)	1 cup	13.5
Pomegranates (R)	1 cup	13.2
Hazelnuts or Filberts	1/4 cup	13.1
Honeydew Melon (R)	1 cup	12.9
Guavas, common (R)	1 cup	12.5
Mangos (R)	1 cup	12.5
Miso	1 tbsp	12.4
Mung Beans (C)	1 cup	12.3
Okra (R)	1 cup	12.3
Blackberries (R)	1 cup	12.2
Cantaloupe (R)	1 cup	12.2
Tangerines (R)	1 large	12.2
Chayote (R)	1 cup	12.1
Red Tomatoes (R)	1 cup	12.1

C = Cooked | R = Raw

VSG Brain

Dopamine	Serotonin	Acetylcholine	GABA

Choline	B1	B5	Manganese

Ingred / Portions / B1 %			Ingred / Portions / B1 %			Ingred / Portions / B1 %		
Granola, homemade	1 cup	60	Brussels Sprouts (C)	1 cup	12	Parsnips (C)	1 cup	8
Lentils (R)	1/2 cup	56	Millet (C)	1 cup	12	Parsnips (R)	1 cup	8
Wheat Germ (R)	1/4 cup	36	Oatmeal (C)	1 cup	12	Pomegranates (R)	1 cup	8
Sunflower Seed Kernels (D)	1/4 cup	34.5	Pecans	1/4 cup	12	Potatoes (C)	1 cup	8
Green Garbanzo Beans (R)	1/2 cup	32	Brown Rice (C)	1 cup	12	Pumpkin Seeds (C)	1/4 cup	8
Wheat Germ (C)	1/4 cup	31.5	Rye	1/3 cup	12	Rutabagas (R)	1 cup	8
Macadamia Nuts (R)	1/4 cup	26.7	Tofu	4 oz	12	Broccoli Raab (C)	1 cup	7.4
Sesame Seeds	2 tbsp	26	Beet Greens (C)	1 cup	11	Dandelion Greens (R)	1 cup	7
Wheat, red (D)	1/2 cup	24.5	Lentils (C)	1/2 cup	11	Grapes, red or green (R)	1 cup	7
Flaxseed	2 tbsp	22	Mung Beans (C)	1/2 cup	11	Guavas (R)	1 cup	7
Spelt (D)	1/2 cup	21	Pinto Beans (C)	1/2 cup	11	Garbanzo Beans (C)	1/2 cup	6.5
Asparagus (C)	1 cup	20	Spinach (C)	1 cup	11	Artichokes (R)	1 med	6
Oats (D)	1/4 cup	19.7	Sugar-Apples (R)	1 ea	11	Broccoli (C)	1 cup	6
Oat Bran (R)	1/4 cup	18.2	Yellow Corn (R)	1/2 cup	10.5	Cabbage (C)	1 cup	6
Pistachio Nuts	1/4 cup	17.7	Soy Beans, Edadame	1/2 cup	10.5	Carrots (C)	1 cup	6
White Rice (C)	1 cup	17	Great Northern Beans (C)	1/2 cup	9.5	Carrots (R)	1 cup	6
Peanuts	1/4 cup	15.5	Kidney Beans (C)	1/2 cup	9.5	Sweet Yellow Corn (C)	1/2 cup	6
Navy Beans (C)	1/2 cup	14.5	Adzuki Beans (C)	1/2 cup	9	Green Beans (C)	1 cup	6
Black Beans (C)	1/2 cup	14	Barley (C)	1 cup	9	Green Beans (R)	1 cup	6
Green Peas (C)	1/2 cup	14	Dandelion Greens (C)	1 cup	9	Lentils, sprouted (R)	1/2 cup	6
Okra (C)	1 cup	14	Pineapple (R)	1 cup	9	Mangos (R)	1 cup	6
Sweet Potato (C)	1 cup	14	Rutabagas (C)	1 cup	9	Mung Beans (R)	1 cup	6
Brazilnuts (D)	1/4 cup	13.7	Taro (C)	1 cup	9	Red Tomatoes (C)	1 cup	6
Asparagus (R)	1 cup	13	Yam (C)	1 cup	9	Walnuts (R)	1/4 cup	6
Green Peas (R)	1/2 cup	13	Cherimoya (R)	1/2 each	8.5	Chestnuts (C)	1/4 cup	5.7
Okra (R)	1 cup	13	Tamarinds (R)	1/4 cup	8.5	Oat Bran (C)	1/4 cup	5.7
Quinoa (C)	1 cup	13	Pine Nuts (D)	1/4 cup	8.2	Fava Beans (C)	1/2 cup	5.5
Split Peas (C)	1/2 cup	12.5	Brussels Sprouts (R)	1 cup	8	Sweet Green Bell Pepper (C)	1 cup	5
Split Peas (C)	1/2 cup	12.5	Lima Beans (C)	1/2 cup	8	Coconut Water	1 cup	5
Hazelnuts or Filberts	1/4 cup	12.2	Oranges	1 med	8	Collard Greens (C)	1 cup	5

(C) Cooked | (R) = Raw | (D) = Dried

 Brain

Dopamine | Serotonin | Acetylcholine | GABA

Choline | B1 | B5 | Manganese

Ingred / Portions / B5 %			Ingred / Portions / B5 %			Ingred / Portions / B5 %		
Shiitake Mushroms (C)	1/2 cup	26	White Rice (C)	1 cup	6	Wheat Germ (C)	1/4 cup	4
Lentils (R)	1/2 cup	20.5	Split Peas (C)	1/2 cup	6	Yam (C)	1 cup	4
Granola, homemade	1 cup	19	Oats (D)	1/4 cup	5.2	Cherimoya (R)	1/2 each	3.5
Sweet Potato (C)	1 cup	18	Adzuki Beans (C)	1/2 cup	5	Oat Bran (R)	1/4 cup	3.5
Green Garbanzo Beans (R)	1/2 cup	16	Beet Greens (C)	1 cup	5	Kumquats (R)	1 cup	3.3
Avocados	1/2 ea	14	Broccoli (R)	1 cup	5	Wheat Bran	1/4 cup	3.2
Broccoli (C)	1 cup	10	Carambola/ Starfruit (R)	1 cup	5	Artichokes (C)	1 med	3
Parsnips (C)	1 cup	10	Pumpkin (C)	1 cup	5	Brussels Sprouts (R)	1 cup	3
Spelt (D)	1/2 cup	9.5	White Mushroom (R)	1/2 cup	5	Carrots (R)	1 cup	3
Wheat (D)	1/2 cup	9	Winter Squash (C)	1 cup	5	Celery (C)	1 cup	3
Crimini Mushrooms (C)	1/2 cup	8.5	Cashew Nuts	1/4 cup	4.2	Chayote Fruit (R)	1 cup	3
Rye	1/3 cup	8.3	Artichokes (R)	1 med	4	Sweet Cherries (R)	1 cup	3
Coriander (cilantro)	2 tbsp	8	Asparagus (C) & (R)	1 cup	4	Honeydew Melon (R)	1 cup	3
Parsnips (R)	1 cup	8	Bananas (R)	1 med	4	Kohlrabi (C)	1 cup	3
White Mushrooms (C)	1/2 cup	8	Blackberries (R)	1 cup	4	Mangos (R)	1 cup	3
Cauliflower (R)	1 cup	7	Brussels Sprouts (C)	1 cup	4	Millet (C)	1 cup	3
Chayote Fruit (C)	1 cup	7	Carrots (C)	1 cup	4	Mung Beans (C)	1 cup	3
Sweet Yellow Corn (C)	1/2 cup	7	Collard Greens (C)	1 cup	4	Nectarines (R)	1 ea	3
Guavas (R)	1 cup	7	Endive (R)	1 cup	4	Oranges	1 med	3
Oatmeal (C)	1 cup	7	Gooseberries (R)	1 cup	4	Papaya (R)	1 cup	3
Lentils (C)	1/2 cup	6.5	Grapefruit, pink red white (R)	1/2 med	4	Pumpkin (R)	1 cup	3
Peanuts	1/4 cup	6.5	Mung Beans (C)	1/2 cup	4	Rutabagas (C)	1 cup	3
Wheat Germ (R)	1/4 cup	6.5	Mung Beans (R)	1 cup	4	Soy Beans, Edadame	1/2 cup	3
Buckwheat Groats (C)	1 cup	6	Okra (C)	1 cup	4	Spinach (C)	1 cup	3
Cauliflower (C)	1 cup	6	Pineapple (R)	1 cup	4	Swiss Chard (C)	1 cup	3
Yellow Corn (R)	1/2 cup	6	Raspberries (R)	1 cup	4	Tangerines (R)	1 large	3
Dates, Medjool	3 pieces	6	Sugar-Apples (R)	1 ea	4	Red Tomatoes (C)	1 cup	3
Pomegranates (R)	1 cup	6	Sunflower Seed Kernels (D)	1/4 cup	4	Turnips (R)	1 cup	3
Potatoes (C)	1 cup	6	Taro (C)	1 cup	4	Watermelon (R)	1 cup	3
Brown Rice (C)	1 cup	6	Turnip Greens (C)	1 cup	4	Hazelnuts or Filberts	1/4 cup	2.7

C = Cooked | R = Raw

VSG Brain

Dopamine	Serotonin	Acetylcholine	GABA

Choline	B1	B5	Manganese

Ingred / Portions / Manganese %			Ingred / Portions / Manganese %			Ingred / Portions / Manganese %		
Pumpkin Seeds (C)	1/4 cup	75.7	Peanuts	1/4 cup	15.2	Fava Beans (C)	1/2 cup	9
Granola, homemade	1 cup	53	Adzuki Beans (C)	1/2 cup	15	Guavas (R)	1 cup	9
Spinach (C)	1 cup	39	Black Beans (C)	1/2 cup	15	Lentils (C)	1/2 cup	9
Swiss Chard (C)	1 cup	38	Coconut Water	1 cup	15	Split Peas (C)	1/2 cup	9
Brazilnuts (D)	1/4 cup	31.2	Okra (C)	1 cup	14	Kumquats (R)	1 cup	8.2
Quinoa (C)	1 cup	30	Okra (R)	1 cup	14	Pecans	1/4 cup	8.2
Wheat (D)	1/2 cup	30	Sweet Potato (C)	1 cup	14	Bananas (R)	1 med	8
Lentils (R)	1/2 cup	29.5	Oat Bran (R)	1/4 cup	13.7	Broccoli (C)	1 cup	8
Spelt (D)	1/2 cup	29.5	Artichokes (C)	1 med	13	Brussels Sprouts (C)	1 cup	8
Green Garbanzo Beans (R)	1/2 cup	29	Soy Beans, Edamame	1/2 cup	12.5	Coriander (cilantro)	2 tbsp	8
Sunflower Seed Kernels (D)	1/4 cup	28.5	Blackstrap Molasses	1 tbsp	12	Green Peas (C)	1/2 cup	8
Almonds, blanched	1/4 cup	25	Mung Beans (C)	1/2 cup	12	Kohlrabi (C)	1 cup	8
Beet Greens (C)	1 cup	24	Navy Beans (C)	1/2 cup	12	Potatoes (C)	1 cup	8
Wheat Germ (C)	1/4 cup	22.5	Parsnips (C)	1 cup	12	Rutabagas (R)	1 cup	8
Cashew Nuts	1/4 cup	22.2	Hazelnuts or Filberts	1/4 cup	11.7	Sesame Seeds	2 tbsp	8
Wheat Bran	1/4 cup	22.2	Great Northern Beans (C)	1/2 cup	11	Sugar-Apples (R)	1 ea	8
Pine Nuts (D)	1/4 cup	21.2	Macadamia Nuts (R)	1/4 cup	11	Turnip Greens (C)	1 cup	8
Buckwheat Groats (C)	1 cup	21	Summer Squash (C)	1 cup	11	Avocados	1/2 ea	7.5
Brown Rice (C)	1 cup	21	Walnuts (R)	1/4 cup	11	Beet Greens (R)	1 cup	7
Cacao	2 tbsp	20	Pinto Beans (C)	1/2 cup	10.5	Blackberries (R)	1 cup	7
Flaxseed	2 tbsp	20	Collard Greens (C)	1 cup	10	Yellow Corn (R)	1/2 cup	7
Artichokes (R)	1 med	19	Garbanzo Beans (C)	1/2 cup	10	Green Beans (R)	1 cup	7
Millet (C)	1 cup	19	Parsnips (R)	1 cup	10	Raspberries (R)	1 cup	7
Oats (D)	1/4 cup	17.2	Rutabagas (C)	1 cup	10	Swiss Chard (R)	1 cup	7
Wheat Germ (R)	1/4 cup	17.2	Taro (C)	1 cup	10	Tamarinds (R)	1/4 cup	7
Rye	1/3 cup	17	Zucchini with skin (C)	1 cup	10	Winter Squash (C)	1 cup	7
Tempeh	1/2 cup	17	Kidney Beans (C)	1/2 cup	9.5	Figs (R) (fresh)	1/4 cup	6.2
Oatmeal (C)	1 cup	16	Pistachio Nuts	1/4 cup	9.2	Asian Pears (R)	1 med	6
Tofu	4 oz	16	Barley (C)	1 cup	9	Asparagus (C)	1 cup	6
Lima Beans (C)	1/2 cup	15.5	Dates, Medjool	3 pieces	9	Cabbage (C)	1 cup	6

(C) Cooked | (R) = Raw | (D) = Dried

Dopamine | Serotonin | Acetylcholine | GABA

Glutamic Acid | Inositol | B1 | B3 | B6

Ingred / Portions / Glut Prec in mg			Ingred / Portions / Glut Prec in mg			Ingred / Portions / Glut Prec in mg		
Spelt (D)	1/2 cup	4047	Fava Beans (C)	1/2 cup	1097.5	Cabbage (C)	1 cup	438
Granola, homemade	1 cup	3893	Quinoa (C)	1 cup	1073	Wheat Bran	1/4 cup	416.7
Wheat (D)	1/2 cup	3838.5	Hazelnuts or Filberts	1/4 cup	1066.7	Okra (C)	1 cup	404
Green Garbanzo Beans (R)	1/2 cup	3374.5	Brazilnuts (D)	1/4 cup	1046.5	Potatoes (C)	1 cup	400
Pumpkin Seeds (C)	1/4 cup	3298.5	Brown Rice (C)	1 cup	1026	Coconut Water	1 cup	396
Tofu	4 oz	3056	Pine Nuts (D)	1/4 cup	987.5	Sweet Potato (C)	1 cup	396
Tempeh	1/2 cup	2732.5	Red Tomatoes (C)	1 cup	943	Beets (C)	1/2 cup	379
Rye	1/3 cup	2062.6	Barley (C)	1 cup	928	Oat Bran (C)	1/4 cup	351.5
Peanuts	1/4 cup	1967.5	Oat Bran (R)	1/4 cup	881	Cantaloupe (R)	1 cup	334
Sunflower Seed Kernels (D)	1/4 cup	1952.7	Buckwheat Groats (C)	1 cup	877	Collard Greens (C)	1 cup	334
Almonds, blanched	1/4 cup	1934.7	Broccoli (C)	1 cup	856	Miso	1 tbsp	329.1
Soy Beans, Edadame	1/2 cup	1565.5	Flaxseed	2 tbsp	828	Pumpkin (C)	1 cup	326
Oatmeal (C)	1 cup	1458	White Rice (C)	1 cup	828	Winter Squash (C)	1 cup	318
Oats (D)	1/4 cup	1447.7	Walnuts (R)	1/4 cup	796	Asparagus (R)	1 cup	312
Wheat Germ (C)	1/4 cup	1419.7	Red Tomatoes (R)	1 cup	776	Cacao	2 tbsp	310
Split Peas (C)	1/2 cup	1397.5	Macadamia Nuts (R)	1/4 cup	759.5	Cauliflower (C)	1 cup	304
Lentils (C)	1/2 cup	1385	Lima Beans (C)	1/2 cup	745.5	Winter Squash (R)	1 cup	295
Adzuki Beans (C)	1/2 cup	1349	Spinach (C)	1 cup	643	Beets (R)	1/2 cup	291
Millet (C)	1 cup	1328	Green Peas (C)	1/2 cup	586.5	Avocados	1/2 ea	288.5
Garbanzo Beans (C)	1/2 cup	1271	Guavas (R)	1 cup	550	Kale (C)	1 cup	281
Mung Beans (C)	1/2 cup	1268.5	Sweet Yellow Corn (C)	1/2 cup	537	Crimini Mushrooms (C)	1/2 cup	280
Cashew Nuts	1/4 cup	1241.2	Green Peas (R)	1/2 cup	537	Okra (R)	1 cup	271
Pinto Beans (C)	1/2 cup	1237	Pecans	1/4 cup	498.2	Cauliflower (R)	1 cup	264
Kidney Beans (C)	1/2 cup	1233	Coconut Cream/Milk (R)	1/4 cup	497.5	Cabbage (R)	1 cup	262
Sesame Seeds	2 tbsp	1192	Broccoli (R)	1 cup	493	Honeydew Melon (R)	1 cup	260
Pistachio Nuts	1/4 cup	1174.2	Yellow Corn (R)	1/2 cup	489.5	Rutabagas (C)	1 cup	258
Black Beans (C)	1/2 cup	1162	Lentils, sprouted (R)	1/2 cup	484.5	Shiitake Mushrooms (C)	1/2 cup	256
Wheat Germ (R)	1/4 cup	1148.5	Asparagus (C)	1 cup	460	Bok Choy (R)	1 cup	252
Navy Beans (C)	1/2 cup	1146	Broccoli Raab (C)	1 cup	450.1	Kale (R)	1 cup	251
Great Northern Beans (C)	1/2 cup	1124	Beet Greens (C)	1 cup	449	Green Beans (C)	1 cup	243

(C) Cooked | (R) = Raw | (D) = Dried

VSG Brain

Dopamine | Serotonin | Acetylcholine | GABA

Glutamic Acid | Inositol | B1 | B3 | B6

Ingred / Portions / Inositol in mg		
Cantaloupe (R)	1 cup	1420
Great Northern Beans (C)	1/2 cup	440
Oranges	1 med	402.2
Blackberries (R)	1 cup	346
Mangos (R)	1 cup	317.2
Lime juice (R)	1/4 cup	266.7
Grapefruit, pink red white (R)	1/2 med	254.7
Kidney Beans (C)	1/2 cup	249
Sweet Potato (C)	1 cup	184
Sweet Cherries (R)	1 cup	175.3
Eggplant (C)	1 cup	168
Nectarines (R)	1 ea	118
Kiwi Fruit	1 med	116.8
Lima Beans (C)	1/2 cup	110
Dates, Medjool	3 pieces	109.4
Turnip Greens (C)	1 cup	86
Honeydew Melon (R)	1 cup	81.4
Pear	1 med	73
Pineapple (R)	1 cup	66
Navy Beans (C)	1/2 cup	65
Pinto Beans (C)	1/2 cup	64
Split Peas (C)	1/2 cup	64
Watermelon (R)	1 cup	62
Peaches (R)	1 med	58
Avocados	1/2 ea	46
Brown Rice (C)	1 cup	45
Romaine Lettuce (R)	1 cup	34
Figs (R) (fresh)	1/4 cup	33.7
Cucumber (R)	1 cup	30
Potatoes (C)	1 cup	28

Ingred / Portions / Inositol in mg		
Apricots (R)	1 med	26
Strawberries (R)	1 cup	26
White Rice (C)	1 cup	24
Lentils (C)	1/2 cup	22.5
Radishes (R)	1 cup	20
Plums	1 fruit	19.8
Apples (R)	1 med	17.5
Parsley (R)	2 tbsp	4.4
Endive (R)	1 cup	4.3
Papaya (R)	1 cup	2.4
Barley (C)	1 cup	1

(C) Cooked | (R) = Raw | (D) = Dried

| Dopamine | Serotonin | Acetylcholine | GABA |

| Glutamic Acid | Inositol | B1 | B3 | B6 |

Ingred / Portions / B1 %			Ingred / Portions / B1 %			Ingred / Portions / B1 %		
Granola, homemade	1 cup	60	Brussels Sprouts (C)	1 cup	12	Parsnips (C) & (R)	1 cup	8
Lentils (R)	1/2 cup	56	Millet (C)	1 cup	12	Pomegranates (R)	1 cup	8
Wheat Germ (R)	1/4 cup	36	Oatmeal (C)	1 cup	12	Potatoes (C)	1 cup	8
Sunflower Seed Kernels (D)	1/4 cup	34.5	Pecans	1/4 cup	12	Pumpkin Seeds (C)	1/4 cup	8
Green Garbanzo Beans (R)	1/2 cup	32	Brown Rice (C)	1 cup	12	Rutabagas (R)	1 cup	8
Wheat Germ (C)	1/4 cup	31.5	Rye	1/3 cup	12	Broccoli Raab (C)	1 cup	7.4
Macadamia Nuts (R)	1/4 cup	26.7	Tofu	4 oz	12	Dandelion Greens (R)	1 cup	7
Sesame Seeds	2 tbsp	26	Beet Greens (C)	1 cup	11	Grapes, red or green (R)	1 cup	7
Wheat, red (D)	1/2 cup	24.5	Lentils (C)	1/2 cup	11	Guavas (R)	1 cup	7
Flaxseed	2 tbsp	22	Mung Beans (C)	1/2 cup	11	Garbanzo Beans (C)	1/2 cup	6.5
Spelt (D)	1/2 cup	21	Pinto Beans (C)	1/2 cup	11	Artichokes (R)	1 med	6
Asparagus (C)	1 cup	20	Spinach (C)	1 cup	11	Broccoli (C)	1 cup	6
Oats (D)	1/4 cup	19.7	Sugar-Apples (R)	1 ea	11	Cabbage (C)	1 cup	6
Oat Bran (R)	1/4 cup	18.2	Yellow Corn (R)	1/2 cup	10.5	Carrots (C) & (R)	1 cup	6
Pistachio Nuts	1/4 cup	17.7	Soy Beans, Edadame	1/2 cup	10.5	Sweet Yellow Corn (C)	1/2 cup	6
White Rice (C)	1 cup	17	Great Northern Beans (C)	1/2 cup	9.5	Green Beans (C) & (R)	1 cup	6
Peanuts	1/4 cup	15.5	Kidney Beans (C)	1/2 cup	9.5	Lentils, sprouted (R)	1/2 cup	6
Navy Beans (C)	1/2 cup	14.5	Adzuki Beans (C)	1/2 cup	9	Mangos (R)	1 cup	6
Black Beans (C)	1/2 cup	14	Barley (C)	1 cup	9	Mung Beans (R)	1 cup	6
Green Peas (C)	1/2 cup	14	Dandelion Greens (C)	1 cup	9	Red Tomatoes (C)	1 cup	6
Okra (C)	1 cup	14	Pineapple (R)	1 cup	9	Walnuts (R)	1/4 cup	6
Sweet Potato (C)	1 cup	14	Rutabagas (C)	1 cup	9	Chestnuts (C)	1/4 cup	5.7
Brazilnuts (D)	1/4 cup	13.7	Taro (C)	1 cup	9	Oat Bran (C)	1/4 cup	5.7
Asparagus (R)	1 cup	13	Yam (C)	1 cup	9	Fava Beans (C)	1/2 cup	5.5
Green Peas (R)	1/2 cup	13	Cherimoya (R)	1/2 each	8.5	Sweet Green Bell Pepper (C)	1 cup	5
Okra (R)	1 cup	13	Tamarinds (R)	1/4 cup	8.5	Coconut Water	1 cup	5
Quinoa (C)	1 cup	13	Pine Nuts (D)	1/4 cup	8.2	Collard Greens (C)	1 cup	5
Split Peas (C)	1/2 cup	12.5	Brussels Sprouts (R)	1 cup	8	Eggplant (C)	1 cup	5
Split Peas (C)	1/2 cup	12.5	Lima Beans (C)	1/2 cup	8	Kale (C) & (R)	1 cup	5
Hazelnuts or Filberts	1/4 cup	12.2	Oranges	1 med	8	Kohlrabi (C)	1 cup	5

(C) Cooked | (R) = Raw | (D) = Dried

VSG Brain

Dopamine	Serotonin	Acetylcholine	GABA

Glutamic Acid	Inositol	B1	B3	B6

Ingred / Portions / B3 %			Ingred / Portions / B3 %			Ingred / Portions / B3 %		
Spelt (D)	1/2 cup	30	Pine Nuts (D)	1/4 cup	7.5	Summer Squash (C)	1 cup	5
Wheat (D)	1/2 cup	26	Artichokes (C) & (R)	1 med	7	Red Tomatoes (R)	1 cup	5
Peanuts	1/4 cup	22	Asparagus (R)	1 cup	7	Winter Squash (C)	1 cup	5
Crimini Mushrooms (C)	1/2 cup	18	Sugar-Apples (R)	1 ea	7	Cherimoya (R)	1/2 each	4.5
Barley (C)	1 cup	16	Broccoli Raab (C)	1 cup	6.8	Lima Beans (C)	1/2 cup	4.5
Brown Rice (C)	1 cup	15	Almonds, blanched	1/4 cup	6.7	Split Peas (C)	1/2 cup	4.5
Sweet Potato (C)	1 cup	15	Sweet Yellow Corn (C)	1/2 cup	6.5	Split Peas (C)	1/2 cup	4.5
Sunflower Seed Kernels (D)	1/4 cup	14.5	Yellow Corn (R)	1/2 cup	6.5	Macadamia Nuts (R)	1/4 cup	4.2
Granola, homemade	1 cup	13	White Mushroom (R)	1/2 cup	6.5	Adzuki Beans (C)	1/2 cup	4
Lentils (R)	1/2 cup	12.5	Cantaloupe (R)	1 cup	6	Bananas (R)	1 med	4
Millet (C)	1 cup	12	Carrots (C)	1 cup	6	Beet Greens (C)	1 cup	4
White Rice (C)	1 cup	12	Carrots (R)	1 cup	6	Broccoli (C)	1 cup	4
Rye	1/3 cup	12	Dates, Medjool	3 pieces	6	Brussels Sprouts (C)	1 cup	4
Tomatillos (R)	1 cup	12	Lychee (R)	1 cup	6	Flaxseed	2 tbsp	4
Tempeh	1/2 cup	11	Okra (C)	1 cup	6	Green Beans (C)	1 cup	4
White Mushrooms (C)	1/2 cup	11	Parsnips (C)	1 cup	6	Green Beans (R)	1 cup	4
Asparagus (C)	1 cup	10	Peaches (R)	1 med	6	Honeydew Melon (R)	1 cup	4
Wheat Bran	1/4 cup	9.7	Rutabagas (C)	1 cup	6	Mung Beans (R)	1 cup	4
Wheat Germ (R)	1/4 cup	9.7	Red Tomatoes (C)	1 cup	6	Pineapple (R)	1 cup	4
Guavas (R)	1 cup	9	Shiitake Mushrooms (C)	1/2 cup	5.5	Quinoa (C)	1 cup	4
Avocados	1/2 ea	8.5	Blackberries (R)	1 cup	5	Raspberries (R)	1 cup	4
Buckwheat Groats (C)	1 cup	8	Collard Greens (C)	1 cup	5	Spinach (C)	1 cup	4
Coriander (cilantro)	2 tbsp	8	Lentils (C)	1/2 cup	5	Tofu	4 oz	4
Green Peas (C)	1/2 cup	8	Mangos (R)	1 cup	5	Yam (C)	1 cup	4
Nectarines (R)	1 ea	8	Mung Beans (C)	1 cup	5	Zucchini with skin (C)	1 cup	4
Potatoes (C)	1 cup	8	Okra (R)	1 cup	5	Soy Beans, Edadame	1/2 cup	3.5
Sesame Seeds	2 tbsp	8	Parsnips (R)	1 cup	5	Kumquats (R)	1 cup	3.3
Wheat Germ (C)	1/4 cup	8	Pumpkin Seeds (C)	1/4 cup	5	Asian Pears (R)	1 med	3
Green Garbanzo Beans (R)	1/2 cup	7.5	Pumpkin (C)	1 cup	5	Sweet Green Bell Pepper (C)	1 cup	3
Green Peas (R)	1/2 cup	7.5	Rutabagas (R)	1 cup	5	Blueberries (R)	1 cup	3

(C) Cooked | (R) = Raw | (D) = Dried

VSG·Brain

Ingred / Portions / B6 %			Ingred / Portions / B6 %			Ingred / Portions / B6 %		
Sweet Potato with Skin (C)	1 cup	29	Okra (R)	1 cup	11	Cabbage (C)	1 cup	8
Green Garbanzo Beans (R)	1/2 cup	27	Quinoa (C)	1 cup	11	Coriander (cilantro)	2 tbsp	8
Pistachio Nuts	1/4 cup	26.2	Beet Greens (C)	1 cup	10	Dandelion Greens (C)	1 cup	8
Sunflower Seed Kernels (D)	1/4 cup	23.5	Green Bell Pepper (R)	1 cup	10	Hazelnuts or Filberts	1/4 cup	8
Bananas (R)	1 med	22	Brussels Sprouts (R)	1 cup	10	Lima Beans (C)	1/2 cup	8
Spinach (C)	1 cup	22	Cauliflower (C)	1 cup	10	Parsnips (C)	1 cup	8
Taro (C)	1 cup	22	Kohlrabi (R)	1 cup	10	Walnuts (R)	1/4 cup	8
Wheat Germ (R)	1/4 cup	18.7	Lychee (R)	1 cup	10	Broccoli Raab (C)	1 cup	7.4
Granola, homemade	1 cup	18	Pinto Beans (C)	1/2 cup	10	Artichokes (R)	1 med	7
Potatoes (C)	1 cup	18	Spelt (D)	1/2 cup	10	Blackstrap Molasses	1 tbsp	7
Winter Squash (C)	1 cup	17	Wheat Bran	1/4 cup	9.5	Bok Choy (R)	1 cup	7
Cherimoya (R)	1/2 each	16.5	Barley (C)	1 cup	9	Dandelion Greens (R)	1 cup	7
Sweet Green Bell Pepper (C)	1 cup	16	Carrots (R)	1 cup	9	Honeydew Melon (R)	1 cup	7
Broccoli (C)	1 cup	16	Chayote Fruit (C)	1 cup	9	Mustard Greens (C)	1 cup	7
Yam (C)	1 cup	16	Chestnuts (C)	1/4 cup	9	Onions (C)	1/2 cup	7
Sugar-Apples (R)	1 ea	15	Dates, Medjool	3 pieces	9	White Rice (C)	1 cup	7
Wheat, hard red (D)	1/2 cup	14.5	Guavas (R)	1 cup	9	Rutabagas (R)	1 cup	7
Brussels Sprouts (C)	1 cup	14	Kale (C)	1 cup	9	Swiss Chard (C)	1 cup	7
Okra (C)	1 cup	14	Kale (R)	1 cup	9	Red Tomatoes (R)	1 cup	7
Brown Rice (C)	1 cup	14	Lentils (C)	1/2 cup	9	Turnip Greens (R)	1 cup	7
Zucchini (R)	1 cup	14	Millet (C)	1 cup	9	Zucchini with skin (C)	1 cup	7
Wheat Germ (C)	1/4 cup	13.7	Pineapple (R)	1 cup	9	Navy Beans (C)	1/2 cup	6.5
Avocados	1/2 ea	13	Rutabagas (C)	1 cup	9	Peanuts	1/4 cup	6.2
Kohlrabi (C)	1 cup	13	Tempeh	1/2 cup	9	Asparagus (R)	1 cup	6
Turnip Greens (C)	1 cup	13	Red Tomatoes (C)	1 cup	9	Buckwheat Groats (C)	1 cup	6
Carrots (C)	1 cup	12	Winter Squash (R)	1 cup	9	Cabbage (R)	1 cup	6
Collard Greens (C)	1 cup	12	Green Peas (C)	1/2 cup	8.5	Cantaloupe (R)	1 cup	6
Summer Squash (R)	1 cup	12	Rye	1/3 cup	8.3	Celery (C)	1 cup	6
Cauliflower (R)	1 cup	11	Asparagus (C)	1 cup	8	Figs (R) (fresh)	2 med	6
Mangos (R)	1 cup	11	Broccoli (R)	1 cup	8	Garlic (R)	3 cloves	6

(C) Cooked | (R) = Raw | (D) = Dried

VSG·Immune·Boost

Vitamin C | Zinc | Other Immune Boosting Nutrients

Ingred / Portions / Vita C %			Ingred / Portions / Vita C %			Ingred / Portions / Vita C %		
Guavas (R)	1 cup	628	Mustard Greens (R)	1 cup	65	Dandelion Greens (R)	1 cup	32
Lychee (R)	1 cup	226	Sweet Potato with Skin (C)	1 cup	65	Summer Squash (R)	1 cup	32
Pummelo (R)	1 cup	193	Beet Greens (C)	1 cup	60	Lime Juice (R)	1/4 cup	30.5
Broccoli (C)	1 cup	168	Mustard Greens (C)	1 cup	59	Cherimoya (R)	1/2 each	30
Sweet Green Bell Pepper (C)	1 cup	167	Collard Greens (C)	1 cup	58	Green Beans (R)	1 cup	30
Brussels Sprouts (C)	1 cup	162	Rutabagas (R)	1 cup	58	Pomegranates (R)	1 cup	30
Kohlrabi (C)	1 cup	149	Turnip Greens (R)	1 cup	55	Turnips (C)	1 cup	30
Strawberries (R)	1 cup	149	Cabbage (R)	1 cup	54	Radishes (R)	1 cup	29
Papaya (R)	1 cup	144	Raspberries (R)	1 cup	54	Spinach (C)	1 cup	29
Kohlrabi (R)	1 cup	140	Rutabagas (C)	1 cup	53	Grapes, red or green (R)	1 cup	27
Broccoli (R)	1 cup	135	Swiss Chard (C)	1 cup	53	Persimmons, native (R)	1 each	27
Kale (R)	1 cup	134	Tangerines (R)	1 large	53	Yam (C)	1 cup	27
Pineapple (R)	1 cup	131	Bok Choy (R)	1 cup	52	Potatoes (C)	1 cup	26
Brussels Sprouts (R)	1 cup	125	Coriander (cilantro)	2 tbsp	52	Tomatillos (R)	1 cup	26
Green Bell Pepper (R)	1 cup	123	Honeydew Melon (R)	1 cup	51	Artichokes (R)	1 med	25
Kumquats (R)	1 cup	120.4	Blackberries (R)	1 cup	50	Asparagus (C)	1 cup	24
Kiwi Fruit	1 med	117	Green Peas (R)	1/2 cup	48.5	Blueberries (R)	1 cup	24
Oranges (R)	1 med	116	Lemon Juice (R)	1/4 cup	46.7	Mung Beans (C)	1 cup	24
Cantaloupe (R)	1 cup	98	Daikon Radish (R)	1 cup	46.2	Watercress (R)	1 cup	24
Cauliflower (C)	1 cup	96	Turnips (R)	1 cup	46	Winter Squash (R)	1 cup	24
Cabbage (C)	1 cup	94	Okra (C)	1 cup	44	Dill Weed, fresh	1 tsp	21.3
Sugar-Apples (R)	1 ea	94	Broccoli Raab (C)	1 cup	42.1	Chayote Fruit (C)	1 cup	21
Red Tomatoes (C)	1 cup	91	Jicama (R)	1 cup	40	Collards (R)	1 cup	21
Kale (C)	1 cup	89	Parsnips (R)	1 cup	38	Watermelon (R)	1 cup	21
Cauliflower (R)	1 cup	77	Red Tomatoes (R)	1 cup	38	Green Beans (C)	1 cup	20
Carambola/ Starfruit (R)	1 cup	76	Daikon Radishes (C)	1 cup	37	Beet Greens (R)	1 cup	19
Mangos (R)	1 cup	76	Okra (R)	1 cup	35	Green Peas (C)	1/2 cup	19
Grapefruit, pink red white (R)	1/2 med	73	Zucchini (R)	1 cup	35	Pumpkin (C)	1 cup	19
Gooseberries (R)	1 cup	69	Parsnips (C)	1 cup	34	Romaine Lettuce (R)	1 cup	19
Turnip Greens (C)	1 cup	66	Winter Squash (C)	1 cup	33	Swiss Chard (R)	1 cup	18

(C) Cooked | (R) = Raw | (D) = Dried

VSG Immune Boost

| Vitamin C | Zinc | Other Immune Boosting Nutrients |

Ingred / Portions / Zinc %			Ingred / Portions / Zinc %			Ingred / Portions / Zinc %		
Granola, homemade	1 cup	33	Buckwheat Groats (C)	1 cup	7	Brussels Sprouts (C)	1 cup	4
Wheat Germ (C)	1/4 cup	31.5	Chayote Fruit (R)	1 cup	7	Cacao	2 tbsp	4
Pumpkin Seeds (C)	1/4 cup	28.2	Soy Beans, Edadame	1/2 cup	7	Lentils, sprouted (R)	1/2 cup	4
Wheat Germ (R)	1/4 cup	23.5	Wheat Bran	1/4 cup	7	Mung Beans (C)	1 cup	4
Green Garbanzo Beans (R)	1/2 cup	23	Black Beans (C)	1/2 cup	6.5	Okra (C) & (R)	1 cup	4
Spelt (D)	1/2 cup	19	Green Peas (C)	1/2 cup	6.5	Pomegranates (R)	1 cup	4
Pistachio Nuts	1/4 cup	18	Shiitake Mushroms (C)	1/2 cup	6.5	Pumpkin (C)	1 cup	4
Wheat (D)	1/2 cup	17	Split Peas (C)	1/2 cup	6.5	Rutabagas (C)	1 cup	4
Oatmeal (C)	1 cup	16	Tempeh	1/2 cup	6.5	Sweet Potato with Skin (C)	1 cup	4
Pine Nuts (D)	1/4 cup	14.5	Flaxseed	2 tbsp	6	Swiss Chard (C)	1 cup	4
Rye	1/3 cup	14	Green Peas (R)	1/2 cup	6	Coconut Cream/Milk (R)	1/4 cup	3.7
Adzuki Beans (C)	1/2 cup	13.5	Maple Syrup	1 tbsp	6	Yellow Sweet Corn (C)	1 cup	3.5
Quinoa (C)	1 cup	13	Navy Beans (C)	1/2 cup	6	Chayote Fruit (C)	1 cup	3
Cashew Nuts (R)	1/4 cup	12.7	Walnuts (R)	1/4 cup	6	Collard Greens (C)	1/2 cup	3
Tofu	4 oz	12	Fava Beans (C)	1/2 cup	5.5	Crimni Mushrooms (C)	1/2 cup	3
Sunflower Seed Kernels (D)	1/4 cup	11.7	Mung Beans (C)	1/2 cup	5.5	Dates, Medjool	3 pieces	3
Millet (C)	1 cup	11	Pinto Beans (C)	1/2 cup	5.5	Guavas (R)	1 cup	3
Oats (D)	1/4 cup	10.2	Asparagus (R)	1 cup	5	Kohlrabi (C)	1 cup	3
Sesame Seeds	2 tbsp	10	Beet Greens (C)	1 cup	5	Macadamia Nuts (R)	1 cup	3
Kidney Beans (C)	1/2 cup	9.5	Blackberries (R)	1 cup	5	Raspberries (R)	1 cup	3
Barley (C)	1 cup	9	Great Northern Beans (C)	1/2 cup	5	Rutabagas (R)	1 cup	3
Brazilnuts (D)	1/4 cup	9	Parsnips (R)	1 cup	5	Winter Squash (C)	1 cup	3
Spinach (C)	1 cup	9	White Rice (C)	1 cup	5	Miso	1 tbsp	2.9
Garbanzo Beans (C)	1/2 cup	8.5	Summer Squash (C)	1 cup	5	Broccoli Raab (C)	1 cup	2.7
Lentils (C)	1/2 cup	8.5	Hazelnuts or Filberts	1/4 cup	4.7	Yellow Corn (R)	1/2 cup	2.5
Pecans	1/4 cup	8.2	Oat Bran (R)	1/4 cup	4.7	Alfalfa Seeds, sprouted (R)	1 cup	2
Asparagus (C)	1 cup	8	Avocados	1/2 ea	4.5	Beets (C)	1/2 cup	2
Peanuts	1/4 cup	8	Lima Beans (C)	1/2 cup	4.5	Blueberries (R)	1 cup	2
Brown Rice (C)	1 cup	8	Artichokes (R)	1 med	4	Broccoli (R)	1 cup	2
Almonds, blanched	1/4 cup	7.5	Broccoli (C)	1 cup	4	Brussels Sprouts (R)	1 cup	2

(C) Cooked | (R) = Raw | (D) = Dried

| Vitamin C | Zinc | Other Immune Boosting Nutrients |

Betaglucane	Lauric Acid	Allicin	Vitamin D
Barley Mushrooms Oats	Coconut Meat Coconut Oil Coconut Milk (Culinary) Palm Kernel Oil *(Best to avoid chemically extracted)*	Garlic, chopped and exposed to air 10-15 min	Mushrooms sliced and exposed to sun for 12 hrs before drying

C = Cooked | R = Raw

Calcium | Magnesium | Potassium | Iron | Vitamin C | Zinc | Selenium

Ingred / Portions / Calcium %			Ingred / Portions / Calcium %			Ingred / Portions / Calcium %		
Tofu	4 oz	76	Brussels Sprouts (C)	1 cup	6	Papaya (R)	1 cup	3
Collard Greens (C)	1 cup	27	Celery (C)	1 cup	6	Quinoa (C)	1 cup	3
Spinach (C)	1 cup	24	Coconut Water	1 cup	6	Radishes (R)	1 cup	3
Turnip Greens (C)	1 cup	20	Dates, Medjool	3 pieces	6	Raspberries (R)	1 cup	3
Beet Greens (C)	1 cup	16	Figs (D)	1/4 cup	6	Spinach (R)	1 cup	3
Dandelion Greens (C)	1 cup	15	Flaxseed	2 tbsp	6	Red Tomatoes (C)	1 cup	3
Okra (C)	1 cup	12	Great Northern Beans (C)	1/2 cup	6	Walnuts (R)	1/4 cup	3
Sesame Seeds	2 tbsp	12	Mustard Greens (R)	1 cup	6	Wheat (D)	1/2 cup	3
Green Garbanzo Beans (R)	1/2 cup	10.5	Parsnips (C)	1 cup	6	Winter Squash (R)	1 cup	3
Dandelion Greens (R)	1 cup	10	Brazilnuts (D)	1/4 cup	5.2	Macadamia Nuts (R)	1/4 cup	2.7
Granola, homemade	1 cup	10	Collards (R)	1 cup	5	Sunflower Seed Kernels (D)	1/4 cup	2.7
Mustard Greens (C)	1 cup	10	Green Beans (C)	1 cup	5	Black Beans (C)	1/2 cup	2.5
Rhubarb (R)	1 cup	10	Oranges (R)	1 med	5	Leeks (R)	1/2 cup	2.5
Swiss Chard (C)	1 cup	10	Parsnips (R)	1 cup	5	Lima Beans (C)	1/2 cup	2.5
Turnip Greens (R)	1 cup	10	Soy Beans, Edadame	1/2 cup	5	Mung Beans (C)	1/2 cup	2.5
Kumquats (R)	1 cup	9.9	Summer Squash (C)	1 cup	5	Onions (C)	1/2 cup	2.5
Kale (C) & (R)	1 cup	9	Turnips (C)	1 cup	5	Pumpkin Seeds (C)	1/4 cup	2.5
Tempeh	1/2 cup	9	Winter Squash (C)	1 cup	5	Spelt (D)	1/2 cup	2.5
Broccoli Raab (C)	1 cup	8.1	Adzuki Beans (C)	1/2 cup	3	Tamarinds (R)	1/4 cup	2.2
Cabbage (C)	1 cup	8	Artichokes (C)	1 med	3	Barley (C)	1 cup	2
Coriander (cilantro)	2 tbsp	8	Asparagus (R)	1 cup	3	Cauliflower (C) & (R)	1 cup	2
Okra (R)	1 cup	8	Black Pepper	1 tsp	3	Chayote Fruit (C) & (R)	1 cup	2
Rutabagas (C)	1 cup	8	Cinnamon, ground	1 tsp	3	Sweet Cherries (R)	1 cup	2
Sweet Potato with Skin (C)	1 cup	8	Fava Beans (C)	1/2 cup	3	Cacao	2 tbsp	2
Almonds, blanched	1/4 cup	7.7	Garlic (R)	3 cloves	3	Cucumber (R)	1 cup	2
Bok Choy (R)	1 cup	7	Guavas (R)	1 cup	3	Cumin Seed	1 tsp	2
Rutabagas (R)	1 cup	7	Kidney Beans (C)	1/2 cup	3	Daikon Radishes (C)	1 cup	2
Navy Beans (C)	1/2 cup	6.5	Kiwi Fruit	1 med	3	Endive (R)	1 cup	2
Artichokes (R)	1 med	6	Kohlrabi (R)	1 cup	3	Grapefruit (R)	1/2 med	2
Broccoli (C)	1 cup	6	Napa Cabbage (C)	1 cup	3	Grapes (R)	1 cup	2

(C) Cooked | (R) = Raw | (D) = Dried

Calcium | **Magnesium** | Potassium | Iron | Vitamin C | Zinc | Selenium

Ingred / Portions / Magnesium %			Ingred / Portions / Magnesium %			Ingred / Portions / Magnesium %		
Pumpkin Seeds (C)	1/4 cup	75.7	Black Beans (C)	1/2 cup	15	Guavas (R)	1 cup	9
Granola, homemade	1 cup	53	Coconut Water	1 cup	15	Lentils (C)	1/2 cup	9
Spinach (C)	1 cup	39	Cacao	2 tbsp	14	Split Peas (C)	1/2 cup	9
Swiss Chard (C)	1 cup	38	Okra (C)	1 cup	14	Kumquats (R)	1 cup	8.2
Brazilnuts (D)	1/4 cup	31.2	Okra (R)	1 cup	14	Pecans	1/4 cup	8.2
Quinoa (C)	1 cup	30	Sweet Potato w/ Skin (C)	1 cup	14	Bananas (R)	1 med	8
Wheat (D)	1/2 cup	30	Oat Bran (R)	1/4 cup	13.7	Broccoli (C)	1 cup	8
Spelt (D)	1/2 cup	29.5	Artichokes (C)	1 med	13	Brussels Sprouts (C)	1 cup	8
Green Garbanzo Beans (R)	1/2 cup	29	Soy Beans, Edadame	1/2 cup	12.5	Coriander (cilantro)	2 tbsp	8
Sunflower Seed Kernels (D)	1/4 cup	28.5	Blackstrap Molasses	1 tbsp	12	Green Peas (C)	1/2 cup	8
Almonds, blanched	1/4 cup	25	Mung Beans (C)	1/2 cup	12	Kohlrabi (C)	1 cup	8
Beet Greens (C)	1 cup	24	Navy Beans (C)	1/2 cup	12	Potatoes (C)	1 cup	8
Wheat Germ (C)	1/4 cup	22.5	Parsnips (C)	1 cup	12	Rutabagas (R)	1 cup	8
Cashew Nuts (R)	1/4 cup	22.2	Hazelnuts or Filberts	1/4 cup	11.7	Sesame Seeds	2 tbsp	8
Wheat Bran	1/4 cup	22.2	Great Northern Beans (C)	1/2 cup	11	Sugar-Apples (R)	1 ea	8
Pine Nuts (D)	1/4 cup	21.2	Macadamia Nuts (R)	1/4 cup	11	Turnip Greens (C)	1 cup	8
Buckwheat Groats (C)	1 cup	21	Summer Squash (C)	1 cup	11	Avocados	1/2 ea	7.5
Brown Rice (C)	1 cup	21	Walnuts (R)	1/4 cup	11	Beet Greens (R)	1 cup	7
Flaxseed	2 tbsp	20	Pinto Beans (C)	1/2 cup	10.5	Blackberries (R)	1 cup	7
Artichokes (R)	1 med	19	Collard Greens (C)	1 cup	10	Yellow Corn (R)	1/2 cup	7
Millet, cooked	1 cup	19	Garbanzo Beans (C)	1/2 cup	10	Green Beans (R)	1 cup	7
Oats (D)	1/4 cup	17.2	Parsnips (R)	1 cup	10	Raspberries (R)	1 cup	7
Wheat Germ (R)	1/4 cup	17.2	Rutabagas (C)	1 cup	10	Swiss Chard (R)	1 cup	7
Rye	1/3 cup	17	Taro (C)	1 cup	10	Tamarinds (R)	1/4 cup	7
Tempeh	1/2 cup	17	Zucchini with skin (C)	1 cup	10	Winter Squash (C)	1 cup	7
Oatmeal (C)	1 cup	16	Kidney Beans (C)	1/2 cup	9.5	Figs (D)	1/4 cup	6.2
Tofu	4 oz	16	Pistachio Nuts	1/4 cup	9.2	Asian Pears (R)	1 med	6
Lima Beans (C)	1/2 cup	15.5	Barley (C)	1 cup	9	Asparagus (C)	1 cup	6
Peanuts	1/4 cup	15.2	Dates, Medjool	3 pieces	9	Cabbage (C)	1 cup	6
Adzuki Beans (C)	1/2 cup	15	Fava Beans (C)	1/2 cup	9	Cherimoya (R)	1/2 ea	6

(C) Cooked | (R) = Raw | (D) = Dried

Calcium | Magnesium | **Potassium** | Iron | Vitamin C | Zinc | Selenium

Ingred / Portions / Potassium %			Ingred / Portions / Potassium %			Ingred / Portions / Potassium %		
Beet Greens (C)	1 cup	37	Zucchini with skin (C)	1 cup	13	Spelt (D)	1/2 cup	9.5
Pistachio Nuts	1/4 cup	36	Asparagus (C)	1 cup	12	Cauliflower (R)	1 cup	9
Sweet Potato w/ Skin (C)	1 cup	27	Bananas (R)	1 med	12	Sweet Cherries (R)	1 cup w/ pits	9
Swiss Chard (C)	1 cup	27	Cantaloupe (R)	1 cup	12	Crimni Mushrooms (C)	1/2 cup	9
Yam (C)	1 cup	26	Carrots (R)	1 cup	12	Kale (R)	1 cup	9
Green Garbanzo Beans (R)	1/2 cup	25	Celery (C)	1 cup	12	Lychee (R)	1 cup	9
Spinach (C)	1 cup	24	Cherimoya (R)	1/2 each	12	Okra (R)	1 cup	9
Guavas (R)	1 cup	20	Daikon Radishes (C)	1 cup	12	Quinoa (C)	1 cup	9
Tempeh	1/2 cup	20	Pomegranates (R)	1 cup	12	Zucchini (R)	1 cup	9
Granola, homemade	1 cup	19	Pummelo (R)	1 cup	12	Black Beans (C)	1/2 cup	8.5
Taro (C)	1 cup	18	Red Tomatoes (R)	1 cup	12	Kumquats (R)	1 cup	8.2
Adzuki Beans (C)	1/2 cup	17.5	Winter Squash (R)	1 cup	12	Asparagus (R)	1 cup	8
Coconut Water	1 cup	17	Honeydew Melon (R)	1 cup	11	Beet Greens (R)	1 cup	8
Kohlrabi (C)	1 cup	16	Pumpkin (R)	1 cup	11	Blackstrap Molasses	1 tbsp	8
Parsnips (C)	1 cup	16	Sugar-Apples (R)	1 ea	11	Broccoli (R)	1 cup	8
Pumpkin (C)	1 cup	16	Lentils (C)	1/2 cup	10.5	Cabbage (C)	1 cup	8
Rutabagas (C)	1 cup	16	Pinto Beans (C)	1/2 cup	10.5	Celery (R)	1 cup	8
Dates, Medjool	3 pieces	15	Asian Pears (R)	1 med	10	Chayote Fruit (C)	1 cup	8
Red Tomatoes (C)	1 cup	15	Brussels Sprouts (R)	1 cup	10	Gooseberries (R)	1 cup	8
Artichokes (R)	1 med	14	Carrots (C)	1 cup	10	Grapes, red or green (R)	1 cup	8
Avocados	1/2 ea	14	Great Northern Beans (C)	1/2 cup	10	Kale (C)	1 cup	8
Broccoli (C)	1 cup	14	Navy Beans (C)	1/2 cup	10	Mustard Greens (C)	1 cup	8
Brussels Sprouts (C)	1 cup	14	Papaya (R)	1 cup	10	Nectarines (R)	1 ea	8
Kohlrabi (R)	1 cup	14	Rhubarb (R)	1 cup	10	Peaches (R)	1 med	8
Lima Beans (C)	1/2 cup	14	Split Peas (C)	1/2 cup	10	Radishes (R)	1 cup	8
Parsnips (R)	1 cup	14	Summer Squash (C)	1 cup	10	Summer Squash (R)	1 cup	8
Potatoes (C)	1 cup	14	Split peas, cooked	1/2 cup	10	Tofu	4 oz	8
Winter Squash (C)	1 cup	14	Tomatillos (R)	1 cup	10	Turnip Greens (C)	1 cup	8
Pumpkin Seeds (C)	1/4 cup	13	Wheat (D)	1/2 cup	10	Turnips (C)	1 cup	8
Rutabagas (R)	1 cup	13	Soy Beans, Edadame	1/2 cup	9.5	Wheat Germ (C)	1/4 cup	7.7

(C) Cooked | (R) = Raw | (D) = Dried

Calcium | Magnesium | Potassium | (Iron) | Vitamin C | Zinc | Selenium

Ingred / Portions / Iron %		
Pumpkin Seeds (C)	1/4 cup	47
Spinach (C)	1 cup	36
Green Garbanzo Beans (R)	1/2 cup	34.5
Granola, homemade	1 cup	29
Swiss Chard (C)	1 cup	22
Spelt (D)	1/2 cup	21.5
Lentils (C)	1/2 cup	18.5
Wheat (D)	1/2 cup	17
Asparagus (R)	1 cup	16
Tofu	4 oz	16
Beet Greens (C)	1 cup	15
Quinoa (C)	1 cup	15
Wheat Germ (C)	1/4 cup	14.2
Adzuki Beans (C)	1/2 cup	13
Garbanzo Beans (C)	1/2 cup	13
Tempeh	1/2 cup	12.5
Barley (C)	1 cup	12
Collard Greens (C)	1 cup	12
Coriander (cilantro)	2 tbsp	12
Navy Beans (C)	1/2 cup	12
Oatmeal (C)	1 cup	12
Cashew Nuts (R)	1/4 cup	11.5
Lima Beans (C)	1/2 cup	11.5
Kidney Beans (C)	1/2 cup	11
White Rice (C)	1 cup	11
Great Northern Beans (C)	1/2 cup	10.5
Oats (D)	1/4 cup	10.2
Pine Nuts (D)	1/4 cup	10.2
Sunflower Seed Kernels (D)	1/4 cup	10.2
Asparagus (C)	1 cup	10

Ingred / Portions / Iron %		
Black Beans (C)	1/2 cup	10
Black Pepper	1 tsp	10
Brussels Sprouts (C)	1 cup	10
Dandelion Greens (C)	1 cup	10
Pinto Beans (C)	1/2 cup	10
Soy Beans, Edadame	1/2 cup	10
Wheat Germ (R)	1/4 cup	10
Peanuts	1/4 cup	9.2
Artichokes (R)	1 med	9
Dandelion Greens (R)	1 cup	9
Red Tomatoes (C)	1 cup	9
Wheat Bran	1/4 cup	8.5
Rye	1/3 cup	8.3
Kumquats (R)	1 cup	8.2
Cacao	2 tbsp	8
Mung Beans (C)	1/2 cup	8
Olives	4 tbsp	8
Pumpkin (C)	1 cup	8
Sweet Potato with Skin (C)	1 cup	8
Almonds, blanched	1/4 cup	7.5
Coconut Cream/Milk (R)	1/4 cup	7.5
Hazelnuts or Filberts	1/4 cup	7.5
Brussels Sprouts (R)	1 cup	7
Buckwheat Groats (C)	1 cup	7
Cumin seed	1 tsp	7
Fava Beans (C)	1/2 cup	7
Green Peas (C)	1/2 cup	7
Lentils, sprouted (R)	1/2 cup	7
Oat Bran (R)	1/4 cup	7
Pistachio Nuts	1/4 cup	7

Ingred / Portions / Iron %		
Split Peas (C)	1/2 cup	7
Thyme (D)	1 tsp	7
Macadamia Nuts (R)	1/4 cup	6.7
Broccoli (C)	1 cup	6
Flaxseed	2 tbsp	6
Green Beans (R)	1 cup	6
Green Peas (R)	1/2 cup	6
Kale (C) & (R)	1 cup	6
Millet (C)	1 cup	6
Parsnips (C)	1 cup	6
Turnip Greens (C)	1 cup	6
Dill Weed, fresh	1 tsp	5.5
Beet Greens (R)	1 cup	5
Blackberries (R)	1 cup	5
Blackstrap Molasses	1 tbsp	5
Broccoli Raab (R)	1 cup	5
Green Beans (C)	1 cup	5
Leeks (R)	1/2 cup	5
Mustard Greens (C) & (R)	1 cup	5
Pumpkin (R)	1 cup	5
Raspberries (R)	1 cup	5
Brown Rice (C)	1 cup	5
Rutabagas (C)	1 cup	5
Spinach (R)	1 cup	5
Sugar-Apples (R)	1 ea	5
Taro (C)	1 cup	5
Turmeric, ground	1 tsp	5
Walnuts (R)	1/4 cup	5
Winter Squash (C)	1 cup	5
Broccoli Raab (C)	1 cup	4.7

(C) Cooked | (R) = Raw | (D) = Dried

VSG-Athlete

Ingred / Portions / Vitamin C %		
Guavas (R)	1 cup	628
Lychee (R)	1 cup	226
Pummelo (R)	1 cup	193
Broccoli (C)	1 cup	168
Sweet Green Bell Pepper (C)	1 cup	167
Brussels Sprouts (C)	1 cup	162
Kohlrabi (C)	1 cup	149
Strawberries (R)	1 cup	149
Papaya (R)	1 cup	144
Kohlrabi (R)	1 cup	140
Broccoli (R)	1 cup	135
Kale (R)	1 cup	134
Pineapple (R)	1 cup	131
Brussels Sprouts (R)	1 cup	125
Green Bell Pepper (R)	1 cup	123
Kumquats (R)	1 cup	120.4
Kiwi Fruit	1 med	117
Oranges (R)	1 med	116
Cantaloupe (R)	1 cup	98
Cauliflower (C)	1 cup	96
Cabbage (C)	1 cup	94
Sugar-Apples (R)	1 ea	94
Red Tomatoes (C)	1 cup	91
Kale (C)	1 cup	89
Cauliflower (R)	1 cup	77
Carambola/ Starfruit (R)	1 cup	76
Mangos (R)	1 cup	76
Grapefruit, pink red white (R)	1/2 med	73
Gooseberries (R)	1 cup	69
Turnip Greens (C)	1 cup	66

Ingred / Portions / Vitamin C %		
Mustard Greens (R)	1 cup	65
Sweet Potato with Skin (C)	1 cup	65
Beet Greens (C)	1 cup	60
Mustard Greens (C)	1 cup	59
Collard Greens (C)	1 cup	58
Rutabagas (R)	1 cup	58
Turnip Greens (R)	1 cup	55
Cabbage (R)	1 cup	54
Raspberries (R)	1 cup	54
Rutabagas (C)	1 cup	53
Swiss Chard (C)	1 cup	53
Tangerines (R)	1 large	53
Bok Choy (R)	1 cup	52
Coriander (cilantro)	2 tbsp	52
Honeydew Melon (R)	1 cup	51
Blackberries (R)	1 cup	50
Green Peas (R)	1/2 cup	48.5
Lemon Juice (R)	1/4 cup	46.7
Daikon Radish (R)	1 cup	46.2
Turnips (R)	1 cup	46
Okra (C)	1 cup	44
Broccoli Raab (C)	1 cup	42.1
Jicama (R)	1 cup	40
Parsnips (R)	1 cup	38
Red Tomatoes (R)	1 cup	38
Daikon Radishes (C)	1 cup	37
Okra (R)	1 cup	35
Zucchini, raw	1 cup	35
Parsnips (C)	1 cup	34
Winter Squash (C)	1 cup	33

Ingred / Portions / Vitamin C %		
Dandelion Greens (C) & (R)	1 cup	32
Summer Squash (R)	1 cup	32
Lime Juice (R)	1/4 cup	30.5
Cherimoya (R)	1/2 each	30
Green Beans (R)	1 cup	30
Pomegranates (R)	1 cup	30
Turnips (C)	1 cup	30
Radishes (R)	1 cup	29
Spinach (C)	1 cup	29
Grapes, red or green (R)	1 cup	27
Persimmons, native (R)	1 each	27
Yam (C)	1 cup	27
Potatoes (C)	1 cup	26
Tomatillos (R)	1 cup	26
Artichokes (R)	1 med	25
Asparagus (C)	1 cup	24
Blueberries (R)	1 cup	24
Mung Beans (C)	1 cup	24
Watercress (R)	1 cup	24
Winter Squash (R)	1 cup	24
Dill Weed, fresh	1 tsp	21.3
Chayote Fruit (C)	1 cup	21
Collards (R)	1 cup	21
Watermelon (R)	1 cup	21
Green Beans (C)	1 cup	20
Beet Greens (R)	1 cup	19
Green Peas (C)	1/2 cup	19
Pumpkin (C)	1 cup	19
Romaine Lettuce (R)	1 cup	19
Swiss Chard (R)	1 cup	18

(C) Cooked | (R) = Raw | (D) = Dried

Calcium | Magnesium | Potassium | Iron | Vitamin C | Zinc | Selenium

Ingred / Portions / Zinc %		
Granola, homemade	1 cup	33
Wheat Germ (C)	1/4 cup	31.5
Pumpkin Seeds (C)	1/4 cup	28.2
Wheat Germ (R)	1/4 cup	23.5
Green Garbanzo Beans (R)	1/2 cup	23
Spelt (D)	1/2 cup	19
Pistachio Nuts	1/4 cup	18
Wheat (D)	1/2 cup	17
Oatmeal (C)	1 cup	16
Pine Nuts (D)	1/4 cup	14.5
Rye	1/3 cup	14
Adzuki Beans (C)	1/2 cup	13.5
Quinoa (C)	1 cup	13
Cashew Nuts (R)	1/4 cup	12.7
Tofu	4 oz	12
Sunflower Seed Kernels (D)	1/4 cup	11.7
Millet (C)	1 cup	11
Oats (D)	1/4 cup	10.2
Sesame Seeds	2 tbsp	10
Kidney Beans (C)	1/2 cup	9.5
Barley (C)	1 cup	9
Brazilnuts (D)	1/4 cup	9
Spinach (C)	1 cup	9
Garbanzo Beans (C)	1/2 cup	8.5
Lentils (C)	1/2 cup	8.5
Pecans	1/4 cup	8.2
Asparagus (C)	1 cup	8
Peanuts	1/4 cup	8
Brown Rice (C)	1 cup	8
Almonds, blanched	1/4 cup	7.5

Ingred / Portions / Zinc %		
Buckwheat Groats (C)	1 cup	7
Chayote Fruit (R)	1 cup	7
Soy Beans, Edadame	1/2 cup	7
Wheat Bran	1/4 cup	7
Black Beans (C)	1/2 cup	6.5
Green Peas (C)	1/2 cup	6.5
Shiitake Mushroms (C)	1/2 cup	6.5
Split Peas (C)	1/2 cup	6.5
Tempeh	1/2 cup	6.5
Flaxseed	2 tbsp	6
Green Peas (R)	1/2 cup	6
Maple Syrup	1 tbsp	6
Navy Beans (C)	1/2 cup	6
Walnuts (R)	1/4 cup	6
Fava Beans (C)	1/2 cup	5.5
Mung Beans (C)	1/2 cup	5.5
Pinto Beans (C)	1/2 cup	5.5
Asparagus (R)	1 cup	5
Beet Greens (C)	1 cup	5
Blackberries (R)	1 cup	5
Great Northern Beans (C)	1/2 cup	5
Parsnips (R)	1 cup	5
White Rice (C)	1 cup	5
Summer Squash (C)	1 cup	5
Hazelnuts or Filberts	1/4 cup	4.7
Oat Bran (R)	1/4 cup	4.7
Avocados	1/2 ea	4.5
Lima Beans (C)	1/2 cup	4.5
Artichokes (R)	1 med	4
Broccoli (C)	1 cup	4

Ingred / Portions / Zinc %		
Brussels Sprouts (C)	1 cup	4
Cacao	2 tbsp	4
Lentils, sprouted (R)	1/2 cup	4
Mung Beans (C)	1 cup	4
Okra (C) & (R)	1 cup	4
Pomegranates (R)	1 cup	4
Pumpkin (C)	1 cup	4
Rutabagas (C)	1 cup	4
Sweet Potato with Skin (C)	1 cup	4
Swiss Chard (C)	1 cup	4
Coconut Cream/Milk (R)	1/4 cup	3.7
Yellow Sweet Corn (C)	1 cup	3.5
Chayote Fruit (C)	1 cup	3
Collard Greens (C)	1/2 cup	3
Crimni Mushrooms (C)	1/2 cup	3
Dates, Medjool	3 pieces	3
Guavas (R)	1 cup	3
Kohlrabi (C)	1 cup	3
Macadamia Nuts (R)	1 cup	3
Raspberries (R)	1 cup	3
Rutabagas (R)	1 cup	3
Winter Squash (C)	1 cup	3
Miso	1 tbsp	2.9
Broccoli Raab (C)	1 cup	2.7
Yellow Corn (R)	1/2 cup	2.5
Alfalfa Seeds, sprouted (R)	1 cup	2
Beets (C)	1/2 cup	2
Blueberries (R)	1 cup	2
Broccoli (R)	1 cup	2
Brussels Sprouts (R)	1 cup	2

(C) Cooked | (R) = Raw | (D) = Dried

Calcium | Magnesium | Potassium | Iron | Vitamin C | Zinc | Selenium

Ingred / Portions / Selenium %			Ingred / Portions / Selenium %			Ingred / Portions / Selenium %		
Wheat Germ (C)	1/4 cup	282	Almonds, blanched	1/4 cup	40.5	Sesame Seeds	2 tbsp	22
Granola, homemade	1 cup	247	Soy Beans, Edadame	1/2 cup	39.5	Chestnuts (C)	1/4 cup	21
Wheat (D)	1/2 cup	191.5	Beet Greens (C)	1 cup	37	Green Peas (C)	1/2 cup	21
Wheat Germ (R)	1/4 cup	191.2	Parsnips (R)	1 cup	37	Brazilnuts (D)	1/4 cup	20.2
Pine Nuts (D)	1/4 cup	148.5	White Rice (C)	1 cup	37	Barley (C)	1 cup	20
Spelt (D)	1/2 cup	130	Peanuts	1/4 cup	35.2	Tofu	4 oz	20
Blackstrap Molasses	1 tbsp	115	Buckwheat Groats (C)	1 cup	34	Pinto Beans (C)	1/2 cup	19.5
Green Garbanzo Beans (R)	1/2 cup	110	Sunflower Seed Kernels (D)	1/4 cup	34	Split Peas (C)	1/2 cup	19.5
Oats (D)	1/4 cup	95.7	Adzuki Beans (C)	1/2 cup	33	Black Beans (C)	1/2 cup	19
Hazelnuts or Filberts	1/4 cup	88.7	Maple Syrup	1 tbsp	33	Kidney Beans (C)	1/2 cup	19
Brown Rice (C)	1 cup	88	Coconut Cream/Milk (R)	1/4 cup	31.4	Mustard Greens (C)	1 cup	19
Pumpkin Seeds, (C)	1/2 cup	85.5	Cloves, ground	1 tsp	30	Summer Squash (C)	1 cup	19
Spinach (C)	1 cup	84	Taro (C)	1 cup	30	Winter Squash (C)	1 cup	19
Wheat Bran	1/4 cup	83.2	Strawberries (R)	1 cup	29	Pistachio Nuts	1/4 cup	18.5
Pineapple (R)	1 cup	76	Swiss Chard (C)	1 cup	29	Black Pepper	1 tsp	18
Rye	1/3 cup	75.3	Kale (C)	1 cup	27	Brussels Sprouts (C)	1 cup	18
Macadamia Nuts (R)	1/4 cup	69.2	Oat Bran (C)	1/4 cup	26.5	Fava Beans (C)	1/2 cup	18
Oatmeal (C)	1 cup	68	Flaxseed	2 tbsp	26	Green Beans (C)	1 cup	18
Oat Bran (R)	1/2 cup	66.2	Kale (R)	1 cup	26	Coconut Water	1 cup	17
Pecans	1/4 cup	61.2	Blueberries (R)	1 cup	25	Artichokes (R)	1 med	16
Quinoa (C)	1 cup	58	Yam (C)	1 cup	25	Bananas (R)	1 med	16
Tempeh	1/2 cup	54	Lentils (C)	1/2 cup	24.5	Broccoli (C)	1 cup	16
Lima Beans (C)	1/2 cup	53	Coriander (cilantro)	2 tbsp	24	Cabbage (C)	1 cup	16
Okra (R)	1 cup	50	Millet (C)	1 cup	24	Zucchini with skin (C)	1 cup	16
Sweet Potato with Skin (C)	1 cup	50	Navy Beans (C)	1/2 cup	24	Brussels Sprouts (R)	1 cup	15
Walnuts (R)	1/4 cup	48	Okra (C)	1 cup	24	Coconut Meat (R)	1/4 cup	15
Blackberries (R)	1 cup	47	Turnip Greens (C)	1 cup	24	Green Peas (R)	1/2 cup	15
Garbanzo Beans (C)	1/2 cup	42	Great Northern Beans (C)	1/2 cup	23	Mung Beans (C)	1/2 cup	15
Collard Greens (C)	1 cup	41	Cinnamon, ground	1 tsp	22	Rutabagas (C)	1 cup	15
Raspberries (R)	1 cup	41	Parsnips (C)	1 cup	22	Cashew Nuts	1/4 cup	14.2

(C) Cooked | (R) = Raw | (D) = Dried

VSG Detoxification

Sulfur Compounds | Polyphenols | Selenium | Zinc

Arugula	Horseradish
Bok Choy	Kale
Broccoli	Mustard Seeds
Brussels Sprouts	Radish
Cabbage	Rapini (Broccoli Rabe)
Cauliflower	Rutabaga
Collard Greens	Turnips
Daikon	Wasabi
Garlic	Watercress

Sulfur Compounds | Polyphenols | Selenium | Zinc

Apple	Green Tea
Artichoke	Hazelnut
Blackberry	Plum
Black Currant	Pomegranate
Black Tea	Raspberry
Blueberry	Strawberry
Cacao	
Cherry	
Dark Chocolate	
Flaxseed	

VSG Detoxification

Sulfur Compounds | **Polyphenols** | **Selenium** | **Zinc**

Ingred / Portions / Selenium %			Ingred / Portions / Selenium %			Ingred / Portions / Selenium %		
Wheat Germ (C)	1/4 cup	282	Almonds, blanched	1/4 cup	40.5	Sesame Seeds	2 tbsp	22
Granola, homemade	1 cup	247	Soy Beans, Edadame	1/2 cup	39.5	Chestnuts (C)	1/4 cup	21
Wheat (D)	1/2 cup	191.5	Beet Greens (C)	1 cup	37	Green Peas (C)	1/2 cup	21
Wheat Germ (R)	1/4 cup	191.2	Parsnips (R)	1 cup	37	Brazilnuts (D)	1/4 cup	20.2
Pine Nuts (D)	1/4 cup	148.5	White Rice (C)	1 cup	37	Barley (C)	1 cup	20
Spelt (D)	1/2 cup	130	Peanuts	1/4 cup	35.2	Tofu	4 oz	20
Blackstrap Molasses	1 tbsp	115	Buckwheat Groats (C)	1 cup	34	Pinto Beans (C)	1/2 cup	19.5
Green Garbanzo Beans (R)	1/2 cup	110	Sunflower Seed Kernels (D)	1/4 cup	34	Split Peas (C)	1/2 cup	19.5
Oats (D)	1/4 cup	95.7	Adzuki Beans (C)	1/2 cup	33	Black Beans (C)	1/2 cup	19
Hazelnuts or Filberts	1/4 cup	88.7	Maple Syrup	1 tbsp	33	Kidney Beans (C)	1/2 cup	19
Brown Rice (C)	1 cup	88	Coconut Cream/Milk (R)	1/4 cup	31.4	Mustard Greens (C)	1 cup	19
Pumpkin Seeds, (C)	1/2 cup	85.5	Cloves, ground	1 tsp	30	Summer Squash (C)	1 cup	19
Spinach (C)	1 cup	84	Taro (C)	1 cup	30	Winter Squash (C)	1 cup	19
Wheat Bran	1/4 cup	83.2	Strawberries (R)	1 cup	29	Pistachio Nuts	1/4 cup	18.5
Pineapple (R)	1 cup	76	Swiss Chard (C)	1 cup	29	Black pepper	1 tsp	18
Rye	1/3 cup	75.3	Kale (C)	1 cup	27	Brussels Sprouts (C)	1 cup	18
Macadamia Nuts (R)	1/4 cup	69.2	Oat Bran (C)	1/4 cup	26.5	Fava Beans (C)	1/2 cup	18
Oatmeal (C)	1 cup	68	Flaxseed	2 tbsp	26	Green Beans (C)	1 cup	18
Oat Bran (R)	1/2 cup	66.2	Kale (R)	1 cup	26	Coconut Water	1 cup	17
Pecans	1/4 cup	61.2	Blueberries (R)	1 cup	25	Artichokes (R)	1 med	16
Quinoa (C)	1 cup	58	Yam (C)	1 cup	25	Bananas (R)	1 med	16
Tempeh	1/2 cup	54	Lentils (C)	1/2 cup	24.5	Broccoli (C)	1 cup	16
Lima Beans (C)	1/2 cup	53	Coriander (cilantro)	2 tbsp	24	Cabbage (C)	1 cup	16
Okra (R)	1 cup	50	Millet (C)	1 cup	24	Zucchini with skin (C)	1 cup	16
Sweet Potato with Skin (C)	1 cup	50	Navy Beans (C)	1/2 cup	24	Brussels Sprouts (R)	1 cup	15
Walnuts (R)	1/4 cup	48	Okra (C)	1 cup	24	Coconut Meat (R)	1/4 cup	15
Blackberries (R)	1 cup	47	Turnip Greens (C)	1 cup	24	Green Peas (R)	1/2 cup	15
Garbanzo Beans (C)	1/2 cup	42	Great Northern Beans (C)	1/2 cup	23	Mung Beans (C)	1/2 cup	15
Collard Greens (C)	1 cup	41	Cinnamon, ground	1 tsp	22	Rutabagas (C)	1 cup	15
Raspberries (R)	1 cup	41	Parsnips (C)	1 cup	22	Cashew Nuts	1/4 cup	14.2

(C) Cooked | (R) = Raw | (D) = Dried

Sulfur Compounds | Polyphenols | Selenium | Zinc

Ingred / Portions / Zinc %		
Granola, homemade	1 cup	33
Wheat Germ (C)	1/4 cup	31.5
Pumpkin Seeds (C)	1/4 cup	28.2
Wheat Germ (R)	1/4 cup	23.5
Green Garbanzo Beans (R)	1/2 cup	23
Spelt (D)	1/2 cup	19
Pistachio Nuts	1/4 cup	18
Wheat (D)	1/2 cup	17
Oatmeal (C)	1 cup	16
Pine Nuts (D)	1/4 cup	14.5
Rye	1/3 cup	14
Adzuki Beans (C)	1/2 cup	13.5
Quinoa (C)	1 cup	13
Cashew Nuts (R)	1/4 cup	12.7
Tofu	4 oz	12
Sunflower Seed Kernels (D)	1/4 cup	11.7
Millet (C)	1 cup	11
Oats (D)	1/4 cup	10.2
Sesame Seeds	2 tbsp	10
Kidney Beans (C)	1/2 cup	9.5
Barley (C)	1 cup	9
Brazilnuts (D)	1/4 cup	9
Spinach (C)	1 cup	9
Garbanzo Beans (C)	1/2 cup	8.5
Lentils (C)	1/2 cup	8.5
Pecans	1/4 cup	8.2
Asparagus (C)	1 cup	8
Peanuts	1/4 cup	8
Brown Rice (C)	1 cup	8
Almonds, blanched	1/4 cup	7.5

Ingred / Portions / Zinc %		
Buckwheat Groats (C)	1 cup	7
Chayote Fruit (R)	1 cup	7
Soy Beans, Edadame	1/2 cup	7
Wheat Bran	1/4 cup	7
Black Beans (C)	1/2 cup	6.5
Green Peas (C)	1/2 cup	6.5
Shiitake Mushroms (C)	1/2 cup	6.5
Split Peas (C)	1/2 cup	6.5
Tempeh	1/2 cup	6.5
Flaxseed	2 tbsp	6
Green Peas (R)	1/2 cup	6
Maple Syrup	1 tbsp	6
Navy Beans (C)	1/2 cup	6
Walnuts (R)	1/4 cup	6
Fava Beans (C)	1/2 cup	5.5
Mung Beans (C)	1/2 cup	5.5
Pinto Beans (C)	1/2 cup	5.5
Asparagus (R)	1 cup	5
Beet Greens (C)	1 cup	5
Blackberries (R)	1 cup	5
Great Northern Beans (C)	1/2 cup	5
Parsnips (R)	1 cup	5
White Rice (C)	1 cup	5
Summer Squash (C)	1 cup	5
Hazelnuts or Filberts	1/4 cup	4.7
Oat Bran (R)	1/4 cup	4.7
Avocados	1/2 ea	4.5
Lima Beans (C)	1/2 cup	4.5
Artichokes (R)	1 med	4
Broccoli (C)	1 cup	4

Ingred / Portions / Zinc %		
Brussels Sprouts (C)	1 cup	4
Cacao	2 tbsp	4
Lentils, sprouted (R)	1/2 cup	4
Mung Beans (C)	1 cup	4
Okra (C)	1 cup	4
Okra (R)	1 cup	4
Pomegranates (R)	1 cup	4
Pumpkin (C)	1 cup	4
Rutabagas (C)	1 cup	4
Sweet Potato with Skin (C)	1 cup	4
Swiss Chard (C)	1 cup	4
Coconut Cream/Milk (R)	1/4 cup	3.7
Yellow Sweet Corn (C)	1 cup	3.5
Chayote Fruit (C)	1 cup	3
Collard Greens (C)	1/2 cup	3
Crimni Mushrooms (C)	1/2 cup	3
Dates, Medjool	3 pieces	3
Guavas (R)	1 cup	3
Kohlrabi (C)	1 cup	3
Macadamia Nuts (R)	1 cup	3
Raspberries (R)	1 cup	3
Rutabagas (R)	1 cup	3
Winter Squash (C)	1 cup	3
Miso	1 tbsp	2.9
Broccoli Raab (C)	1 cup	2.7
Yellow Corn (R)	1/2 cup	2.5
Alfalfa Seeds, sprouted (R)	1 cup	2
Beets (C)	1/2 cup	2
Blueberries (R)	1 cup	2
Broccoli (R)	1 cup	2

(C) Cooked | (R) = Raw | (D) = Dried

We'd love to hear from You!

Did you enjoy this book?
If so, please help us spread the word.

Here is how:
Submit your book review at *Amazon.com*
or at your preferred *online store.*
We'd really appreciate you feedback!

Join us on Facebook:
You can also connect with us online at
www.facebook.com/VeganSurvival

Copies are also available at:
www.FunctionalVeganism.com

This book was a dream come true for me!

I thank you for your feedback and support! Your friend, Ursula

Made in the USA
Charleston, SC
12 March 2014